Digital Rights Management

Medical Library Association Books

The Medical Library Association (MLA) features books that showcase the expertise of health sciences librarians for other librarians and professionals.

MLA Books are excellent resources for librarians in hospitals, medical research practice, and other settings. These volumes will provide health care professionals and patients with accurate information that can improve outcomes and save lives.

Each book in the series has been overseen editorially since conception by the Medical Library Association Books Panel, composed of MLA members with expertise spanning the breadth of health sciences librarianship.

Medical Library Association Books Panel

Lauren M. Young, AHIP, chair
Kristen L. Young, AHIP, chair designate
Michel C. Atlas
Dorothy C. Ogdon, AHIP
Karen McElfresh, AHIP
Megan Curran Rosenbloom
Tracy Shields, AHIP
JoLinda L. Thompson, AHIP
Heidi Heilemann, AHIP, board liaison

About the Medical Library Association

Founded in 1898, MLA is a 501(c)(3) nonprofit, educational organization of 3,500 individual and institutional members in the health sciences information field that provides lifelong educational opportunities, supports a knowledgebase of health information research, and works with a global network of partners to promote the importance of quality information for improved health to the health care community and the public.

Books in Series

The Medical Library Association Guide to Providing Consumer and Patient Health Information, edited by Michele Spatz
Health Sciences Librarianship, edited by M. Sandra Wood
Curriculum-Based Library Instruction: From Cultivating Faculty Relationships to Assessment, edited by Amy Blevins and Megan Inman
Mobile Technologies for Every Library, by Ann Whitney Gleason
Marketing for Special and Academic Libraries: A Planning and Best Practices Sourcebook, by Patricia Higginbottom and Valerie Gordon
Translating Expertise: The Librarian's Role in Translational Research, edited by Marisa L. Conte
Expert Searching in the Google Age, by Terry Ann Jankowski
Digital Rights Management: The Librarian's Guide, edited by Catherine A. Lemmer and Carla P. Wale

Digital Rights Management

The Librarian's Guide

Edited by
Catherine A. Lemmer
Carla P. Wale

ROWMAN & LITTLEFIELD
Lanham • Boulder • New York • London

Published by Rowman & Littlefield
A wholly owned subsidiary of The Rowman & Littlefield Publishing Group, Inc.
4501 Forbes Boulevard, Suite 200, Lanham, Maryland 20706
www.rowman.com

Unit A, Whitacre Mews, 26-34 Stannary Street, London SE11 4AB

British Library Cataloguing in Publication Information Available

Library of Congress Cataloging-in-Publication Data Available

ISBN 978-1-4422-6374-1 (hardback : alk. paper)
ISBN 978-1-4422-6375-8 (paperback : alk. paper)
ISBN 978-1-4422-6376-5 (ebook)

∞ The paper used in this publication meets the minimum requirements of American National Standard for Information Sciences Permanence of Paper for Printed Library Materials, ANSI/NISO Z39.48-1992.

Printed in the United States of America

Contents

Contents

Introduction

Unlike for most legal terms and concepts, the meaning of the term *copyright* is self-evident—protecting the right to make copies. Prior to the advent of the digital age, the risk and associated loss of revenues from illegal or unauthorized copies was manageable or perhaps more appropriately characterized as "bearable."

The digital age turned this equation on its head. Illegal copies are now of sufficient quality and number to pose significant financial risk to content creators and owners. Further, unauthorized modifications challenge the content creator's original intent and expression. Enter digital rights management (DRM)—the proposed but overreaching solution to illegal use, modification, and copying of digital content.

Libraries are challenged on a daily basis by DRM's overreach because in fulfilling their missions they stand at the intersection where the rights and demands of users and content owners often collide. As such, libraries need to be more than reluctant, noncomplaining consumers of digital content. The intent of this book is to educate librarians about DRM and, in turn, empower them to influence ever-evolving DRM in ways that enable them to best serve their users.

To this end, we start with an introductory chapter by Frederick Dingledy and Alex Berrio Matamoros that introduces DRM, its impact on libraries, and the DRM debate. Real-life examples are used to illustrate the arguments for and in opposition to the growing reach of DRM. Although we suggest you start with this chapter, the remaining chapters can be read independently and in an order that best serves you, the reader.

Generally, chapters 2–6 deal with operational concepts. In chapter 2, Jasper Tran explores and explains the various DRM technologies and systems that libraries encounter. The explanations, while comprehensive and technical, avoid jargon and are easily understandable. Similarly, in chapter 3, Amanda Watson explains digital authentication and how it is utilized by content owners in providing and limiting access to content. The chapter details a variety of authentication methods and provides guidance for librarians tasked with evaluating the impact of a particular authentication method on the library's users.

Chapters 4 and 5 provide specific advice for libraries on managing DRM. In chapter 4, Ashley Krenelka Chase discusses and advises how best to adapt organizational structures, workflows, and library staffing to seamlessly integrate DRM. Her thorough description of a number of organizational alternatives, including the pros and cons of each, provides library administrators and managers a playbook from which to pick the best option for their library. In chapter 5, Brian Huffman and Victoria Szymczak reflect on how libraries can manage and respond to DRM via their collection development policies. In addition to a review of contract models and best practices, Huffman and Szymczak provide sample language for collection development policies any library will find useful. This section of the book concludes with chapter 6, in which Benjamin Keele and Jere Odell introduce and discuss the innovative idea of a compatible relationship between open access and DRM. Keele and Odell challenge the reader to think beyond the typical battlegrounds and envision an environment in which the use of DRM may work to further the goals of open access.

No work on DRM is complete without reference to the principles of privacy and copyright. Roberta Studwell and Jordan Jefferson provide a thoughtful and thorough discussion in chapter 7, detailing the continuing erosion of privacy, the law surrounding information privacy, and the impact of DRM on library user privacy. The chapter also includes best practices for protecting information in the library environment.

Copyright is the fundamental structure on which DRM relies. In scholarly journal publishing, the push for open access and the rise of peer-to-peer sharing via such mechanisms as Sci-Hub, Library Genesis, and #icanhazpdf are generating conversations that challenge us to reevaluate our long-held understanding of copyright and its goals. In chapter 8, Renate Chancellor and Heather Wiggins provide the reader with the copyright basics needed to fully engage in those conversations.

Lastly, in chapter 9, Dana Neacsu sums up DRM and its impact on libraries and suggests alternative models that better serve our library users. Her chapter serves as a rallying call for all librarians.

Libraries have successfully faced and adapted to changes in technology since the beginning of their existence. Technology is technology—whether it is reflected in the move from handwritten lists of books to typewritten catalogs to online catalogs, print journals to electronic databases, or print books to e-books. In this era, one of the technological challenges is to understand how we can influence the evolution of copyright and DRM to ensure our users have easily accessible digital content in a manner that does not put their privacy at risk.

In the past, libraries successfully weathered technological change by becoming informed partners so they could utilize and manage the technology in a manner that best served their users. Today's technological environment is no different. Libraries need to think proactively and advocate for changes that better reflect what users need in an era in which content is increasingly digital. We hope this book educates, encourages, and helps libraries better understand DRM so they can be active participants in shaping and influencing its evolution.

Chapter One

What Is Digital Rights Management?

Frederick W. Dingledy and Alex Berrio Matamoros

Digital rights management, usually shortened to DRM, is a frequent guest in technology news. Creators of movies, TV shows, books, software, and other content argue that DRM prevents pirates from stealing and profiting from their work and thereby encourages the creation of more content. Users, on the other hand, challenge that DRM is overly aggressive in limiting their ability to use content, thereby punishing legitimate purchasers of content while doing little to discourage thieves. Librarians find themselves negotiating the middle, trying to balance users' and owners' rights. In order to manage this balance, librarians need to understand what DRM is and how it works, what issues are involved with its use, and how to create DRM responses and policies that satisfy the needs of both users and content owners.

Before going any further, let's agree upon this simple definition: DRM is technology that controls access to content on digital devices.[1] Although discussions of DRM are often coupled with copyright, it should be apparent from this definition that DRM is not copyright. Rather, it is technology employed to protect the rights of the copyright holder, whether it be the creator or subsequent owner of the content. Ideally, DRM should equally protect the content owner's, content creator's, and content user's rights under copyright law.

This introduction to the debate surrounding DRM discusses what prompted the development of DRM, how it works, and the ways librarians encounter DRM every day. In doing so, it will introduce you to both sides of the DRM debate.

WHY DIGITAL RIGHTS MANAGEMENT EXISTS

DRM appears on much digital content, whether it is a movie, e-book, research subscription database, website, or some other source of information. Why is this technology used so often?

Preventing Piracy

It seems that as long as humanity has had the technology to publish information and distribute it to the masses, people have been copying other people's work and selling it or giving it away without the creator's permission. In its early days, the United States used piracy to boost its citizens' access to knowledge and to jump-start the fledgling republic's economy. The Copyright Act of 1790 granted protection only to United States citizens. As a result, from the colonial days through the Civil War, many American citizens learned how to read from cheap, pirated copies of works by British authors. The United States was prompted to grant copyright to foreign authors' works when American authors emerged on the world stage and discovered pirated copies of their works were being sold overseas. In response, Congress acted and granted copyright protection to foreign authors in 1891.[2]

Modern technology has made copying even easier than it was for our predecessors. Someone living in the nineteenth century who wanted to make a copy of *Moby Dick* needed access to a printing press. Similarly, manufacturing and reproducing music required phonograph cylinders. Duplication of a song, such as "Oh! Susanna," required musicians to perform the song multiple times to make multiple copies.[3] As technology evolved, mimeographs and photocopiers allowed for easier duplication of written works. VHS and audiocassette tapes allowed for easy at-home copying of movies and TV shows, but the quality degraded as copies were made from earlier copies. Fast-forward to today. Now you can get a free perfect digital copy of a work with a few clicks of a mouse. Within eight hours of airing, 1.5 million pirated copies of the *Game of Thrones* fifth season finale were downloaded.[4]

The creators of books, movies, music, and other entertainment are interested in DRM for more than the prevention of unauthorized copying. They also see DRM as a way to stop other people from changing their works or using them in ways the creator did not intend.

Artistic Control

The protection United States law gives to content creators is known as copyright law. This law gives the creator the exclusive right to reproduce a work, create derivative works (such as translating into a different language, creating a trailer for a movie, or adapting a novel into a movie),[5] distribute copies of a work for sale to the public, or perform or display a work publicly.[6] This is an economic right that can be transferred, wholly or partially, from one person or organization to another.[7]

Many European countries, however, observe an additional idea of control over a work, called *moral rights*, which is a collection of rights that ensures the content's authenticity and protects exploitation of the original artist's vision. Unlike the rights granted under copyright, moral rights cannot be transferred. No matter who officially owns the copyright in a work, the moral rights remain with the original creator. Moral rights are divided into the right of attribution (the right to be recognized as the work's creator), the right of disclosure (the right to decide when and how a work is released), and the right of integrity (the right to prevent a work from being changed without the creator's approval).[8]

Although moral rights have much stronger protection in Europe, the concept has started to make inroads in the United States. In 1990, Congress passed the Visual Artists Rights Act, which grants limited moral rights to creators of "visual art" (defined as a limited-edition painting, drawing, print, sculpture, or photograph).[9] Even though there is not much official legal protection for moral rights in the United States, many people have voiced support for an expansion of its protections.[10]

Just as the Internet has made it much easier to copy a work, it has also simplified the process of altering a work against an artist's will, which violates that artist's moral rights. Kris Straub, author of the web comic *chainsawsuit*, posted an example of a comic he created that was altered to change the comic's meaning and to remove any attribution to Straub. The altered version of the comic was shared ten times more than the original.[11] In the 2000s, movie studios sued companies that sold "clean" versions of the filmmakers' movies. Customers, usually members of the public, would send a DVD of the original movie they bought to a "clean" movie company to have objectionable material, such as profanity, nudity, or violence, edited or covered up. The filmmakers won in court, but then Congress passed the Family Movie Act of 2005,[12] which allowed the sale of equipment and software that can temporarily edit or remove scenes from motion pictures being viewed at home.[13] Now, members of the public can buy DVD/Blu-ray players from companies such as ClearPlay[14] that create "clean" versions of movies on the fly, or install a filter that "cleans" streaming movies.

Violations of copyright law and moral rights drove the need for a new solution to protect content creators and owners. DRM is the perceived solution. But how does it work?

HOW DIGITAL RIGHTS MANAGEMENT WORKS

DRM crafts the relationship between the digital content owner and user. It can be interjected at the very outset by controlling how the content is accessed or during the transfer and use of the content. The following discusses the various means content owners use to control access and use of content.

Access Control

DRM works through a variety of *access controls*. Access control limits the ways a user obtains access to a work. There are several methods content owners can use to control who can access a digital copy, and what users can do with a digital copy to which they have access. Owners may opt to use one of these methods or to combine multiple methods.

Permission Management

The first form of access control restricts how a work is used by *limiting who has permission* to use it. Makers of computer programs may issue *software licenses and keys* that are required in order for the program to work. The key usually takes the form of an alphanumeric code the user has to enter before the program will run. The computer then authenticates the key with the manufacturer via the Internet. Other times, the manufacturer asks the user to make a phone call. Much of Microsoft's software uses this form of DRM.

Another type of permission management is *user authentication*, technology that ensures that the person reading, viewing, or using the product is really the person who is supposed to have access to it, either through purchase or belonging to an identified class of users. There are traditionally three ways to authenticate a user. The first method is described as "something you know," which is usually a password or question based on your unique personal history such as what street you grew up on or the name of your first pet. For library users, it is often their library card number and related PIN that provide access to the subscription database. Next is "something you have," such as a cell phone to which the software maker will text an access code. The third method is "something you are," which might be a fingerprint or retinal scan.[15]

Many libraries use *IP authentication* as their "something you are." Internet Protocol (IP) addresses are like mailing addresses for computers and other devices on the Internet. IP addresses are often tied to physical locations as well, so a person can tell what part of the world you are in by looking at your computer's IP address. Many database companies will work with libraries to identify and automatically authenticate the IP addresses of the library's computers. This allows anyone trying to access the databases from computers with those authenticated IP addresses to automatically access and use the database without having to enter a user ID and password. If a library wants its users to be able to use a database even if the users are not physically there, the library can use a *proxy server* or a *virtual private network* (VPN). The library's users log in to the proxy server or VPN using an ID and/or password (such as their library card number), and the proxy server or VPN makes it look as if the user is accessing the database from the library's IP address (i.e., a computer located in the library).

Another type of permission management is a *regional restriction* (also known as *geoblocking*). Many entertainment companies have the contractual right to sell a movie, TV show, or book only in certain parts of the world. Regional restrictions are added to digital content to ensure that only those users living within the identified region can access and view the content. When you log in to Netflix, they will check the IP address that your computer is using. If that address is not from the United States, Netflix will not allow you to access their streaming videos.[16] The DVD Consortium, a group of ten companies (Hitachi, JVC, Matsushita, Mitsubishi, Philips, Pioneer, Sony, Thomson, Time Warner, and Toshiba) that created the DVD standard,[17] divided the world into seven regions. The United States is in Region 1, Japan and Europe in Region 2, and so on. Most DVDs and DVD players are encoded with the region they are connected to, so a DVD player sold in Region 1 cannot play a DVD sold in Region 2.[18]

A content producer can also design its product so that it will only work on *specialized hardware or software*. Video game consoles, such as the PlayStation and Xbox, are examples of specialized hardware. Bloomberg terminals, specialized computers rented from Bloomberg in order to access Bloomberg's financial reporting service, are another example of this access control. In the alternative, a library can install software on their computers instead of a renting a standalone terminal, but the software needed to access the content is available only from Bloomberg.

Permission management can also come in the form of *tethered content*, also referred to as *trusted computing*. Tethered content scrambles the e-book, movie, or other work so that the content can only be unscrambled by a key attached to a specific device. A program, for example, would only run on a specific computer with a specific serial number.[19]

Content creators have experimented with *disposable media*. One of the earlier efforts reflecting this technology was DIVX, spearheaded by the now defunct Circuit City. DIVX video discs (which have no relation to the DivX video format that exists today) had to be played in special disc players. Once a person began playing a DIVX disc, it deactivated forty-eight hours later unless the user called a billing center to reactivate the disc.[20] Vendors of e-books used by libraries, such as OverDrive, use a variation of this technology. When a library patron checks out an e-book using OverDrive, the e-book effectively self-destructs at the end of the checkout period, disappearing from the patron's account and becoming unreadable by the patron's devices unless renewed. [21]

Copy Protection

DRM also operates through *copy protection*, which prevents the user from making a copy of a work. One of the more commonly encountered forms of copy protection is *encryption*. The digital content is written in a code that can only be read by devices or software with the proper key to unlock the code. DRM often uses a form of encryption called *scrambling*, in which the key to decrypting the content is hardwired into the computer or device that reads the content. [22] Often, people will use the terms *encryption* and *scrambling* interchangeably. The copy protection on DVDs and Blu-ray discs is an example of scrambling. Encryption is frequently used to disable copying features, because the key to decode the encryption often only lets the user make a limited number of copies or prohibits copying completely. User authentication technology often accompanies encryption to make sure that the device attempting to play the content is using a legitimate key to unlock the code.

Another method content makers use to protect against copying is by *disabling or restricting copying features* or *copy equipment*. The DRM that Sony previously placed on its music CDs used this method of access control. This DRM came in the form of a "rootkit," software that hides itself on the computer so that a user will not notice it through ordinary processes. Sony's rootkit installed a program that allowed the user to burn a copy of a disc a maximum of three times. [23]

Instead of using technology that prevents copying, content makers sometimes use *digital watermarks*. Just as a traditional watermark design on a piece of paper is only visible when you hold the paper up to the light, a digital watermark is a file or piece of computer code that the everyday user is unlikely to notice. On the other hand, a person looking for the watermark to verify legitimate use, such as the content maker, will know where to find it. If a content maker uses digital watermarking, usually each copy of a work sold gets a unique watermark. That way, if a program or movie shows up illegally on the Internet, the content owner will know the exact copy of the work that was used to create the illegal copy or copies. Content makers sometimes make the watermarks more obvious. Movie and TV producers often send screener DVDs to the people who vote on the Oscar and Emmy Awards. When playing one of these screener discs, words will appear on the screen notifying the viewer that they are watching a copy of the disc intended for use by award judges only, along with an ID number that is tied to a specific screener recipient. Although it does not prohibit or disable the playing of the content, there is the hope that the notice, which will also be embedded in any illegally created copies, will discourage reproduction and distribution.

While watermarking adds something extra to the content to make it easy to identify the origin of the illegal copy, *fingerprinting* seeks to identify copies by using aspects of a work such as a song's rhythm and tempo, or the colors and hues used in a movie, to create unique identifiers.[24] YouTube's Content ID system is an example of fingerprinting.[25]

As you can see, there are a number of different options available to content owners if they want to include DRM in their product, and those options have the support of the law if someone tries to circumvent them. But what do these technologies look like in everyday life?

DIGITAL RIGHTS MANAGEMENT LIBRARIANS OFTEN ENCOUNTER

DRM is an everyday presence for many people, especially librarians. Whether enjoying entertainment at home or helping patrons access information at work, librarians regularly encounter numerous examples of DRM.

DVDs and Blu-ray Discs

Commercially produced DVDs and Blu-ray discs include DRM. DVDs use a technology called Content Scramble System (CSS), which combines user authentication and disabling of copying with scrambling. A DVD encoded with CSS has a list of keys that are used to unlock the code. The DVD then compares its list of keys with the key the DVD player is using. If the player's key is on the list of valid keys, the DVD plays.[26]

Blu-ray discs have several types of DRM. Advanced Access Content System (AACS) works much the same way as CSS by encrypting the content on the disc and authenticating the user.[27] Cinavia technology acts as a digital watermark.[28] High-Bandwidth Digital Content Protection (HDCP) is an added form of user authentication. A DVD player with a proper key to decode CSS can play the disc on any monitor or TV set, but a Blu-ray player with the right key to decode HDCP must be attached to a TV or monitor that also has a valid HDCP code. Otherwise, the Blu-ray player deliberately downgrades the resolution of the playback.[29]

E-books and Online Journals

DRM appears in many e-books and online subscription journals. With e-books, it often takes the form of specialized hardware and software. Reading a book in Amazon's AZW or KF8 formats requires a Kindle standalone e-reader, Amazon's Kindle program for computers, or Amazon's web browser plugin.[30] Apple's iBooks are protected by Apple's FairPlay technology; iBooks can only be read on Apple devices.[31]

Adobe's Portable Document Format (PDF) is a file format that can be created and read by a variety of programs and devices, but Adobe also has a format called Digital Editions that uses DRM called ADEPT (Adobe Digital Experience Protection Technology). ADEPT combines specialized software with user authentication and watermarking so that a person can install Digital Editions on different devices and read an e-book on all of them as long as they log in with the user ID connected to the book.[32]

DRM is embedded in journal articles in subscription databases such as EBSCO or Elsevier, as well as articles from the *New York Times*'s website. Some databases watermark articles that users download, and they often employ a form of user authentication. NYTimes.com makes you create a user ID and password to confirm you are a subscriber entitled to read all the articles on the website or a nonsubscriber who can only read a certain number of articles per month. If someone does not want to log in, NYTimes.com might use some other way to identify them, such as adding a cookie (a small file) to the browser that lets the website know who the user is and how many articles they have read. Databases designed with institutional access in mind, such as EBSCOHost or Elsevier's ScienceDirect, often use IP authentication.

Software

Software comes wrapped in DRM. Sometimes the DRM is placed there by its maker, such as when Microsoft requires you to agree to a user license and input a key in order to install Windows or Office. Sometimes the DRM is added by a distributor. Valve Software's Steam is a program users install on their computer that acts as a distribution system for game software made by numerous companies, not just Valve. Steam acts as encryption and user authentication, only allowing someone to access and run the games it installs when the user is logged in as the purchaser of those games. Steam also acts as specialized software DRM. If Steam is not installed, the game it installed won't run.[33] Apple uses specialized hardware and user authentication DRM for its iOS devices, such as the iPad and iPhone. If someone wants to use an app for an iOS device, they must install it through Apple's App Store, which requires them to log in with their Apple ID.[34]

Makers of software for video game consoles use several DRM techniques to protect their programs. The console is a classic example of specialized hardware. For example, PlayStation game discs only work on a PlayStation. Sony, Microsoft, and Nintendo also have online stores where you can purchase digital copies of games. These stores employ user identification much like Steam or Apple's App Store; you must log in with your user ID in order to play games you purchased with that ID.[35]

Sometimes, software with DRM will play on as many devices as you like. As long as you have the physical game disc, a Sony PlayStation game will play on any PlayStation console anywhere. As long as you are logged into your Steam account, you can install and play any games you have purchased through that ID.

Other times, the DRM will limit the number of computers or devices on which you can use the software. A specific PlayStation Network user ID can only install downloaded games on a capped number of different PlayStation consoles. Microsoft software keys only work for a specific number of installs before you have to contact Microsoft to ask permission for additional installs.

Streaming Audio and Video

Streaming audio and video services such as Spotify, Netflix, and Hulu are becoming very popular with the general public. Libraries are also subscribing to video streaming services, such as Hoopla, Swank, and Kanopy, in order to provide TV programs and movies for their patrons. More and more people are willing to pay a monthly subscription fee for a large collection of music, TV shows, or movies instead of paying piece by piece to buy individual works. Even YouTube, which allows free access to most of its videos, has a system called Content ID[36] that acts as fingerprinting DRM, as well as Encrypted Media Extensions (EMEs), plugins that allow the website to attach DRM to streaming media and prevent someone from downloading a copy of a video to their computer's hard drive.[37]

Many streaming services contain user authentication and encryption technology to prevent users from downloading and saving a copy of streamed content, only allow a download that lasts for a limited amount of time, or make sure that only subscribers can access the shows or the music. Many streaming sites use Microsoft's Silverlight, DRM that can prevent audio/video streams from being saved to a computer or deactivate permissible downloads after a specified period of time unless the content provider extends the user's access.[38] Microsoft has stopped developing and supporting Silverlight,[39] but other forms of DRM are stepping in to take its place. The World Wide Web Consortium, the primary organization that sets standards for the World Wide Web, recently released recommended standards for HTML5.[40] HTML5 is the latest version of Hypertext Markup Language, the computer language that forms the backbone of websites. One of the features of HTML5 is the ability to add EMEs. Many apps that play media on Android or Apple iOS devices also include proprietary DRM to prevent the user from copying content and to stop unauthorized users from accessing the audio/video stream.[41] Adobe has also created DRM technology called PrimeTime that works in much the same way as Silverlight.[42]

Whether using a database for research, reading an e-book, or watching a video, today's librarian encounters many forms of DRM. But why is it so popular among content owners today? What are the reasons for including DRM in so many products?

ARGUMENTS IN SUPPORT OF DIGITAL RIGHTS MANAGEMENT

Content creators and content owners argue that DRM is vital to protect the rights granted to them by law to control how content is sold, copied, repurposed, modified, and publicly performed. In the United States, the Constitution gives Congress the authority to create copyright law to grant authors "for limited Times . . . the exclusive Right to their respective Writings" in order "to promote the Progress of Science and Useful Arts."[43] U.S. copyright law gives copyright owners several exclusive rights,[44] which they can transfer to others. DRM provides copyright holders with an additional set of tools to limit access to their works and prevent the violation of their copyright.

First and Third Exclusive Rights

> (1) "to reproduce the copyrighted work in copies or phonorecord" and (3) "to distribute copies or phonorecords of the copyrighted work to the public by sale or other transfer of ownership, or by rental, lease, or lending"[45]

From its inception, copyright law's primary function has been to prevent the unauthorized reproduction, or copying, of protected works by imposing civil and criminal penalties on those who violate this exclusive right.[46] The ability to create high-quality, perfect digital reproductions of creative works that will not degrade in quality as these copies are shared has led to a boom in piracy compared to the level of copying that existed when things were done mechanically or with analog technologies.[47] With the proliferation of software copying in the 1980s and 1990s, followed by the advent of peer-to-peer file sharing services such as Napster that led to rampant unauthorized audio MP3 and video file distribution in the 2000s, it seems that the penalties contained in the Copyright Act are not a sufficient deterrent to preventing unauthorized copying.

The ease of copying items found on the Internet may be creating a culture in which people do not see such copying as a bad thing. A 2011 study by the American Assembly at Columbia University found that 46 percent of American adults acquired media through ways other than buying a legal copy, but that number went up to 70 percent for people age eighteen to twenty-nine. Over 70 percent of American adults in the study said that it was "reasonable" to share movies, TV shows, and music with family, while about 60 percent said the same thing about sharing those works with friends. Only

15 percent of all American adults said it was reasonable to upload pirated copies of works to websites where anyone could download them, but again that number increased to 24 percent of Americans age eighteen to twenty-nine.[48]

DRM copy protection technology provides an additional degree of deterrence by making it more difficult to engage in unauthorized copying. Just as there are a variety of ways to store physical goods securely (safe deposit box, house safe, locking the front door of your house), there are several methods of DRM that content creators can use to lock down digital versions of their works. By the same token, DRM is supported by legal penalties just as physical locks are supported by laws against burglary.

The Digital Millennium Copyright Act[49] (DMCA) adds legal weight to DRM's technological controls. The DMCA includes an *anti-circumvention provision*[50] that makes it illegal to work around any DRM measure or to make or offer to the public any technology that circumvents DRM.[51] This provision attempts to increase deterrence for digital copying by imposing hefty fines on those who successfully tamper with the technology and then make and distribute copies. The copyright holder can sue someone who violates this law and get either actual damages (including any profit the violator made) or $200 to $2,500 per violation.[52] Every three years, the Librarian of Congress creates a list of exceptions to this rule, but they are very specific (for example, allowing e-readers to read e-books aloud for people with visual impairment) and expire at the end of the three-year period if they are not renewed.[53] The Librarian of Congress released the latest list of exemptions on October 28, 2015.[54] The U.S. Copyright Office has created a web page that includes a FAQ listing all the approved exemptions, along with exemptions the public asked for but the Librarian of Congress rejected. This page also has public comments on, and transcripts of hearings about, the exemptions.[55]

DRM also allows a content owner or distributor to terminate access to a copy of a work if it is determined the copy or the user infringed copyright. In July 2009, some Kindle readers discovered that Amazon had revoked access to copies of George Orwell's *Animal Farm* and (ironically) *1984*. By 2009, Orwell's books were in the public domain in the UK but not in the United States, and the revoked books were UK editions created under public-domain rights being sold on Amazon US's Marketplace (an eBay-like area for third-party sellers) by an unauthorized dealer.[56]

Major publishers, music labels, movie studios, and software companies have been strong proponents of DRM because piracy of digital media has taken a toll on the profits of authorized distributors and copyright holders of popular creative works. The access controls provided by DRM attempt to limit the use of a work to only those authorized to do so, who are ordinarily those who have paid for access to that work, such as purchasers of FairPlay-protected audio, video, and e-book files from Apple's iTunes and iBooks stores.

It was estimated in 2013 that piracy of digital media costs the related industries $18.5 billion per year.[57] While the music and movie industries have initiated several high-profile lawsuits against the makers of DVD ripping software,[58] peer-to-peer file sharing services,[59] and individual infringers,[60] these lawsuits have resulted in a small recovery of the revenue lost due to piracy.[61] In order to "promote the Progress of Science and Useful Arts,"[62] content creators expect compensation for the use of their work, and that expectation helps encourage other potential creators to dedicate their time toward making original creative works. The threat of legal penalties under copyright law has not slowed the growth of piracy of digital media content, making DRM a more effective deterrent for unauthorized copying by placing a technological barrier between the use of content and copying.

Silicon Valley and Hollywood banded together in 2007 to launch Hulu, an ad-supported video streaming site where viewers could watch content from ABC, Fox, NBC, and several other television networks and movie studios, as a joint venture between the parent companies of those networks. Hulu content is encoded with Microsoft PlayReady DRM to prevent unauthorized saving or copying of the video streams.[63] Through this joint venture, along with many other licensed and DRM-protected streaming video and music services such as Netflix, Pandora, and Spotify, content distributors have been able to monetize the use and distribution of their content while resting assured that the content will not be copied and pirated by users of these services.

Second Exclusive Right

(2) "to prepare derivative works based upon the copyrighted work"[64]

This second exclusive right extends the copyright holder's control beyond how the original creative work is used and grants control over how later works are permitted to build on, borrow from, or modify the original work. The creation of unauthorized derivative works flouts the spirit of the moral rights that some countries have granted creators in order to protect their artistic vision from being distorted by others. Derivative works may be critical of the creator of the original work and harmful to that creator's reputation. Derivative works may also be profitable when they take advantage of the popularity of the original work to create unauthorized content appealing to consumers interested in the original work.

One of the highest-profile examples of the ease of creating a profitable derivative work from a digital original using common software is the now-iconic Barack Obama "Hope" poster created by visual artist Shepard Fairey during the 2008 presidential campaign. Fairey created the poster using an online digital photograph from Associated Press photographer Mannie Garcia. Fairey altered the photograph in Adobe Photoshop, printed it out, hand cut four layers of rubylith film using the printouts as a guide, scanned the result back into Photoshop, and then finished creating the poster in Adobe Illustrator.[65] Fairey went on to earn roughly $1 million from the poster and, in anticipation of a lawsuit from the Associated Press for copyright infringement in the creation of the derivative work, sued seeking a declaratory judgment that his poster was protected as a fair use of the original image.[66] The suit settled in 2011 for an undisclosed amount.[67]

DRM helps creators ensure that their works will be experienced in the form they intended by preventing others from making any changes to the work. DRM also prevents profitable derivative works from being created that could potentially compete with the original work and strip away part of its market share. In the absence of DRM, technology today makes the creation of a derivative work as easy as choosing "Save As" for a digital work and modifying that work in text, image, or video editing software.

Fourth, Fifth, and Sixth Exclusive Rights

> (4) "in the case of literary, musical, dramatic, and choreographic works, pantomimes, and motion pictures and other audiovisual works, to perform the copyrighted work publicly"; (5) "in the case of literary, musical, dramatic, and choreographic works, pantomimes, and pictorial, graphic, or sculptural works, including the individual images of a motion picture or other audiovisual work, to display the copyrighted work publicly"; and (6) "in the case of sound recordings, to perform the copyrighted work publicly by means of a digital audio transmission"[68]

For many creative works, such as film and dramatic works, a large portion of revenue to the copyright holder comes from the performance of those works to a paying audience rather than the sale of copies of the work. These benefits are protected by the exclusive rights to public performance and public display of particular types of work along with the exclusive right to digital audio performance.

For the film industry, the majority of profits come from box office ticket sales at movie theaters.[69] Nearly all movie theaters in the United States use digital cinema technologies to project their movies,[70] and these technologies use DRM to prevent the unauthorized use and copying of the movies. Digital cinema relies on DRM that associates a security key with both a particular movie file and the specific projector intended to display that movie to ensure that a movie file cannot be played on any other projector, even if it is the same make and model.[71] This extremely limiting form of DRM demonstrates how strict the film industry has become in order to combat the digital piracy of movie in venues where the film is intended to be publicly viewed.

In the case of the music industry, public performance of digital audio includes transmission through an online interactive music service, such as Pandora's online radio stations or Spotify's on-demand playing of individual music tracks.[72] Industry revenue from digital music sales and streams is now on par with physical music sales—the sale of CDs and vinyl records.[73] These digital audio streams are protected by DRM to ensure that the streamed music is only used in the manner licensed to the streaming service, making unauthorized transmission or copying difficult to achieve. Similar to the other exclusive rights granted to copyright holders, public performance and display rights are aided by the protection of DRM in industries where digital distribution and sales are making up an ever increasing portion of revenues, soon to become the dominant source of revenue, for the creative works that serve as the lifeblood of that industry.

Content creators and owners have several artistic and financial reasons for including DRM in digital works—reasons that are backed by copyright and moral rights laws—but many users and people in the library community oppose it. What are their reasons?

ARGUMENTS AGAINST DIGITAL RIGHTS MANAGEMENT

Most people agree that content creators and owners should be properly compensated for their work. Many also agree with the idea of protecting an artist's moral rights in their work, even if those rights are not generally protected under United States law. We would frown on someone who copied another person's work and tried to pass it off as their own, even if they didn't make any money doing it. When footage of the late Fred Astaire was photoshopped into an ad for a vacuum cleaner, many people felt it was *wrong*, even if it was legal at the time.

Even though most people agree on that point, many in the content user and librarian community believe that DRM, in its current form at least, is the wrong way to balance the rights of the content owners and users. The American Library Association[74] and digital civil liberties advocacy group Electronic Frontier Foundation[75] have advocated against DRM. Why does DRM face such strong opposition?

Fair Use

Even though the U.S. Constitution describes the right of authors to their "Writings" as an exclusive one for a limited time, American law has developed exceptions to this right in order to strike a balance between an author's private rights and the public interest. DRM threatens this balance.

One of the most well-known exceptions to copyright protection is *fair use*. Anglo-American law developed the concept of fair use so that the exclusive rights the government granted creators would not interfere with copyright's main purpose: promoting science and the useful arts. By allowing authors to excerpt, within reason, copyrighted works, those authors could build on their predecessors' efforts through commentary, criticism, and the creation of new works, adding to the body of public knowledge.[76]

Fair use is often a hard concept to clearly define. When a person is accused of infringing someone else's copyright and claims fair use, the court weighs several factors to determine if fair use applies in the situation or not. The analysis is done on a case-by-case basis; there is no simple formula to tell a person whether or not what they want to do is fair use.[77] American courts have spent many years developing a body of law that protects the rights of both creators and users.

DRM, however, skews the equation in content owners' favor. A content owner can prevent the use of material even if that use would be fair use, and there may be little the user can do about it. For example, in 2009, video remix artist Jonathan McIntosh created a video using clips from the *Twilight* movies and from *Buffy the Vampire Slayer* and posted his video to YouTube. McIntosh's video, a commentary on gender role portrayals in popular media, was specifically cited by the U.S. Copyright Office as an example of fair use worthy of protection. Nevertheless, in 2012, the movie studio that owned the rights to the *Twilight* movies, Lionsgate Pictures, used YouTube's DRM, called Content ID, to identify McIntosh's video as infringing content.

McIntosh disputed the infringement claim twice, but under YouTube's process, the copyright holder considers the disputes and appeals and decides whether to drop their infringement claim or to take down the video.[78] Lionsgate, the copyright holder, rejected McIntosh's initial dispute of the claim but later accepted his appeal, and YouTube reinstated the video. The same day McIntosh's appeal was accepted, though, Lionsgate filed a second claim that the video infringed on its copyright. Lionsgate rejected McIntosh's next dispute and appeal; YouTube pulled the video and put McIntosh's account on probation. Eventually, after McIntosh's troubles went public, YouTube restored his video without comment.[79]

McIntosh was able to get his work of fair use restored in the end, but he was a fair-use activist willing to go through considerable hassle in order to protect his rights and had the help of a nonprofit legal firm. Many other users in the same situation would likely give up and stop exercising their right of fair use. United States copyright law has a section[80] that is supposed to prevent copyright holders from ordering the removal of works that are clearly fair use. Under this section, a copyright holder can be forced to pay litigation costs if it says a work infringes their copyright but knows that it does not. In reality, however, this is hard to prove in court. In a recent case,[81] a federal appellate court said that the copyright holder does not have to thoroughly consider whether fair use applies, they just have to consider it, and the judges opined that using a computer algorithm might satisfy this need.[82]

DRM can stop the exercise of fair use before it even starts. At a hearing on May 27, 2015, officials from the U.S. Copyright Office heard the story of Janine Cook, who is the head teacher at YESPhilly, a nonprofit organization that helps young adults earn their GEDs. Cook wanted her students to use clips from various movies to create their own poetry videos for a project, as allowed under fair use, but they would have to work around the DRM on streaming videos or DVDs to do that. Had YESPhilly been a college program, it would have had a legal exemption allowing it to work around DRM on the videos. Nonprofit GED programs such as YESPhilly, however, do not have an exemption and could be fined for circumventing the DRM.[83] Later that year, the Librarian of Congress created a new exemption for nonprofit organizations such as YESPhilly,[84] but since the exemptions only last three years, organizations such as YESPhilly must rely on the continuing mercy of the Librarian of Congress to avoid returning to the same problem in the future.

Limits Users' Options

DRM effectively punishes people who own legitimate copies of a work by subjecting them to restrictions that owners of pirated copies do not face. A purchased print book comes with certain rights. A person willing to pay for a legitimate copy of the same work in digital format may find that she simply cannot replicate the print owner's rights because she owns the "wrong" e-reader or other device, lives in the wrong area, or does not have the proper Internet connection.

DRM technology often locks users into specific devices. A Nook cannot read an e-book in Kindle format. How about that audiobook you checked out from the local library? For many years, many audiobooks from libraries came from OverDrive, and most of their audiobooks came with DRM that did not let the audiobook play on Apple devices.[85]

Difficult to Use

Sometimes, DRM prevents a person from accessing content no matter how much they would be willing to pay. Regional restrictions coded into a DVD or Blu-ray disc purchased in another country can prevent it from playing on a person's player in their home. Someone who subscribes to Major League Baseball's or the National Football League's game-streaming service will find that games involving the local team are blacked out, courtesy of DRM. For example, the only way a Seattle Seahawks fan can watch their team online is if he or she does not live in the Pacific Northwest.[86] Americans who pay for a Netflix or Hulu subscription discover that regional restriction DRM prevents them from watching their subscription when traveling or living overseas.[87]

People often find that DRM makes it difficult for their device to play the content they are trying to use. Several high-profile video games come with "always-online DRM." This form of DRM requires the computer or console playing the game to have an active Internet connection to help verify that the copy of the game is legitimate. If the player's Internet connection is disrupted for a moment (a realistic possibility for most people), there is a good chance the game will stop and cause the player to lose progress made since the last save.[88]

DRM can make it difficult for a person who is not tech savvy to read or watch the material they want to borrow from the library. A person who checks out an audiobook with DRM using Overdrive might have to decode messages such as "Error:0x80070057: The parameter is incorrect"[89] or "Unable to acquire license to play selected title. The requested license is either invalid or already acquired."[90] A user who is fairly comfortable with troubleshooting technology can easily search the web to find a solution to the error messages, but errors such as these add an extra barrier to users who are less adept at solving technology issues. A web comic called *The Brads* illustrates these problems nicely; the solution the comic comes up with implies that the best way to handle DRM is to avoid it.[91]

Can Be Harmful

DRM can do more than just annoy users. In some cases, DRM can pose a threat to the users' devices. Sony BMG added a rootkit DRM to its CDs in 2004. This rootkit installed a music player and software that would only allow a computer to play the CD using that music player. This software also limited the computer to making three copies of the CD.

In addition to the copy restrictions, though, the rootkit put the user's computer at serious risk. It took over some of a computer's most important processes so that antivirus software cannot detect it. Sony's rootkit, called XCP, was poorly written and created security holes in the computers on which it was installed.[92] At least three different viruses were created to take advantage of these security holes.[93]

Even if the user decided not to play Sony BMG CDs on their computer anymore, XCP made itself very difficult to remove. The rootkit did not display as an entry in the Add/Remove Programs menu, nor did the CD come with a program to uninstall XCP. A user could not remove it through the usual procedures. If a user tried more advanced techniques to remove the rootkit, it would damage the operating system, potentially rendering the CD drive unusable and requiring the user to reinstall the operating system.[94] Sony BMG eventually provided a tool to uninstall XCP, but that tool created a new security vulnerability.[95] By November 2005, Sony BMG stopped including XCP on its CDs, and Microsoft identified it as spyware.[96] As security expert Bruce Schneier put it, "the only thing that [made] this rootkit legitimate is that a multinational corporation put it on your computer, not a criminal organization."[97]

License, not Ownership

Along with making it difficult to use the content they have paid for and potentially damaging a user's equipment, DRM prevents a user from truly owning the copy of the purchased content. At best, a user has bought a license to use the content for as long as the content owner is willing and able to provide it.

As discussed above with the Kindle versions of Orwell's *Animal Farm* and *1984*, a content owner or distributor can revoke access to a copy of a work that a user has purchased. Although in this case Amazon had a legal reason for removing these copies of Orwell's books, Amazon could have just as easily revoked access to any other book. The only thing stopping them is the Kindle terms of service, which Amazon has the right to change at any time.

In 2013, a purchaser of Disney streaming video through Amazon later discovered that Amazon revoked his access to the video at Disney's request. Disney, it turned out, wanted to distribute the video exclusively through its own channels during the holiday season. Amazon restored the purchaser's access to the video after the media reported on it, but it seems as if this action was at its discretion. The terms of service for buying streaming videos from Amazon noted that the purchaser had no recourse if they lost access to the video because Amazon's license to sell it expired.[98]

DRM's ability to create self-destructing copies of a work means that libraries may now find themselves paying repeatedly for the same book. E-books that HarperCollins sells to libraries now come with a DRM-enforced twenty-six-loan cap. If a library wants to lend the book out more than twenty-six times, it has to buy another copy.[99]

Even if the user's license does not have an explicit cap on how long the user can access a copy, a change in the content owner's DRM technology can leave the user with a useless collection of bits and bytes. Boston Red Sox fan Allan Wood bought several hundred dollars' worth of videos from MLB.com (Major League Baseball's online video service), then one day discovered that his videos became unplayable because MLB.com changed the company that provided their DRM. MLB.com's initial response was that the videos were onetime sales—no refunds. Wood, of course, was free to buy the videos again if he wanted to watch them. MLB.com later changed their stance and allowed Wood and other affected customers to redownload the videos for free, but MLB.com was under no obligation to do so. [100]

A licensor of DRM-protected content can also lose access to their copies if the content owner goes out of business. JManga was a website launched by several Japanese publishers to provide legitimate, online English-language translations of manga (Japanese graphic novels). JManga's DRM required users to access the manga using JManga's website; users could not download copies to their local device. The website closed less than two years after it began, and customers lost all access to the manga they had purchased with no refunds. [101]

User Privacy

Along with the restrictions it places on a user's access to purchased content, DRM also has the potential to intrude on a user's privacy. Adobe's Digital Editions DRM keeps track of what books a user has downloaded, how long a user has read a particular book, how far in a book the user has progressed, and where the user is reading that book and sends that information back to Adobe. Additionally, in 2014, users learned that Adobe was transmitting this information unencrypted over the Internet, where it could be easily intercepted. [102] Adobe promised to encrypt the data in the future, but that still leaves a lot of information about reading habits in one location where it could potentially be improperly used or even subpoenaed in a legal action.

DRM restricts customers' ability to exercise their full legal rights to use copies they have legitimately purchased. It turns purchasers from owners into licensors at the content owner's pleasure, potentially harms their devices, and invades their privacy. These circumstances have led many users and librarians to resist DRM.

CONCLUSION

Technological advances make it easy for artists to reach audiences they could have only reached in previous eras with great difficulty. On the other hand, that same technology makes it easier to make unauthorized copies of artists' works, whether pure copies or modified versions. DRM is one of the tools artists, content owners, and content distributors use to reduce unauthorized access, copying, and distribution, but it is a tool that comes with substantial costs to the end users of that content. The debate over DRM is an important one, and we hope you find this book a useful guide to the technology and its use.

NOTES

1. Potts, Holden, and Dobruse, "Fracturing Digital Entertainment," 143.
2. Baldwin, *Copyright Wars*, 112–22.
3. Library of Congress, "History of the Cylinder Phonograph."
4. Ernesto, "Game of Thrones Season Finale."
5. Patry, *Patry on Copyright*, § 12:9.
6. Copyright Act of 1976, 17 U.S.C. § 106 (2013).
7. Patry, *Patry on Copyright*, § 5:2.
8. Baldwin, *Copyright Wars*, 15, 29–30.
9. Visual Artists Rights Act, Pub. L. No. 101-650, §§ 601–10, 104 Stat. 5089 (1990).
10. Baldwin, *Copyright Wars*, 19.
11. Straub, "On Sharing and Attribution."
12. Family Movie Act of 2005, Pub. L. No. 109-9, Title II, 119 Stat. 223 (2005).
13. Liu, "Enabling Copyright Consumers," 1107–9.
14. ClearPlay, "What Is ClearPlay."
15. Brainard et al., "Fourth-Factor Authentication," 169.
16. Turner, "There Are Ways TV-Loving Expats Can Get Around."
17. DVD Demystified, "DVD Frequently Asked Questions," 6.1.
18. Ibid., 1.10.
19. Godwin, *What Every Citizen Should Know*, 8–9.
20. Fost, "DIVX's Death Pleases Opponents."
21. OverDrive Help, "Digital Titles from Your Library Expire."
22. Godwin, *What Every Citizen Should Know*, 7–8.
23. LaBelle, "The 'Rootkit Debacle'," 92–94.
24. Godwin, *What Every Citizen Should Know*, 12.
25. Schlackman, "Google's Content ID Program."
26. DVD Demystified, "DVD Frequently Asked Questions," 1.11.
27. Advanced Access Content System, "Introduction and Common Cryptographic Elements."
28. Cinavia, "What Does Cinavia Technology Do?"
29. DVD Demystified, "DVD Frequently Asked Questions," 1.11.
30. DigitalPublishing101, "EPUB and Kindle formats explained."
31. Aimonetti, "Has Apple's iBooks Fair Play DRM Been Cracked?"
32. Adobe Digital Editions, "FAQ."
33. Valve Business Solutions, "Steamworks Publishing Services." Valve's website describes it as an alternative to DRM, but by our definition it is DRM.
34. Apple, "Mac App Store."
35. For an example, see Sony Computer Entertainment, "PlayStation Store Overview."
36. YouTube Help, "Using Content ID."
37. Doctorow, "YouTube Ditches Flash."
38. Microsoft, "Silverlight Digital Rights Management."
39. Bright, "DRM in HTML5."
40. Bright, "HTML5 Specification Finalized."
41. Bright, "DRM in HTML5."
42. Shankland, "Boosting Browsers."
43. U.S. Const. art. I, § 8, cl. 8.
44. 17 U.S.C. § 106 (2013).
45. 17 U.S.C. § 106 (1), (3) (2013).
46. Patry, *Patry on Copyright*, §§ 1:2, 1:6, 1:8, 1:17, 1:21, 1:23, 1:41, 1:45.
47. Verrier, "Online Piracy of Entertainment Content."
48. Karaganis and Renkema, *Copy Culture in the US & Germany*, 6, 30, 36.
49. Digital Millennium Copyright Act, Pub. L. No. 105-304, 112 Stat. 2860 (1998).
50. Digital Millennium Copyright Act, 17 U.S.C. § 1201 (2013).
51. Ibid.
52. Ibid., § 1203(c).

53. Ibid., § 1201(a)(C)–(D).

54. Exemption to Prohibition on Circumvention of Copyright Protection Systems for Access Control Technologies, 80 Fed. Reg. 65944 (Oct. 28, 2015) (to be codified at 37 C.F.R. 201.40).

55. Copyright.gov, "Section 1201 Exemptions."

56. Fisher, "Why Amazon Went Big Brother."

57. Bialik, "Putting a Price Tag on Film Piracy."

58. *RealNetworks, Inc. v. DVD Copy Control Ass'n, Inc.*, 641 F. Supp. 2d 913 (N.D. Cal. 2009).

59. *MGM Studios, Inc. v. Grokster, Ltd.*, 545 U.S. 913 (2005).

60. *Capitol Records, Inc. v. Thomas-Rasset*, 692 F.3d 899 (8th Cir. 2012).

61. Bangeman, "RIAA Anti-P2P Campaign a Real Money Pit."

62. U.S. Const. art. I, § 8, cl. 8.

63. Microsoft, "Approved Microsoft PlayReady Licensees."

64. 17 U.S.C. § 106(2) (2013).

65. Fisher et al., "Reflections on the Hope Poster Case," 250–52.

66. Kennedy, "Artist Sues the A.P."

67. Kennedy, "Shepard Fairey and the A.P. Settle."

68. 17 U.S.C. § 106(4), (5), (6) (2013).

69. Lang, "Digital Home Entertainment."

70. Brenneman, "Cinema Technologies."

71. MKPE Consulting, "How Digital Cinema Works."

72. 17 U.S.C. § 114 (2013).

73. International Federation of the Phonographic Industry, "Facts & Stats."

74. American Library Association, "Digital Rights Management."

75. Electronic Frontier Foundation, "DRM."

76. Patry, *Patry on Fair Use*, §§ 1:2, 1:3.

77. Ibid., §§ 2:1, 2:2.

78. YouTube Help, "Dispute a Content ID Claim."

79. Higgins, "Copyright Vampires Attempt to Suck the Lifeblood."

80. Digital Millennium Copyright Act, 17 U.S.C. § 512(f) (2013).

81. *Lenz v. Universal Music Corp.*, 801 F.3d 1126 (9th Cir. 2015).

82. Ibid., 1135. The current court amended this decision the next year, but it did not change the earlier decision's language about whether a computer algorithm would suffice for considering fair use. *Lenz v. Universal Music Corp.*, 815 F.3d 1145 (9th Cir. 2016).

83. Library of Congress, United States Copyright Office, "Sixth Triennial 1201 Rulemaking Hearings," May 27, 2015, 231–34, http://copyright.gov/1201/2015/hearing-transcripts/1201-Rulemaking-Public-Roundtable-05-27-2015.pdf, archived at http://perma.cc/R3PH-SD7R.

84. Exemption to Prohibition on Circumvention of Copyright Protection Systems for Access Control Technologies, 80 Fed. Reg. 65944, 65962 (Oct. 28, 2015) (to be codified at 37 C.F.R. 201.40(b)(1)(vi)).

85. West, "Overdrive and Audiobooks."

86. Plante, "The Best Way to Enjoy Baseball."

87. Turner, "There Are Ways TV-Loving Expats Can Get Around."

88. B, "The Video Game Industry and DRM."

89. Albuquerque and Bernalillo County Library, "Q. When I Try to Download Audiobooks."

90. OverDrive Help, "What to Do."

91. Colbow, "Why DRM Doesn't Work."

92. Schneier, "Sony's DRM Rootkit."

93. BBC News, "Viruses Use Sony Anti-piracy CDs."

94. Russinovich, "Sony, Rootkits and Digital Rights Management."

95. Schneier, "Sony's DRM Rootkit."

96. BBC News, "Microsoft to Remove Sony CD Code."

97. Schneier, "Sony's DRM Rootkit."

98. Farivar, "Can't Stream That Christmas Movie."

99. Kelley, "One Year Later."

100. Bangeman, "Major League Baseball's DRM Change."
101. MacDonald, "JManga Shuts Down."
102. Gallagher, "Adobe's E-book Reader."

REFERENCES

Adobe Digital Editions. "FAQ." http://www.adobe.com/solutions/ebook/digital-editions/faq.html. Archived at http://perma.cc/ZU4N-H25V.

Advanced Access Content System. "Introduction and Common Cryptographic Elements." February 17, 2006. http://www.aacsla.com/specifications/specs091/AACS_Spec_Common_0.91.pdf. Archived at http://perma.cc/Y9RB-SNJ7.

Aimonetti, Joe. "Has Apple's iBooks Fair Play DRM Been Cracked?" CNET, February 24, 2012. http://www.cnet.com/news/has-apples-ibooks-fair-play-drm-been-cracked/. Archived at http://perma.cc/EDB7-3ADG.

Albuquerque and Bernalillo County Library. "Q. When I Try to Download Audiobooks with Overdrive Media Console I Get the Message 'Error:0x80070057: The Parameter Is Incorrect.' Can You Help?" December 18, 2014. http://libanswers.abclibrary.org/downloads/faq/27987. Archived at http://perma.cc/W8UF-9FAD.

American Library Association. "Digital Rights Management (DRM) & Libraries." http://www.ala.org/advocacy/copyright/digitalrights. Archived at http://perma.cc/5DP7-D3J7.

Apple. "Mac App Store, App Store, and iBooks Terms and Conditions." http://www.apple.com/legal/internet-services/itunes/us/terms.html#APPS. Archived at http://perma.cc/85WG-KU8P.

Association of Research Libraries. "Copyright Timeline: A History of Copyright in the United States." http://www.arl.org/focus-areas/copyright-ip/2486-copyright-timeline. Archived at http://perma.cc/RZ2H-E4H9.

B, Ryan. "The Video Game Industry and DRM—Time for a Change." *Yale Law & Technology*, March 18, 2010. http://www.yalelawtech.org/ip-in-the-digital-age/the-video-game-industry-and-drm-time-for-a-change/. Archived at http://perma.cc/W284-QCLF.

Baldwin, Peter. *The Copyright Wars: Three Centuries of Trans-Atlantic Battle.* Princeton, NJ: Princeton University Press, 2014.

Bangeman, Eric. "Major League Baseball's DRM Change Strikes Out with Fans." *Ars Technica*, November 7, 2007. http://arstechnica.com/uncategorized/2007/11/major-league-baseballs-drm-change-strikes-out-with-fans/. Archived at http://perma.cc/Q67E-WQ54.

———. "RIAA Anti-P2P Campaign a Real Money Pit, according to Testimony." *Ars Technica*, October 2, 2007. http://arstechnica.com/tech-policy/2007/10/music-industry-exec-p2p-litigation-is-a-money-pit/. Archived at http://perma.cc/8NHB-9VTJ.

BBC News. "Microsoft to Remove Sony CD Code." November 14, 2005. http://news.bbc.co.uk/2/hi/technology/4434852.stm. Archived at http://perma.cc/B3AM-RKVW.

———. "Viruses Use Sony Anti-Piracy CDs." November 11, 2005. http://news.bbc.co.uk/2/hi/technology/4427606.stm. Archived at http://perma.cc/EFL6-QJH2.

Bialik, Carl. "Putting a Price Tag on Film Piracy." *Wall Street Journal*, April 5, 2013. http://blogs.wsj.com/numbers/putting-a-price-tag-on-film-piracy-1228/. Archived at http://perma.cc/6P6L-SVDT.

Brainard, John, Ari Juels, Ronald L. Rivest, Michael Szydlo, and Moti Yung. "Fourth-Factor Authentication: Somebody You Know." In *CCS '06: Proceedings of the 13th ACM Conference on Computer and Communications Security*, 168–78 New York: ACM, 2006. doi:10.1145/1180405.1180427.

Brenneman, Jackie. "Cinema Technologies." National Association of Theater Owners, March 31, 2015. http://natoonline.org/initiatives/cinema-technologies/. Archived at http://perma.cc/3X65-FY3Y.

Bright, Peter. "DRM in HTML5 Is a Victory for the Open Web, not a Defeat." *Ars Technica*, May 10, 2013. http://arstechnica.com/business/2013/05/drm-in-html5-is-a-victory-for-the-open-web-not-a-defeat/. Archived at http://perma.cc/F4UK-EUCR.

————. "HTML5 Specification Finalized, Squabbling over Specs Continues." *Ars Technica*, October 28, 2014. http://arstechnica.com/information-technology/2014/10/html5-specification-finalized-squabbling-over-who-writes-the-specs-continues/. Archived at http://perma.cc/TAV5-4SCG.

Cinavia. "What Does Cinavia Technology Do?" http://www.cinavia.com/languages/english/pages/technology.html. Archived at http://perma.cc/4EFQ-E95G.

ClearPlay. "What Is ClearPlay." https://www.clearplay.com/t-about2.aspx. Archived at https://perma.cc/NZF3-SZYB.

Colbow, Brad. "Why DRM Doesn't Work." *The Brads*, March 1, 2010. http://bradcolbow.com/archive/view/the_brads_why_drm_doesnt_work/?p=205. Archived at http://perma.cc/YB6M-YK74.

Copyright.gov. "Section 1201 Exemptions to Prohibition against Circumvention of Technological Measures Protecting Copyrighted Works." http://copyright.gov/1201/. Archived at http://perma.cc/6EK4-EGC8.

DigitalPublishing101. "EPUB and Kindle formats explained." http://digitalpublishing101.com/digital-publishing-101/digital-publishing-basics/epub-kindle-formats/. Archived at https://perma.cc/8AH6-BQ3G.

Doctorow, Cory. "YouTube Ditches Flash, and It Hardly Matters: Meet the New Boss, Same as the Old Boss." Electronic Frontier Foundation, February 6, 2015. http://www.eff.org/deeplinks/2015/01/new-drm-boss-same-old-boss. Archived at http://perma.cc/EPK8-Y886.

DVD Demystified. "DVD Frequently Asked Questions (and Answers)." http://www.dvddemystified.com/dvdfaq.html. Archived at http://perma.cc/9LN5-HYQG.

Electronic Frontier Foundation. "DRM." https://www.eff.org/issues/drm. Archived at https://perma.cc/YBB4-S4B4.

Ernesto. "Game of Thrones Season Finale Breaks Piracy Records." *TorrentFreak*, June 15, 2015, http://torrentfreak.com/game-of-thrones-season-finale-breaks-piracy-record-150615/. Archived at http://perma.cc/8FM8-27ER.

Farivar, Cyrus. "Can't Stream That Christmas Movie You 'Bought' on Amazon? Blame Disney." *Ars Technica*, December 16, 2013. http://arstechnica.com/business/2013/12/cant-stream-that-christmas-movie-you-bought-on-amazon-blame-disney/. Archived at http://perma.cc/DS3U-BRV5.

Fisher, Ken. "Why Amazon Went Big Brother on Some Kindle E-books." *Ars Technica*, July 17, 2009. http://arstechnica.com/gadgets/2009/07/amazon-sold-pirated-books-raided-some-kindles/. Archived at http://perma.cc/9WAE-WF43.

Fisher, William W., III, Frank Cost, Shepard Fairey, Meir Feder, Edwin Fountain, Geoffrey Stewart, and Marita Sturken. "Reflections on the Hope Poster Case." *Harvard Journal of Law & Technology* 25, no. 1 (Fall 2012): 243–338.

Fost, Dan. "DIVX's Death Pleases Opponents." *SFGate*, June 18, 1999. http://www.sfgate.com/business/article/Divx-s-Death-Pleases-Opponents-2924407.php. Archived at http://perma.cc/XH66-6R6M.

Gallagher, Sean. "Adobe's E-book Reader Sends Your Reading Logs Back to Adobe—in Plain Text." *Ars Technica*, October 7, 2014. http://arstechnica.com/security/2014/10/adobes-e-book-reader-sends-your-reading-logs-back-to-adobe-in-plain-text/. Archived at http://perma.cc/J9AU-5YQJ.

Godwin, Mike. *What Every Citizen Should Know about DRM, a.k.a. "Digital Rights Management."* Washington, DC: Public Knowledge and New America Foundation, 2004. https://www.publicknowledge.org/pdf/citizens_guide_to_drm.pdf. Archived at https://perma.cc/SK7H-ET8G.

Higgins, Parker. "Copyright Vampires Attempt to Suck the Lifeblood out of Fair Use Video." Electronic Frontier Foundation, January 10, 2013. https://www.eff.org/deeplinks/2013/01/copyright-vampires-attempt-suck-lifeblood-out-fair-use-video. Archived at http://perma.cc/9EL3-DZQ9.

International Federation of the Phonographic Industry. "Facts & Stats." http://www.ifpi.org/facts-and-stats.php. Archived at http://perma.cc/58P8-L3N9.

Karaganis, Joe, and Lennart Renkema. *Copy Culture in the US & Germany.* New York: American Assembly, 2013. http://piracy.americanassembly.org/wp-content/uploads/2013/01/Copy-Culture.pdf. Archived at http://perma.cc/UP45-UUMQ.

Kelley, Michael. "One Year Later, HarperCollins Sticking to 26-Loan Cap, and Some Librarians Rethink Opposition." *Digital Shift,* February 17, 2012. http://www.thedigitalshift.com/2012/02/ebooks/one-year-later-harpercollins-sticking-to-26-loan-cap-and-some-librarians-rethink-opposition/. Archived at http://perma.cc/B4JZ-D2AM.

Kennedy, Randy. "Artist Sues the A.P. over Obama Image." *New York Times,* February 2, 2009. http://www.nytimes.com/2009/02/10/arts/design/10fair.html. Archived at http://perma.cc/2AS9-34YS.

———. "Shepard Fairey and the A.P. Settle Legal Dispute." *New York Times,* January 12, 2011. http://www.nytimes.com/2011/01/13/arts/design/13fairey.html. Archived at https://perma.cc/KR93-VRBL.

LaBelle, Megan M. "The 'Rootkit Debacle': The Latest Chapter in the Story of the Recording Industry and the War on Music Piracy." *Denver University Law Review* 84 (2006): 79–134.

Lang, Brent. "Digital Home Entertainment to Exceed Physical by 2016, Study Finds." *Variety,* June 3, 2014. http://variety.com/2014/digital/news/digital-home-entertainment-to-exceed-physical-by-2016-study-finds-1201207708/. Archived at http://perma.cc/96WV-WU4S.

Library of Congress. "History of the Cylinder Phonograph." *Inventing Entertainment: The Early Motion Pictures and Sound Recordings of the Edison Companies.* http://www.loc.gov/collections/edison-company-motion-pictures-and-sound-recordings/articles-and-essays/history-of-edison-sound-recordings/history-of-the-cylinder-phonograph/. Archived at http://perma.cc/K7ZT-M6QY.

Liu, Joseph P. "Enabling Copyright Consumers." *Berkeley Technology Law Journal* 22 (2007): 1099–1118.

MacDonald, Heidi. "JManga Shuts Down, Taking All the Manga You Bought with It." *The Beat,* March 14, 2013. http://www.comicsbeat.com/jmanga-shuts-down-taking-all-the-manga-you-bought-with-it/. Archived at http://perma.cc/794K-BQT3.

Microsoft. "Approved Microsoft PlayReady Licensees." https://www.microsoft.com/playready/licensing/list/, archived at https://perma.cc/X36S-6TEW.

———. "Silverlight Digital Rights Management." http://msdn.microsoft.com/en-us/subscriptions/cc838192%28v=vs.95%29.aspx. Archived at http://perma.cc/PHR9-DMFV.

MKPE Consulting. "How Digital Cinema Works." http://mkpe.com/digital_cinema/works/dc_technology4.php. Archived at http://perma.cc/L3SG-LMEP.

OverDrive Help. "Digital Titles from Your Library Expire at the End of the Lending Period." May 20, 2015. http://help.overdrive.com/customer/portal/articles/1483894-digital-titles-from-your-library-expire-at-the-end-of-the-lending-period. Archived at http://perma.cc/E4AN-ZE5D.

———. "What to Do If You Get an 'Unable to Acquire License' Error in OverDrive's Desktop App." October 2, 2015. http://help.overdrive.com/customer/portal/articles/1481126-what-to-do-if-you-get-an-%22unable-to-acquire-license%22-error-in-overdrive-s-desktop-app. Archived at http://perma.cc/9MSN-2AD6.

Patry, William F. *Patry on Copyright.* St. Paul, MN: Thomson/West, 2015.

———. *Patry on Fair Use.* St. Paul, MN: Thomson/West, 2015.

Plante, Chris. "The Best Way to Enjoy Baseball Is to Live Far Away from Your Favorite Team." *Verge,* July 1, 2015. http://www.theverge.com/2015/7/1/8872659/mlb-tv-nfl-sunday-ticket-sports-streaming-apps. Archived at http://perma.cc/UPD9-C2AE.

Potts, Liza, Dean Holden, and Katie Dobruse. "Fracturing Digital Entertainment by Kindling Rivalries and Blowing Steam." In *Cultures of Copyright,* edited by Dànielle Nicole DeVoss and Martine Courant Rife, 140–53. New York: Peter Lang, 2015.

Russinovich, Mark. "Sony, Rootkits and Digital Rights Management Gone Too Far." *Mark's Blog,* October 31, 2005. http://blogs.technet.com/b/markrussinovich/archive/2005/10/31/sony-rootkits-and-digital-rights-management-gone-too-far.aspx. Archived at http://perma.cc/UV69-N78J.

Schlackman, Steve. "Google's Content ID Program Allows Infringements on YouTube." *Art Law Journal*, October 26, 2014. http://artlawjournal.com/googles-content-id-program-infringements-youtube/. Archived at http://perma.cc/9P28-ZVSX.

Schneier, Bruce. "Sony's DRM Rootkit: The Real Story." *Schneier on Security*, November 17, 2005. http://www.schneier.com/blog/archives/2005/11/sonys_drm_rootk.html. Archived at http://perma.cc/44HB-AF72.

Shankland, Stephen. "Boosting Browsers, Adobe Extends Its DRM to Web Video." CNET, September 8, 2014. http://www.cnet.com/news/boosting-browsers-adobe-extends-its-drm-to-web-video/. Archived at http://perma.cc/5BVG-XUUQ.

Sony Computer Entertainment. "PlayStation Store Overview." http://manuals.playstation.net/document/en/ps3/current/store/store.html. Archived at http://perma.cc/RA4X-CLEU.

Straub, Kris. "On Sharing and Attribution." *chainsawsuit*, December 11, 2012. http://chainsawsuit.com/2012/12/11/on-sharing-and-attribution/. Archived at http://perma.cc/G6QT-4X2F.

Turner, Taos. "There Are Ways TV-Loving Expats Can Get around the Dreaded 'Geo-Block.'" *Wall Street Journal Expat*, April 14, 2015. http://blogs.wsj.com/expat/2015/04/14/firms-circumvent-geo-blocking-helping-expats-watch-favorite-shows-abroad/. Archived at http://perma.cc/5MS2-AEZM.

Valve Business Solutions. "Steamworks Publishing Services." http://www.steampowered.com/steamworks/publishingservices.php. Archived at http://perma.cc/7BE4-S5HE.

Verrier, Richard. "Online Piracy of Entertainment Content Keeps Soaring." *Los Angeles Times*, September 23, 2013. http://articles.latimes.com/print/2013/sep/17/business/la-fi-ct-piracy-bandwith-20130917. Archived at http://perma.cc/D594-6Y8V.

West, Jessamyn. "Overdrive and Audiobooks and the Pervasive iPod." *librarian.net*, August 17, 2007. http://www.librarian.net/stax/2117/overdrive-and-audiobooks-and-the-pervasive-ipod/. Archived at http://perma.cc/WA9C-YPLH.

YouTube Help. "Dispute a Content ID Claim." https://support.google.com/youtube/answer/2797454?hl=en. Archived at https://perma.cc/KB64-ECQH.

———. "Using Content ID." https://support.google.com/youtube/answer/3244015?hl=en&ref_topic=4515467. Archived at https://perma.cc/C6QL-ASQ7.

Chapter Two

A Primer on Digital Rights Management Technologies

Jasper L. Tran

DRM is not a single technology and it is not even a single philosophy . . .
DRM is not thin copyright, and it isn't even thick copyright; DRM is potentially a nearly absolute protection of the works.—Karen Coyle[1]

There are a variety of digital rights management (DRM) technologies employed by content owners and publishers to protect creators, owners, and the
integrity of the content itself. DRM technologies prevent unauthorized use by
controlling access to and use of information. As such, DRM can hinder or
threaten the effectiveness of information intermediaries such as libraries
when they provide digital content controlled by DRM technologies that they
themselves do not employ or manage. Therefore, librarians need to be aware
of commercial DRM applications and understand the various DRM technologies in this increasingly protected digital information age.

This chapter is structured in three parts. First, it explores the four DRM
schemes of prevention, restriction, deterrence, and detection. The various
DRM tools and DRM systems and how they work are then explained. The
discussion, while technical, avoids jargon and is easily accessible. The chapter concludes with advice for libraries on how to protect their digital resource
investment when they do not control the related DRM.

DRM SCHEMES

DRM schemes are categorized based on four functions: prevention, restriction, deterrence, and detection.[2] Prevention prevents unauthorized access,
use, or damage to protected sources. Restriction restricts use by limiting the

manner in which users interact with the information. Deterrence deters by making inappropriate or illegal use not worth the time, money, or effort to circumvent DRM protections. Detection detects unapproved use of content after it is distributed through the use of forensic technologies, such as watermark, pattern matching, and plagiarism-detection software.

Prevention

Prevention is the traditional function of DRM systems and is often referred to as copy protection or copy control. Prevention prevents unauthorized access, use, or damage to protected sources. The concept of prevention in DRM systems was initially drawn from other sources, such as computer security. Three attributes traditionally define computer security: (1) confidentiality— the "prevention of unauthorized disclosure of information"; (2) integrity— the "prevention of unauthorized modification of information"; and (3) availability—the "prevention of unauthorized withholding of information or resources."[3]

Restriction

Restriction is why DRM is often referred to as "digital restrictions management."[4] The goal is to give content owners the most control over their protected assets possible. Restriction restricts use by limiting the manner in which users interact with the information. For instance, DRM can restrict a user "from copying or sharing a song, reading an e-book on another device, or playing a single-player game without an Internet connection."[5] A common example of restriction occurs when information is accessible only in a read-only document file to prevent downloading and copying. In a way, "DRM creates damaged goods, preventing [users] from doing what would be possible without it."[6]

Deterrence

Deterrence is the primary rights protection method in the analog space. It is easier to understand deterrence in terms of nuisance: making inappropriate use not worth an individual's time, money, or effort to circumvent DRM protections. Deterrence works when people view the costs for authorized access, in terms of time, money, or effort, as reasonable and a fair trade for the resource. For example, photocopying a book costs time and printing resources and produces a copy of lesser quality compared to an authorized copy—an individual is deterred from violating DRM if photocopying a book would likely cost just as much as buying an authorized copy of the same book at a bookstore. However, deterrence becomes less effective when an individual only wants a small portion of the protected source and not the entire protected source, such as a chapter in a book rather the whole book—now, photocopying a chapter in a book would likely be cheaper than buying a new (or even used) book.[7]

Detection

Detection is a cost-effective strategy because it allows unprotected distribution but then detects unapproved use of content after its distribution (after the fact) through forensic technologies (e.g., watermark, pattern matching, plagiarism-detection software). For instance, the Internet allows easy integration of copyright-protected sources into content creators' websites and not all content users create and distribute a "perfect copy" to other unauthorized users, thus undermining the right holders' potential benefits.[8] Without available detection technologies, content owners would have a difficult time detecting which derivatives of the content were made from the original owned by the content owner. Thus content owners prefer this DRM scheme.

The DRM systems and tools discussed in the next section reflect the technologies that belong to these four functional categories.

DRM SYSTEMS AND TOOLS

There are at least four steps in each DRM system: content identification, encryption, decryption, and licensing. A DRM system may employ one or more individual DRM technologies. These technologies can attach to any step of the particular DRM system. In addition, DRM can be affixed to hardware to create a close-universe content communication and transmission system between two or more DRM-enabled specialized hardware units.[9]

Content Identification

Content owners identify (mark) content by embedding watermarks, digital fingerprints, digital signature, and time stamps into the content or by viewing the metadata. For example, news organizations can determine the source of archived footage—a staff reporter, a freelancer, or a third party—based on the embedded information.[10] Content identification is very useful in the areas of antipiracy and usage tracking.[11] Content identification falls under DRM detection.

Watermarking and Digital Fingerprints

Watermarks insert information into content to detail creation and establish ownership, copyright, and use permissions and limitations. The insertion generally uses spread spectrum techniques (i.e., adding an embedded signal pseudo-noise watermark pattern, recoverable by correlation)[12] that result in an embedded watermark undetectable to content users but detectable with watermark recognition applications.[13]

Watermarks are added during production or distribution, such as when embedded within audio or video data.[14] Watermarks can be used to record the copyright owner, the distributor, or the distribution chain, or to identify the purchaser of the music.[15] Watermarking helps secure prosecution evidence for legal disputes.[16] For example, after police secure allegedly pirated DVDs recovered from a raid, the police's forensics team could use available computer software to detect the underlying watermark of the DVD to identify the content owners of the original DVD. Watermarks can be distorted, deleted, or otherwise interfered with by software used to edit video or audio.[17] Researchers have been investigating and developing new methods to make watermarking technologies resistant to watermark copy attack.[18]

Content owners evaluate the effectiveness of watermarks in terms of capacity and original signal fidelity.[19] Capacity measures the amount of information that a watermark can contain, and fidelity measures the distortion between the unmarked file and the watermarked file.[20] Any distortion is rather minimal and does not impact users' experience with the protected source.[21] An effective watermark would be imperceptible (not altering the content or aesthetics of the content), robust (can withstand any manipulation, whether editing, compressing, altering, or removing the watermark), reversible (removable without affecting the source's content), and secure (only authorized parties can apply, detect, and remove the watermark).[22]

Hackers can nonetheless defeat watermark protections through collusion or through reverse engineering.[23] In collusion, hackers combine and analyze multiple copies of the original signal for small noise variations to develop a composite copy that resembles an unmarked source.[24] To reverse engineer, hackers use watermark detection applications to determine the watermark signal's specific type and location.[25] Once the watermark's type and location are identified, the hackers have an easier time in removing the watermark from the source's content.[26]

Although watermarks can be compromised, they remain an effective and efficient means of communicating ownership and use information to DRM devices and applications.[27] Watermarks are a common example of DRM detection. But most importantly, watermarks also qualify as DRM deterrence because they are "not easily broken without significant time, effort and technological sophistication."[28]

Digital fingerprints are a form of forensic or individualized watermarking most often used for digital video content on the Internet—for example, Google's video fingerprinting technology for YouTube videos.[29] Digital fingerprints are embedded data in the digital content to track content use and unauthorized distribution.[30] Two files with even a single character different would have completely different digital fingerprints.[31] For example, when employees use firm-issued computers, employers can utilize digital fingers to block the employees' access to unauthorized materials on the Internet.[32]

There are three types of digital fingerprints: (1) symmetric (i.e., a content owner can identify unauthorized reuse or redistribution to a customer based on each customer's unique assigned fingerprint), (2) asymmetric (i.e., an interactive protocol where the fingerprint is based on each customer's unique information and the content owner knows the customer's identity), and (3) anonymous asymmetric (i.e., a merchant must apply to a registration authority based on a need to identify an unauthorized copy to learn of the customer's identity or else the customer remains anonymous).[33]

Digital Signatures and Time Stamps

Digital signatures verify identities and authenticate the transactional participants—content owner and user. Digital signatures are also used to verify that the content is authentic and unmodified. Digital signatures often contain a hash and a signature.[34] The hash is a unique numeric value created by calculating the content's length such that any change to the content invalidates the hash.[35] This makes the hash's presence very valuable in the transactional world, where both parties want to ensure that they are contracting the same content—as previously agreed upon—without worrying about unknown one-sided changes.

The transactional parties can digitally sign the hash using private encryption keys. The parties then use a public key to validate the private key's signature. Verification can occur at any point in the transaction—for example, when licensing the content.[36] One example is the XML signature in XML content, which is the standard schema for assigning signatures in XML to any content to ensure content integrity or to authenticate the content signer.[37] Digital signatures qualify as DRM detection.

Digital time stamps identify and guarantee a document's age through cryptographic information.[38] Digital objects are time-stamped in batches in a manner that guarantees that the time stamps cannot be repudiated. Group support logic is the underlying foundation of digital time stamp.[39] The time stamp of a challenged document is compared with the other documents in the same time-stamped batch.[40] Because tampering with all documents of the same batch is statistically unlikely, users rely on the identical dates of time stamps within the same batch to validate the content dating of the challenged document. In other words, users can reliably match up the dates of digital content via viewing digital time stamps to identify the age of the document.[41]

Digital time stamps reinforce digital signatures.[42] For instance, digital time stamps contain two features that enhance the digital signature system's integrity: (1) digital time stamps cannot be compromised by a disclosure of an encryption key because digital time stamps do not rely on keys, and (2) digital time stamp certificates can be renewed to remain valid indefinitely. [43]

Encryption and Decryption

Encryption and decryption often use one or more of the following: keys, digital certificates, broadcast encryption, broadcast flag (or simple mark), or content scrambling. [44]

Keys

Encryption scrambles content, rendering the source unintelligible until a user utilizes a key to decrypt and make the content usable. [45] One can think of encryption and decryption as accessing an email box. Although anyone can send messages to an email box, only authenticated users can read or delete the emails. Likewise, although people can view the encrypted (i.e., un-decrypted) messages, only the users with the encryption keys can read the decrypted messages. [46]

There is a range of encryption strategies. Simple systems may encrypt all content under a single key, while more complex systems may encrypt individual units of content each with a unique key. The more complex the system, the less likely the entire system will fail because more than one key will need to fail to gain access to all the content. In short, a hacker gains access to the entire system under a single master key versus gaining access to only a section or segment of the system when multiple keys are used. [47]

Encryption cryptography includes private key encryption (symmetric encryption) and public key encryption (asymmetric encryption). Private key encryption is the most secure form of key encryption because it requires both parties to know the private key to transact or to exchange a secured message. For instance, private encryption can be used when two parties want to communicate secretly through a secured message using a mode of communication that could be susceptible to the public's eye. [48] Public key encryption requires the use of both a public key and a private key—where everyone, including users, has access to the public key, but only the content owner knows the private key. [49] In this latter scenario, only the private key is able to decrypt the content. [50]

Though public key encryption can maintain some confidentiality and security through the private key's use, hackers can break the key through brute-force attacks (i.e., repeated attempts until successful) or through intercepting public communication channels. [51] One form of brute-force attacks is side-channel attack, which measures the amount of time known hardware takes to encrypt plain text then compares that finding with the amount of efforts (called "work factors") needed for encryption to search for a decryption key. [52]

Key size or key length indicates the size measured in bits of the key used in encryption cryptography.[53] Owners prefer larger key encryptions over shorter keys because the more efforts required, the less likely a hacker would successfully break a key.[54] Meanwhile, a common form of interception attack is the "man-in-the-middle" attack, where a third party intercepts then modifies a public key to enable a hacker to intercept, decrypt, and re-encrypt the messages.[55]

A key generally binds to a certificate that validates the key's authenticity. A trusted third party, most commonly the certificate authority (CA), assigns all parties the keys (key assignment), verifies the certificate holder's identity before issuing a certificate (key escrow), and promptly revokes any compromised certificate to guard against corrupted public keys (key revocation). Once assigned, a key is bound to a user. The CA maintains the user's identity, public key, key binding, and other information.[56]

Given how key use and management could lead to cryptography failure, the public key infrastructure (PKI) was formed to govern key management through its policy, technology, and practice. These practices and policies enable key holders to encrypt and exchange information.[57] A stable key distribution scheme needs to be obscure (not interceptable), diverse (one successful attack would not compromise the entire system), and renewable (the PKI can easily recover from successful attacks without complete replacement).[58] Keys are a common example of DRM prevention.

Digital Certificates

A digital certificate is a form of public key. A digital certificate is comparable to a driver's license in that both contain the owner's identification information. Digital certificates verify the content owner's identity as documented in the certificate, creating a trusted level of proof. Digital certificates exist only for a defined period of time. Once expired, digital certificates are revoked and periodically published by the CA in the certificate revocation list (CRL) to give notice (inform users) that the certificates can no longer be relied upon.[59] Prior to relying on a specific CRL, a user can validate it by using the certificate of its corresponding CA, which can usually be found in a public directory (e.g., preinstalled in web browsers).[60]

Digital certificates contain digital signatures of the owner and issuer, a validity period, unique identifiers for issuers and subject, and further extensions that may include additional information regarding the owner or the content.[61] One widely accepted international digital certificate is the X.509 certificate used in the PKI digital certificate standard.[62] Like keys, digital certificates are an example of DRM prevention.

Broadcast Encryption

For transactions involving more than two parties, broadcast encryption allows the content owner to distribute encrypted content to a larger audience through public telecommunication channels.[63] One can think of broadcast encryption as participating in a teleconference, where only the invited participants have access to the telephone call to enter the teleconference. In this type of distribution, the encryption is based on what is known as a secret session encrypting key (SEK). After the selected keys are encrypted, the keys encrypt the SEK and distribute the encrypted SEK to the valid group members. These users must decrypt the SEK to access the source's content.[64]

To reduce the inherent risk of exposing the encrypted content to unauthorized users, content owners can also create time-bound keys embedded with specific activation and expiration times to make the encrypted content available only within the transaction's constraints.[65] For instance, such time-bound keys are common in pay-per-view transactions, where paid users are given access to view encrypted content for a limited amount of time.[66] Broadcast encryption is another example of DRM prevention.

Content Scrambling System

Content Scrambling System (CSS)—developed by Matsushita and Toshiba—encrypts DVD content using a series of keys for encryption and decryption.[67] CSS is similar to locking your car and leaving it in the parking lot. Your car is safe because only the right key can open it. Similarly, CSS prevents the use of information unless you have the right key. Most DVD players incorporate a CSS decryption module to read the keys stored on the DVD.[68] The keys are passed to the decryption module through a secure handshake.[69] Decrypting CSS occurs in a multistage process using title keys, disc keys, and player keys.[70] CSS developers envisioned that system administrators could shut out or turn off compromised systems (i.e., prevent compromised or unauthenticated DVD players from playing new content).[71]

CSS has been compromised many times, and CSS decryption software (DeCSS) is widely available on the Internet to rip protected DVD content.[72] Nonetheless, content producers continue to use CSS to protect content primarily because a new encryption scheme would be incompatible with the vast number of DVDs currently in circulation—the market consequences resulting from the anticipated adverse consumer backlash are not worth it for the DVD industry to increase its content protection to a stronger, uncompromised encryption standard.[73] Though CSS is a form of DRM prevention, it is also a common example of DRM deterrence because DVDs are relatively inexpensive versus a hacker's opportunity costs in downloading DVD ripping software to decrypt protected video content.[74]

Broadcast Flag

The broadcast flag, also known as a simple mark, is defined as binary data bits (or flags) functioning as an on/off switch in digital TV streaming to indicate whether the content can be recorded and whether other usage restrictions should apply.[75] One can think of the broadcast flag as including information inside (in addition to labeling the receiver's name and address on) a mail package for the receiver to read. In other words, the broadcast flag system embeds digital code into a digital broadcasting stream to signal the program's protection level to the receiver (e.g., HDTV, recorder, any digital device).[76] All receivers must be able to decrypt and protect flagged content to limit how and when users may play, record, or distribute the content.[77] For example, the CSS encryption for DVD and Blu-ray disks contains region codes as broadcast flags to limit playback to the region or regions encoded on the content copy.[78] However, just like CSS, DVD region codes and broadcast flags in general can be easily compromised by Web applications overriding region codes.[79] Initially, Federal Communications Commission (FCC) regulations required all new television receivers using the Advanced Television Systems Committee standard to incorporate the broadcast flag system by 2005.[80] However, courts found that the FCC exceeded its authority in doing so, and as of 2011 the FCC officially eliminated the broadcast flag regulations.[81] The broadcast flag is an example of DRM detection.

Licenses

Licenses, also known as end-user license agreements, are contracts between two or more parties documenting and controlling the permissions provided to the end user to access and use the protected content.[82] Licenses are an example of DRM restriction. An example of a user license is when a viewer pays Amazon for a one-account access to stream an on-demand video for an agreed time period. Amazon's license is set to expire after the agreed time period ends.[83]

We contract every day without realizing it,[84] from the purchase of a cup of Starbucks coffee to pulling out a parking ticket when entering a parking garage. Similarly, content providers and intermediaries often contract licenses on behalf of users, but many users are not aware of the licenses.[85] Sometimes user licenses are entered into unknowingly or without full understanding of the terms and conditions by the actual end user.[86] A common example is the "Click Through" license that accompanies the installation of a software product. A "Click Through" license describes what happens when a user does not realize he or she consented to the license because the user is unaware of the terms of services because he or she didn't read them.[87]

Metadata

The U.S. National Institute of Standards and Technology divides metadata into five categories,[88] two of which are relevant here: (1) library and preservation metadata and (2) rights management metadata. Library and preservation metadata is used for archiving purposes to "ensure that when the asset is accessed or restored sometime in the future, there is adequate information that can identify it."[89] Rights management metadata (or DRM metadata) is "the protection data for distribution and includes copyright, intellectual property, and distribution rights, carrying the expiration rules, encryption policies, and tracking metadata used in watermarking for piracy protection."[90]

In other words, DRM metadata records information such as the purchaser's name, account information, or email address and possibly the file's publisher, author, creation date, download date, and various notes.[91] Unlike watermark, DRM metadata is not embedded in the played content; rather, it is kept separate but within the file. One can think of metadata as all the extra information of an email (who the senders and receivers were, what their email addresses were, the date and time of when the email was sent) in addition to the email's content.[92] Being visible to users, metadata results in many benefits, such as putting users on notice whether the content is published or unpublished, providing users with information about the content's ownership, and allowing users to quickly calculate the content's copyright term.[93] Metadata is another example of DRM detection.

DRM metadata is very useful in license acquisition.[94] For instance, unlike usual metadata, Adobe Access DRM Metadata (Adobe Metadata) is "an encrypted opaque blob (to client devices) that can only be fully parsed and decrypted by an Adobe Access license server."[95] To the licensee, Adobe Metadata includes the following:

- The URL of the Adobe Access license server that can generate a license for this content.
- The transport encryption key, which is used to encrypt all data sent to the Adobe Access license server.
- Adobe Access DRM policies associated with the content during Adobe Access packaging.
- The date/time the content was packaged (which is used to determine license/caching durations that are based on the packaging time).[96]

Conversely, to the license server, Adobe Metadata generates a license response including the following:

- The transport decryption key, which is used to decrypt the message sent by the client device.

- The license server decryption key, which is used to decrypt the content encryption key from the metadata.
- Adobe Access DRM policies associated with the content during Adobe Access encryption/packaging.
- The client device's encryption key, which the server can use to secure the license.[97]

Specialized Hardware

DRM can be affixed to hardware to create a close-universe content communication and transmission between two or more DRM-enabled hardware systems. A daily example of specialize hardware is the VHS player (i.e., Video Home System), which is needed to read VHS tapes. Some of the prominent examples of DRM hardware are trust system, secured hardware, and secured transmission. Specialized hardware is an example of DRM restriction.

Trust System and Secured Hardware

Trust system is the traditional close-universe system for a DRM transaction, requiring reliable nodes in each step of the DRM process to enforce and obey the system's rules.[98] A trusted system can ensure content protection from creation to packaging through purchase and delivery and even through downstream uses. Trust system has evolved from tethering content to a single user device—by using a secret key known only to the consumer (e.g., software CD key)—to transferring content across all devices and platforms owned and used by a particular consumer (e.g., desktop computers, digital playback equipment, cell phones, portable music players). This evolution from single device to personal network reflects today's users, who require the ability to move protected content with ease across many devices and platforms.[99]

One common trust system is secured hardware, which is a DRM-embedded hardware to support a DRM-controlled system. Prominent examples of secured hardware include SD memory cards, Trusted Platform Module (TPM) microcontrollers, and Secure Video Process (SVP).[100] An SD memory card contains integrated Content Protection for Record Media (CPRM) to control the copying, playback, transfer, and deletion of digital media and also key revocation and copy-counting technology to restrict the number of copies that can be transferred from the SD memory card to a computer.[101] TPM microcontrollers are generally affixed to a computer's motherboard to store keys, passwords, and digital certificates through hashing, random number generation, asymmetric key generation, and asymmetric encryption or decryption.[102] SVP is a DRM-enabled video-processing chip that can be embedded in any consumer electronics device.[103] Each SVP has a unique device certificate that allows decryption, decompression, and playback only within the chip.[104]

Secured Transmission

Secured transmission protects content communications and transport between devices and across networks through an end-to-end DRM system.[105] Some examples of secured transmission methods are Transport Layer Security (TLS), High-Bandwidth Digital Content Protection (HDCP), and Digital Transmission Content Protection (DTCP).[106] TLS, the modern version of Secure Sockets Layer (SSL), allows encrypted messaging across the Internet through (1) algorithm negotiation, (2) key exchange and authentication, and (3) symmetric encryption and message authentication.[107] TLS and SSL are commonly used in email and File Transfer Protocol (FTP).[108]

HDCP, licensed by Intel's Digital Content Protection, uses authentication, encryption, and key revocation to protect content transmission across cable using high-definition interfaces, such as DVI (Digital Visual Interface), HDMI (High-Definition Multimedia Interface), and UDI (Unified Display Interface).[109] Meanwhile, DTCP (and DTCP-IP), licensed by the 5C[110] / Digital Transmission Licensing Administrator, protects content transmission over cable between two communicating devices, such as USB and FireWire, by using authentication and key exchange protocol (AKE) to verify connection, content control information, content encryption, and renewability.[111] DTCP-IP extends DTCP to support content transmission over IP network using 128-bit encryption.[112]

LIBRARIES AND DRM TECHNOLOGIES

DRM technologies directly affect libraries and their role as an intermediary between content owners and end users. DRM technologies commonly control the use of journal and reference databases, e-books, and downloadable audiobooks.[113]

The use of DRM technologies challenges the traditional library-lending model. In the past, if a library wished to share a physical book with a reader, there was little to prevent that reader from enjoying the work. Today, for that reader to enjoy an electronic work, there are significant technical hurdles to overcome. For instance, readers must use download services and own devices that are supported by the download services that have contracted with content owners (authors, publishers, and content consolidators), or else the users are out of luck.[114]

Libraries purchase digital content but do not control the DRM that governs the content. A thorough understanding of various DRM schemes, systems, and technologies enables libraries to protect their investments and serve all patrons. As discussed below, this understanding includes but is not limited to understanding not only the "nature of DRM" but also how to prevent damage to content, addressing electronic content in budget and acquisition functions, and educating users.

Prevent Damage to Content

Libraries should be aware of the DRM technologies embedded in a source's content and other DRM-compliant software and hardware applications to guard against unauthorized copying of the protected content. Because licenses, watermarks, and simple marks are imperceptible, libraries may loan DVD or Blu-ray disks without knowledge of the embedded DRM. If library patrons attempt to tamper with a protected disk, the device keys that enable the compliant devices to use protected media may be revoked. To prevent such tampering, libraries can install protection software on library computers to disable or at least limit users from running unauthorized applications on library computers. [115]

Budget Implications

Libraries need to be conscious of the impact on the budget when evaluating electronic resources. Most libraries face the reality of decreasing budgets. Yet libraries must pay not only for the electronic publications to add to their collection but also for overall access to the download service that provides those works—to help maintain DRM's hold over an electronic work. This particular cost is extremely high—sometimes prohibitively high—for many libraries. For those libraries able to afford access to the download service, they might be suddenly "sticker shocked" when they find out that individual e-books cost many times the price of their physical counterparts. [116]

Limited Access

Libraries should be aware of the limits of the "pay-per-use" model of information dissemination (e.g., Amazon's on-demand video), where the content essentially disappears after a specific period of time or number of uses. For instance, some e-books have a shelf life of fifty-two weeks, after which they become unusable. [117] DRM technologies can prevent copying content into new formats. Such controls from the content owner could prevent libraries from preserving and providing long-term access to our society's knowledge products. [118]

Educate Librarians

To fully educate users, the librarians themselves must be knowledgeable about available DRM technologies. DRM is currently like a minefield where those who do not know where the mines are could easily step on one (such as by repaying for more access to DRM-locked works or inadvertently violating the content owners' rights). Librarians should keep up with what is going on in the DRM, e-book, e-resource, and vendor worlds.[119] This discussion serves as a good start, but curious librarians should seek out other resources available on DRM technologies to be well versed in current and emerging DRM technologies.[120] For instance, the American Library Association website has many downloadable resources on DRM technologies.[121]

It is worth noting that some authors have released their works DRM free, and some download services share electronic audiobooks in non-DRM format.[122] For example, Tor/Forge (an imprint of Macmillan) and Momentum (an imprint of Pan Macmillan) recently announced that their future releases will be sold without publisher DRM, though retailers may still add their own.[123] Keeping current on DRM trends and updates is important work for librarians. Doing so ensures great service to the library's patrons and enables librarians to be active advocates in the DRM debate.

Educate Users

Copyright laws govern not only print texts but also digital multimedia. DRM technologies can prevent normal uses of copyrighted works, such as printing or excising portions for quotation.[124] DRM technologies can interfere with the "first sale" doctrine in copyright law.[125] For centuries, the first sale doctrine has allowed libraries to loan lawfully acquired works to the public.[126] Now, DRM technologies can limit secondary transfer of works to others.[127]

For libraries to serve their educational, research, and information roles, the public should be able to use works in the full range of ways subject to copyright limitations and exceptions. As the intermediary party between content owners and users, libraries should provide copyright and DRM information to patrons to inform users of the use restrictions and shield themselves from liability.[128]

Disabled Patrons

Aside from annoying and frustrating users, DRM technologies may also disadvantage disabled users. For instance, disabled patrons' needs could include access to captioning, the ability to enlarge file display size, and the ability to convert text to speech or speech to text. Libraries should be on notice of this concern to negotiate a special provision for the disabled—for content to be accessible to disabled patrons in some manner—when purchasing content.[129]

Role of the Parent Institution

Libraries are often part of larger organizations, such as universities or the government. Libraries should consult with their parent institutions about risk management in the event of compromising users' private information (e.g., identity theft occurring in libraries that accept credit card payment for library-related fees) or incurring liability from content owners' lawsuits.[130] Oftentimes, the larger organizations are better equipped to handle such risks.

Renewability

When purchasing content, libraries should think about renewability when DRM systems are compromised. Successfully breaking an encryption creates an analog hole, which is a disruption in the end-to-end transmission and delivery of protected content.[131] An example of an analog hole is when users capture a YouTube music video and convert it into a music file for future replay without having to access YouTube. While some DRM systems include technologies to address the analog hole, others do not.[132]

To deal with compromised DRM technologies, content owners can require upgrades to DRM periodically, such as requiring software or hardware upgrades or providing new devices. However, some new devices are incompatible with the prior DRM system, causing problems with device performance and content playback. Thus libraries should negotiate for an option to renew when purchasing the content. This is especially relevant for libraries that routinely purchase DRM-protected content to avoid incompatibility with their computers' operating system and other applications whenever a DRM is automatically renewed.[133]

CONCLUSION

This chapter demonstrates the various DRM technologies and systems that libraries, as content purchasers and intermediaries between content owners and users, should be familiar with.

Whether DRM technologies are here to stay is far from clear. For instance, major publishers are eliminating DRM technologies on their e-books. DRM technologies are evidently ineffective in preventing unauthorized uses of digital technologies and often serve to anger consumers.[134] Regardless, librarians well versed in DRM will be better equipped to successfully utilize and manage DRM-embedded sources to their full potential.

NOTES

1. Coyle, "Technology of Rights."

2. See Bygrave, *Digital Rights Management*, 441.
3. Bhatt, "Computer & Network Security Threats."
4. Brown and Boulderstone, *Impact of Electronic Publishing*, 231.
5. Defective by Design, "What Is DRM?"
6. Ibid.
7. Digital Watermarking Alliance, "Forensics and Piracy Deterrence."
8. Agnew, *Digital Rights Management*, 298.
9. See Becker et al., *Digital Rights Management*, 155–57.
10. Milano, "Content Control."
11. Rosenblatt, "Content Identification Technologies."
12. Hartung et al., "Spread Spectrum Watermarking."
13. Hartung and Ramme, "Digital Rights Management and Watermarking."
14. Wikipedia, "Digital Rights Management."
15. Ibid.
16. See, for example, Schellekens, "Digital Watermarks as Legal Evidence."
17. Wikipedia, "Digital Rights Management."
18. Kuttera et al., "Watermark Copy Attack."
19. Kim, "Watermark and Data Hiding Evaluation," xi–xii.
20. Ibid.
21. See Doerr, Dugelay, and Grange, "Exploiting Self-Similarities."
22. See Kim, "Watermark and Data Hiding Evaluation," 20–24; Mintzer, Lotspiech, and Morimoto, "Safeguarding Digital Library Contents."
23. Furon and Duhamel, "Asymmetric Watermarking Method," 985.
24. Agnew, *Digital Rights Management*, 307.
25. Furon and Duhamel, "Asymmetric Watermarking Method," 985.
26. Sunesh, "Watermark Attacks and Applications."
27. Furon and Duhamel, "Asymmetric Watermarking Method," 985.
28. Agnew, *Digital Rights Management*, 307.
29. Johnson, "How Will YouTube's Video Fingerprinting Work?"
30. Yong and Lee, "Efficient Fingerprinting Scheme," 192.
31. Business Dictionary, "Digital Fingers."
32. Ibid.
33. Yong and Lee, "Efficient Fingerprinting Scheme," 122; Agnew, *Digital Rights Management*, 309.
34. See Rouse, "Digital Signature."
35. Ibid.
36. Ibid.
37. Bartel et al., "XML Signature Syntax."
38. See Haber and Stornetta, "How to Time-Stamp," 100–11.
39. See Maniatis, Giuli, and Baker, "Enabling the Long-Term Archival of Signed Documents."
40. See RSA Laboratories, "7.11 What Is Digital Timestamping?"
41. Ibid.
42. X5 Networks, "Cryptography."
43. Osari and Roy, "Improving Security and Reducing Computation Time," 109.
44. See Zhang, "Survey of Digital Rights Management Technologies."
45. See Vellante, "Data Encryption Strategies."
46. Ibid.
47. Abelson et al., "Risks of Key Recovery."
48. Ibid.
49. See Microsoft Support, "Description of Symmetric and Asymmetric Encryption."
50. Ibid.
51. Kessler, "Overview of Cryptography."
52. See, for example, Wikipedia, "Side-Channel Attack."
53. Kessler, "Overview of Cryptography."
54. Ibid.

55. Ibid.; Agnew, *Digital Rights Management*, 300.
56. Kessler, "Overview of Cryptography."
57. Ibid.
58. See Net Security Training, "What Is a Public Key Infrastructure?"
59. Microsoft Technet, "How Certificates Work."
60. Wikipedia, "Revocation List."
61. Microsoft Technet, "How Certificates Work."
62. See Rouse, "X.509 Certificate."
63. Ramkumar, "Broadcast Encryption."
64. Zhu, "Cryptanalysis of Two Group Key Management Protocols," 37.
65. See IBM, "Improved Remote Key Distribution."
66. Mihaljević, Fossorier, and Imai, "Novel Broadcast Encryption," 258–59.
67. Rouse, "Content Scrambling System."
68. Ibid.
69. Taylor, "DVD Frequently Asked Questions."
70. ExtremeTech, "Digital Content Protection."
71. Godwin, "Digital Rights Management," 11.
72. Ibid.; Agnew, *Digital Rights Management*, 303.
73. See Godwin, "Digital Rights Management," 25.
74. Agnew, *Digital Rights Management*, 324.
75. Center for Democracy and Technology, "Implications of Broadcast Flag," 6.
76. Ibid.
77. CyberLink, "TV and the Entertainment PC."
78. Wikipedia, "DVD Region Code."
79. Ibid.
80. 47 C.F.R. § 73.9002(b) (2005); Eskicioglu, "Key Management," 144.
81. See *American Library Association v. FCC*, 406 F.3d 689 (D.C. Cir. 2005) (holding that the FCC had exceeded its authority in prohibiting the manufacture of computer or video hardware without copy protection technology because the FCC only has authority to regulate transmissions, not devices that receive communications); Boliek, "FCC Finally Kills Off Fairness Doctrine."
82. See, for example, Tran, "Rethinking Intellectual Property Transactions," 152–54.
83. Farivar, "Can't Stream That Christmas Movie."
84. See Bakos, Marotta-Wurgle, and Trossen, "Does Anyone Read the Fine Print?," 2.
85. Ibid.
86. Ibid.; Tran, "Right to Attention" (many "do not pay attention in reviewing contracts").
87. Coyle, "Automation of Rights," 326.
88. The five types of metadata are descriptive, structural, administrative, rights management, and library and preservation; Olson, "Demystifying and Debunking Metadata."
89. Ibid.
90. Ibid.
91. See, for example, Breen, "Watermarked iTunes Files."
92. EDRM, "Email Metadata."
93. See, generally, Whalen, "Introduction to Metadata 3.0."
94. See H., "What Is DRM Metadata."
95. Ibid.
96. Ibid.
97. Ibid.
98. Wikipedia, "Trusted System"; Agnew, *Digital Rights Management*, 311–12.
99. Agnew, *Digital Rights Management*, 311–12.
100. Mullick, "Tools, Techniques and Standards," slide 10.
101. Petkovic and Jonker, *Security, Privacy, and Trust*, 281, n. 7.
102. See Trusted Computing Group, "Trusted Platform Module."
103. See Business Wire, "SVP Alliance Launched."
104. See Continental Automated Buildings Association, "Standard Approach to Digital Content Protection."

Jasper L. Tran

105. Mullick, "Tools, Techniques and Standards," slide 11; Wikipedia, "Secured Transmission."

106. Harte, *Introduction to Digital Rights Management*, 52, 83.

107. See Rouse, "Transport Layer Security."

108. Wikipedia, File Transfer Protocol."

109. See Rouse, "HDCP."

110. The 5C group denotes the five companies who created DTCP: Hitachi, Intel, Matsushita, Sony, and Toshiba. See Intel, "Intel and DTCP."

111. Intel, "Intel and DTCP"; Agnew, *Digital Rights Management*, 314–15.

112. See Andre, "Digital Transmission Content Protection."

113. Young, "Chilling Impact of Digital Restrictions."

114. Ibid.

115. Agnew, *Digital Rights Management*, 346.

116. Young, "Chilling Impact of Digital Restrictions."

117. Ibid.

118. American Library Association, "Digital Rights Management."

119. American Library Association, "DRM Tip Sheet."

120. The author has made a similar recommendation to librarians regarding the emerging field of 3D printing and law; Tran, "Law and 3D Printing," 511. For a general background discussion on 3D printing, see Tran, "To Bioprint or Not to Bioprint," 133–40; Tran, "Press Clause and 3D Printing," 78.

121. See, generally, American Library Association, "Digital Rights Management."

122. Young, "Chilling Impact of Digital Restrictions."

123. Senior, "Will We Ever Find." See also Doctorow, "Tor Books Goes Completely DRM-Free."

124. Harvard University Office of General Counsel, "Copyright and Fair Use."

125. Wolf, *Digital Millennium Copyright Act*, 463.

126. American Library Association, "Digital Rights Issues."

127. American Library Association, "Digital Rights Management."

128. Ibid.

129. Agnew, *Digital Rights Management*, 347.

130. Ibid., 348.

131. Wikipedia, "Digital Rights Management."

132. See Electronic Frontier Foundation, "Analog Hole."

133. Senoh et al., "DRM Renewability and Interoperability."

134. American Library Association, "DRM Tip Sheet," 2.

REFERENCES

Abelson, Harold, et al. "The Risks of Key Recovery, Key Escrow, and Trusted Third-Party Encryption." *Schneier on Security*, 1998. https://www.schneier.com/cryptography/archives/1997/04/the_risks_of_key_rec.html.

Agnew, Grace. *Digital Rights Management: A Librarian's Guide to Technology and Practise* (2008).

American Library Association. "Digital Rights Issues." http://www.ala.org/advocacy/sites/ala.org.advocacy/files/content/copyright/digitalrights/DRMissues.pdf.

———."Digital Rights Management (DRM) & Libraries." http://www.ala.org/advocacy/copyright/digitalrights.

———. "DRM Tip Sheet." July 2012. http://www.ala.org/transforminglibraries/drm-tip-sheet.

Andre, Michael. "Digital Transmission Content Protection ('DTCP')." TEACH Act Hearing Transcripts. http://www.uspto.gov/web/offices/dcom/olia/teachcomments/digital-transmn.pdf.

Bakos, Yannis, Florencia Marotta-Wurgler, and David R. Trossen. "Does Anyone Read the Fine Print? Consumer Attention to Standard-Form Contracts." 43 *J. Legal Stud.* 1 (2014).

Bartel, Mark, et al. "XML Signature Syntax and Processing." 2008. https://www.w3.org/TR/xmldsig-core/.

Becker, Eberhard, et al., eds. *Digital Rights Management: Technological, Economic, Legal and Political Aspects* (2004).

Bhatt, Abhishek P. "Computer & Network Security Threats." 1 *Int'l J. Advance Res. in Computer Sci. & Mgmt. Stud.* (2013). http://www.ijarcsms.com/docs/paper/volume1/issue1/V1I1-0002.pdf.

Boliek, Brooks. "FCC Finally Kills Off Fairness Doctrine." *Politico*, August 22, 2011. http://www.politico.com/news/stories/0811/61851.html.

Breen, Christopher. "Watermarked iTunes Files." *MacWorld*, June 1, 2007. http://www.macworld.com/article/1058178/ituneswatermark.html.

Brown David J., and Richard Boulderstone. *The Impact of Electronic Publishing: The Future for Publishers and Librarians* (2008).

Business Dictionary. "Digital Fingers." www.businessdictionary.com/definition/digital-fingerprint.html.

Business Wire. "SVP Alliance Launched to Promote Adoption of Content Protection Technology." Press Release, September 9, 2004. http://www.businesswire.com/news/home/20040909005677/en/SVP-Alliance-Launched-Promote-Adoption-Content-Protection.

Bygrave, Lee A. *Digital Rights Management and Privacy: Legal Aspects in the European Union* (2003).

Center for Democracy and Technology. "Implications of Broadcast Flag: A Public Interest Primer (Version 2.0)." December 2003. https://cdt.org/files/copyright/broadcastflag.pdf.

Continental Automated Buildings Association. "A Standard Approach to Digital Content Protection." March 2004. http://www.caba.org/CABA/DocumentLibrary/Public/IS-2004-17.aspx.

Coyle, Karen. "The Automation of Rights." 32 *J. Acad. Librarianship* 326 (2006).

———. "The Technology of Rights: Digital Rights Management." Based on a talk originally given at the Library of Congress, November 19, 2003. http://www.kcoyle.net/drm_basics1.html.

CyberLink. "TV and the Entertainment PC." http://www.cyberlink.com/stat/product-tutorial/enu/digital-home/tv-tech.jsp.

Defective by Design. "What Is DRM?" http://www.defectivebydesign.org/what_is_drm_digital_restrictions_management.

Digital Watermarking Alliance. "Forensics and Piracy Deterrence." http://www.digitalwatermarkingalliance.org/app_forensics.asp.

Doctorow, Cory. "Tor Books Goes Completely DRM-Free." *Boing Boing*, April 24, 2012. http://boingboing.net/2012/04/24/tor-books-goes-completely-drm.html.

Doerr, Gwenael, Jean-Luc Dugelay, and Lucas Grange. "Exploiting Self-Similarities to Defeat Digital Watermarking Systems: A Case Study on Still Images." Paper presented at ACM Multimedia and Security Workshop, September 20–21, 2004. http://www.eurecom.fr/en/publication/1561/detail/exploiting-self-similarities-to-defeat-digital-watermarking-systems-a-case-study-on-still-images.

EDRM. "Email Metadata." www.edrm.net/resources/glossaries/glossary/e/email-metadata.

Electronic Frontier Foundation. "Analog Hole." https://www.eff.org/issues/analog-hole.

Eskicioglu, Ahmet M. "Key Management for Multimedia Access and Distribution." In *Multimedia Security Technologies for Digital Rights Management*, ed. Wenjun Zeng et al. (2006).

ExtremeTech. "Digital Content Protection, Part III." August 25, 2003. http://www.extremetech.com/computing/54912-digital-content-protection-part-iii.

Farivar, Cyrus. "Can't Stream That Christmas Movie You 'Bought' on Amazon? Blame Disney." *Ars Technica*, December 16, 2013. http://arstechnica.com/business/2013/12/cant-stream-that-christmas-movie-you-bought-on-amazon-blame-disney/. Archived at https://perma.cc/DS3U-BRV5.

Furon, Teddy, and Pierre Duhamel. "An Asymmetric Watermarking Method." 51 *IEEE Transactions on Signal Processing* 981 (2003). https://hal.inria.fr/inria-00080829/file/Asym_ieee_v2.pdf.

Godwin, Michael. "Digital Rights Management: A Guide for Librarians (Version 1)." Am. Lib. Ass'n. *OITP Tech. Pol'y Brief*, January 2006. http://www.cs.yale.edu/homes/jf/Godwin-Libraries.pdf.

H., Eric. "What Is DRM Metadata (.drmmeta)?" Adobe Forums, November 4, 2013. https://forums.adobe.com/thread/1328226.

Haber, Stuart, and W. Scott Stornetta. "How to Time-Stamp a Digital Document." 3 *J. Cryptology* 99 (1991).

Harte, Lawrence. *Introduction to Digital Rights Management (DRM): Identifying, Tracking, Authorizing and Restricting Access to Digital Media* (2006).

Hartung, Frank, and Friedhelm Ramme. "Digital Rights Management and Watermarking of Multimedia Content for M-Commerce Applications." *IEEE Com. Mag.* 82 (2000).

Hartung, Frank, et al. "Spread Spectrum Watermarking: Malicious Attacks and Counterattacks." 3657 *Proc. SPIE: Sec. & Watermarking Multimedia Contents* (April 1999).

Harvard University Office of General Counsel. "Copyright and Fair Use." http://ogc.harvard.edu/pages/copyright-and-fair-use.

IBM. "Improved Remote Key Distribution." *z/OS Cryptographic Services ICSF Application Programmer's Guide.* http://www.ibm.com/support/knowledgecenter/SSLTBW_2.1.0/com.ibm.zos.v2r1.csfb400/improve.htm%23improve.

Intel. "Intel and DTCP: Protecting Premium Content and Its Use in the Digital Home." www.intel.com/content/dam/www/public/us/en/documents/white-papers/intel-and-dtcp.pdf.

Johnson, Bobbie. "How Will YouTube's Video Fingerprinting Work?" *Guardian*, June 18, 2007. https://www.theguardian.com/technology/blog/2007/jun/18/howwillyoutub.

Kessler, Gary C. "An Overview of Cryptography." GaryKessler.net, March 3, 2016. http://www.garykessler.net/library/crypto.html.

Kim, Hyung Cook. "Watermark and Data Hiding Evaluation: The Development of a Statistical Analysis Framework." Ph.D. thesis, Purdue University (May 2006). https://engineering.purdue.edu/~ace/thesis/kim/hyung-cook-thesis.pdf.

Kuttera, Martin, et al. "The Watermark Copy Attack." 3971 *Proc. SPIE: Sec. & Watermarking Multimedia Contents* 1, 9 (January 2000).

Maniatis, Petros, T. J. Giuli, and Mary Baker. "Enabling the Long-Term Archival of Signed Documents through Time Stamping." June 28, 2001. http://arxiv.org/abs/cs/0106058.

Microsoft Support. "Description of Symmetric and Asymmetric Encryption." October 26, 2007. https://support.microsoft.com/en-us/kb/246071.

Microsoft Technet. "How Certificates Work." March 28, 2003. https://technet.microsoft.com/en-us/library/cc776447(v=ws.10).aspx.

Mihaljević, Miodrag J., Marc P. C. Fossorier, and Hideki Imai. "A Novel Broadcast Encryption Based on Time-Bound Cryptographic Keys." In *Digital Rights Management: Technologies, Issues, Challenges and Systems*, ed. Reihaneh Safavi-Naini and Moti Yung (2006).

Milano, Dominic. "Content Control: Digital Watermarking and Fingerprinting." Rhoznet White Paper. https://www.digimarc.com/docs/default-source/technology-resources/white-papers/rhozet_wp_fingerprinting_watermarking.pdf.

Mintzer, Fred, Jeffrey Lotspiech, and Norishige Morimoto. "Safeguarding Digital Library Contents and User: Digital Water Markings." *D-Lib Mag.*, May 1997. http://www.dlib.org/dlib/may97/ibm/05gladney.html.

Mullick, Jayeeta. "Tools, Techniques and Standards of Digital Rights Management Systems." Slidegur. http://slidegur.com/doc/1210714/jayeeta-mullick_drm_1.

Net Security Training. "What Is a Public Key Infrastructure?" www.net-security-http://training.co.uk/what-is-a-public-key-infrastructure/.

Olson, Gary. "Demystifying and Debunking Metadata." Broadcast Bridge, May 6, 2015. https://www.thebroadcastbridge.com/content/entry/2729/demystifying-and-debunking-metadata.

Osari, Ranjeet, and Bhola Nath Roy. "Improving Security and Reducing Computation Time Using the ECDSA and PHAL." 1 *Int'l J. Computational Intelligence & Info. Sec.* 106, 109 (2010).

Petkovic, Milan, and Willem Jonker, eds. *Security, Privacy, and Trust in Modern Data Management* (2007).

Ramkumar, Mahalingam. "Broadcast Encryption Using Probabilistic Key Distribution and Applications." 1 *J. Computers* 1 (June 2006).

Rosenblatt, Bill. "Content Identification Technologies: Business Benefits for Content Owners." GiantStep White Paper, April 15, 2008, http://www.giantstepsmts.com/Content%20ID%20Whitepaper.pdf.

Rouse, Margaret. "Content Scrambling System (CSS)." TechTarget, April 2005. http://searchsecurity.techtarget.com/definition/Content-Scrambling-System.

―――. "Digital Signature." TechTarget, November 2014. http://searchsecurity.techtarget.com/definition/digital-signature.

―――. "HDCP (High-Bandwidth Digital Content Protection)." TechTarget, June 2007. http://searchsecurity.techtarget.com/definition/HDCP.

―――. "Transport Layer Security (TLS)." TechTarget, July 2006. http://searchsecurity.techtarget.com/definition/Transport-Layer-Security-TLS.

―――. "X.509 Certificate." TechTarget, January 2014. http://searchsecurity.techtarget.com/definition/X509-certificate.

RSA Laboratories. "7.11 What Is Digital Timestamping?" *PKCS 11: Cryptographic Token Interface Standard*. http://www.emc.com/emc-plus/rsa-labs/standards-initiatives/what-is-digital-timestamping.htm.

Schellekens, Maurice. "Digital Watermarks as Legal Evidence." 8 *Digital Evidence & Electronic Signature L. Rev.* 152 (2011).

Senior, Antonia. "Will We Ever Find the Kindle's Achilles Heel? Book Migration to Digital Is Utterly Dominated by Amazon and Its E-reader." *Guardian*, June 4, 2012.

Senoh, T., et al. "DRM Renewability and Interoperability." Paper presented at the Consumer Communications and Networking Conference, January 5, 2004.

Sunesh, Harish Kumar. "Watermark Attacks and Applications in Watermarking." *Int'l J. Computer Applications* 1 (2011). http://research.ijcaonline.org/rtmc/number10/rtmc1081.pdf.

Taylor, Jim. "DVD Frequently Asked Questions (and Answers)." DVD Demystified. http://www.dvddemystified.com/dvdfaq.html.

Tran, Jasper L. "The Law and 3D Printing." 31 *J. Marshall J. Info. Tech. & Privacy L.* 505 (2015).

―――. "Press Clause and 3D Printing." 14 *Nw. J. Tech. & Intell. Prop.* 75 (2015).

―――. "Rethinking Intellectual Property Transactions." 43 *S. U. L. Rev.* 149 (2016).

―――. "The Right to Attention." 91 *Ind. L. J.* (forthcoming, 2016). http://papers.ssrn.com/sol3/papers.cfm?abstract_id=2600463.

―――. "To Bioprint or Not to Bioprint." 17 *N.C. J. L. & Tech.* 123 (2015).

Trusted Computing Group. "Trusted Platform Module (TPM) Summary." http://www.trustedcomputinggroup.org/resources/trusted_platform_module_tpm_summary.

Vellante, David. "Data Encryption Strategies." Wikibon, September 29, 2009. http://wikibon.org/wiki/v/Data_encryption_strategies.

Whalen, Maureen. "Introduction to Metadata 3.0: Rights Metadata Made Simple." J. Paul Getty Trust, 2008. http://www.getty.edu/research/publications/electronic_publications/intrometadata/rights.pdf.

Wikipedia. "Digital Rights Management." https://en.wikipedia.org/wiki/Digital_rights_management.

―――. "DVD Region Code." https://en.wikipedia.org/wiki/DVD_region_code.

―――. "File Transfer Protocol." https://en.wikipedia.org/wiki/File_Transfer_Protocol.

―――. "Revocation List." https://en.wikipedia.org/wiki/Revocation_list.

―――. "Secured Transmission." https://en.wikipedia.org/wiki/Secure_transmission.

―――. "Side-Channel Attack." https://en.wikipedia.org/wiki/Side-channel_attack.

―――. "Trusted System." https://en.wikipedia.org/wiki/Trusted_system.

Wolf, Christopher. *The Digital Millennium Copyright Act: Text, History, and Caselaw* (2003).

X5 Networks. "Cryptography: How Do Digital Timestamps Support Digital Signatures?" http://x5.net/faqs/crypto/q108.html.

Yong, Seunglim, and Sang-Ho Lee. "An Efficient Fingerprinting Scheme with Secret Sharing." In *Digital Rights Management: Technologies, Issues, Challenges and Systems*, ed. Reihaneh Safavi-Naini and Moti Yung (2005).

Young, Georgia. "The Chilling Impact of Digital Restrictions Management in Libraries." Defective by Design, May 5, 2015. http://www.defectivebydesign.org/drm-in-libraries.

Zhang, Xiao, "A Survey of Digital Rights Management Technologies." November 28, 2011. http://www.cse.wustl.edu/~jain/cse571-11/ftp/drm/.

Zhu, Wen Tao. "Cryptanalysis of Two Group Key Management Protocols for Secure Multicast." In *Cryptology and Network Security: 4th International Conference*, ed. Yvo G. Desmedt et al. (2005).

Chapter Three

Understanding and Utilizing Digital Authentication

Amanda T. Watson

I recently received an email from a faculty member who wanted to have access to an e-book available through a common vendor. She had already provided proxy credentials to use the library's online catalog but was prompted for another set of credentials at the e-book access point. After guiding her through the process of creating those credentials, she expressed frustration when prompted to download a proprietary reader. Many steps later she was rewarded with a seven-day checkout. The faculty member was now very frustrated. Somehow, after all this effort, she could only use the downloaded book for seven days. I had to explain e-books are still library books with lending periods. Even after all this signing in and proving who you are, you are still just borrowing the material. She nodded, but her sentiment remained.

Why did she have to go to so much trouble to borrow an e-book? She had to authenticate to prove her rights to borrow the materials in question. Why was the process cumbersome? That is a more complicated question to answer.

In a digital rights management (DRM) transaction, authentication is the process that allows a user to prove they are entitled to access and use the material in question.[1] If properly authorized, the material is released to the user. This process can be quite simple or very complicated.

Authentication should balance the necessity of protecting the authority and fair use of digitized material with the ever-present needs of the user to access materials. For the rights holder, authentication communicates that the user in question is properly licensed to use the material. For the user, this step takes place almost entirely on the rights holder's side and should be as transparent and reliable as possible.

A useful analogy may be when an individual pays a bill at a restaurant using a credit card. The user simply hands over the card and waits. Of course, the card must be valid, meaning the user has acquired the proper authority to use it to pay for the meal. On the restaurant side of the transaction, the server runs the card and a complicated but automated system checks to make sure the card is valid and reflects the correct amount. For the restaurant diner, this transaction should be as simple as taking a sip of wine and waiting a few moments. And although we don't usually provide wine for the library user, our hope as librarians is to provide a similar low-effort, low-wait process for authentication. For this to happen, the restaurant server (here the library) and the credit card company (here the rights holder) must utilize a practiced and reliable method of authentication. The user's participation (here a patron of the library) should mostly, if not totally, have taken place prior to the transaction in question.

THE BASICS OF AUTHENTICATION

There are basically three types of authentication methods: authentication based on identification as a member with an account, authentication based on the device being used, and authentication based on individual user input.[2] The ways these methods are applied are many and varied, and they will continue to develop as authentication technology evolves.

Libraries can play a role by being aware of the ways users may be affected by the use of various authentication methods. This awareness can help do the following:

- Ensure that users are able to access the materials to the fullest legal extent possible
- Keep access as simple and open as possible
- Protect the user from any unnecessary collection of personal information[3]

MULTIPERSON MULTILEVEL DRM

Often material needs to be accessed for different reasons by different users. For instance, a distributor, a consumer, and a redistributor might all need to access the same material. When a DRM system is put into place to handle this type of situation, it is called multiperson multilevel DRM or MPML DRM. It is important to note that multiple types of DRM authentication might be used within this type of system.[4] Libraries should specifically be aware of these types of complicated structures because often systems that are set up specifically for libraries are MPML DRM systems.[5] The relevant levels include at a minimum the library and the patron.

COMMERCIAL MARKETS

Generally, whatever the task at hand, a librarian has the ability to research methods and choose the best fit for the library. When we are considering DRM, however, it is traditionally the content and not the system that drives our choice as librarians. In other words, we are choosing the information, not the authentication method. In digital materials there are certainly systems that might cover some of the same content, but different systems often allow access to different containers of content. Even if the librarian considers DRM when choosing a container, that container may change over time.

Since the content rights holders are the drivers, or at least the decision makers, of DRM systems, they are generally designed in favor of the rights holders. The ease of use for a library system is simply not on the forefront of developers' minds in creating these systems. Take, for example, a public library instruction sheet for patrons to check out Amazon Kindle books.[6] After executing the catalog search for the book, a user must complete about nine steps before ever touching their Kindle device. The user will have to log into both their library and Amazon accounts and enter a personal email address. Obviously, this is not close to a best practice for a library.

How can a librarian best serve the patron when it comes to DRM authentication? First, librarians must educate themselves on the many different DRM authentication methods. Second, we must discern if there are some methods that are simply too complicated or otherwise problematic to offer to our patrons and find other less challenging information sources.

READER WARS

Librarians have in some part always dealt with the concept of different modes of reading. Braille and large print are two obvious examples. But digital materials bring a new challenge. Patrons choose an e-book reader completely independent from their library. While libraries may recommend a reader, it is certain that libraries will be faced with different types of digital readers.[7] Why is this important? As we learn about the types of DRM, we understand that certain DRM systems only work on certain readers.[8] The authentication process for a library patron using licensed material will in some part be determined by the type of reading device used.[9] Even if the library makes an administrative decision to only purchase materials on certain systems, reference librarians will inevitably be called upon to talk about and support other systems.[10]

Note that most systems offer both a stand-alone reader and a portable reading application that can be loaded on computers, tablets, and phones. [11] However, this isn't always true. Some systems do not have a stand-alone reader (Adobe is the most obvious example).

Another distinction to remember is that there are reader devices (like Kindle or Nook) and then there are tablets (like iPad or Surface). [12] Tablets may allow multiple portable reading applications to be used but are not themselves a stand-alone reader. For instance, Amazon's Kindle Fire tablet allows you to download Barnes and Noble's portable reader application Nook so your Fire tablet use both Kindle and Nook materials. [13]

As librarians, we need to understand the restrictions common e-readers might place on our users and develop training materials for how to use library resources on different reader platforms.

TYPES OF AUTHENTICATION

Because one of the most important tools in a librarian's skill set concerning DRM should be an understanding of the types of authentication in play at their library and how these affect users, a description of different methods, examples of each method, and the benefits and determents of each method follows.

Keys

Perhaps one of the simplest concepts and certainly one of the most established is the key method. Aptly named, because it unlocks the material in question, a key is a system of numbers and letters given to the individual user at the time of purchase. At some point, the user is prompted to enter the key. If entered correctly, the material is unlocked for the user. [14]

On the rights holder's side, either an algorithm is used both to generate and verify the key or a completely random key is generated and stored in a database. [15] This is often called security through obscurity, meaning it is possible to guess the proper key, but it would be very difficult. [16]

Example: Anyone who has purchased a copy of a piece of software has likely encountered this method. Technology giant Microsoft uses a twenty-five-digit letter and number key code authentication method to allow users to unlock their software. [17] Microsoft actually embeds information into these codes—for instance, the version (home, professional, etc.) of the software. The key is printed on the packing material of the product or delivered via email to the user. At a certain point during installation, the user is prompted to enter the key. Once entered, the software verifies the key and gathers the information embedded. If correct, the software is unlocked. [18]

Benefits and determents: Keys are easily generated and are easy for users to navigate. The benefits generally end here. The concept of cracking keys or hacking keys is a very real problem for rights holders. If the algorithm used to create the key is discovered, users can simply take advantage of the same algorithm to crack the key. On the user side, codes can be easily misplaced. If reinstalling the software for a valid reason, such as the purchase of a new computer, one must be careful to retain the key to use the product on the new computer without needing to repurchase the software.

Limited Installation

Limited installation authentication allows users to access material only on specific machines or for a specified number of times. Limited installation is sometimes used in conjunction with other forms of DRM authentication. The thought behind limited installation is that a user can access the material but would be challenged if they attempted to transfer the material to another user.[19]

Sometimes limited installations have activation switches, meaning one account can be deactivated and another activated. This allows the user to have a certain number of installations active at any given time. The alternative is that the total number is limited, and deactivation is not an option.[20]

Limited installation is one of the most criticized forms of authentication by users. Rights holders contend that it helps avoid piracy, while users claim that it chills the ability to legally share or pass on items purchased by the user.[21]

Example: The Apple iTunes platform has many types of DRM in place. Limited installation is one of them. In this instance, each user's Apple ID can be used on up to ten devices, with an added limit that only five of those devices can be computers.[22] Apple goes another step to say certain Apple devices (like iPads and iPods) don't count toward your number of authorized devices.[23] Apple does allow you to deactivate devices to stay below your required number.[24] Music, movies, books, and other content can be shared across these active devices freely.[25]

Benefits and determents>: At least initially, one benefit is that the installation is very simple for the user. One large determent is that a user might be forced to reinstall content in a way that has nothing to do with piracy or reuse. For instance, if a user experiences a hard drive crash, they will likely have to reinstall the software. Obviously, this would be a permitted use, the same user with only one access point to the material. However, it would in theory take up two installations.

Persistent Online Authentication

Persistent online authentication, sometimes called always-on authentication, requires a user to be constantly connected to the Internet to use a resource. The user is logged into an authentication server on the rights holder's side that ensures the user is within their legal use of the product.[26] This type of authentication might use a number of methods to verify the user on its server.

Example: Popular game developer Maxis required persistent online authentication for its 2013 release of its hit game SimCity. Although some game functionality required the connection, the obvious purpose of the demand for Internet connectivity was DRM.[27]

Benefits and determents: There are no obvious benefits for the user. It has been said that if the material somehow requires constant Internet connection anyway, this method does not require any additional effort. However, this argument has not generally held up to scrutiny.[28] The most obvious determent is the need for an Internet connection. This is also matched by the need for the right holder's server to be constantly available. Any downtime interrupts the user's legal access to the material.

Digital Watermarking

Digital watermarking is the process of digitally adding a specific mark to material that passes information to the rights holder.[29] Watermarking is a traditional practice in print material, and digital watermarking builds off the same premise. The added information can tell the rights holder any number of things, including who the authorized user is and how the material was accessed.[30] Digital watermarks can sometimes be seen by the user and are sometimes concealed within the material. Steganography is the proper term for creating a concealed message like a digital watermark.[31]

Most often, digital watermarks do not act as a complete DRM solution for rights holders. Instead, they aide in providing information to the rights holder and sometimes even to the user about the material.

Example: Upon printing, an article from digital provider Gale Cengage will have a mark on each page identifying both the user and the license holder of the material. This not only identifies the source of any illegal use, but it also informs the user that she or he is responsible for the use of the document in question.

An example of a concealed watermark is publishing company HarperCollins's use of Guardian Watermarking for Publishing.[32] E-books from HarperCollins may contain a concealed watermark that is embedded and invisible to the reader. The watermark is unique to each individual e-book and allows the publisher to match it to a database containing customer information. Meanwhile, HarperCollins uses a search engine to scour the web for illegal use of its e-books.

Benefits and determents: For the user, digital watermarking happens without any prompt or input. The ease of use makes it attractive, at least initially. It allows legal use without any accidental interference by the rights holder. The main determent from the user side is that personal information is sometimes gathered and printed or embedded into the material.

Encryption Algorithms

Encryption algorithms are systems that use a specific player or device to decrypt the encryption placed on material.[33] Many systems are based on encryption algorithms, most often on DVDs. A system like this might control what device can access the material, the number of times it can be played, or whether the material can be copied in any way.[34]

The device must license the specific encryption algorithm system in order to display the material. Unlike with key authentication, the user does not provide any information.[35] The strength of the system lies in the complexity and thus the general impossibility that the algorithms can be discovered or guessed.[36]

There are generally two types of encryption: Symmetric key (or private key) encryption uses secret codes that are decoded by the device in question. Asymmetric (or public key) encryption uses a combination of codes, one public and one private. Basically, the public key encrypts the message and the private key decrypts it. Although different, the keys are mathematically linked.[37]

Example: Windows Media DRM employs a symmetric encryption algorithm system. Since Windows also has its own media player, it is a fairly straightforward proposition. Windows media is played on its player, which can read the encrypted information about the material.[38] The encrypted information includes the usual information about not only whether the material can be saved or copied but also if it can be played in certain regions. There is also a subscription music service that allows unlimited downloads of certain materials. But the encryption algorithm allows the player to discover if the subscription is active. If not, the media will not play.

Benefits and determents: One of the most developed types of authentication, encryption algorithms are generally considered reliable. The user has no complicated key to enter or retain; in fact, the key is generally never seen by the user. The largest determent is that there must be a system in place both to encode the data and to decode the data. These systems must be licensed. Also, sometimes certain devices are required to access the content.

Metadata and Identifiers

Metadata, in part, is like an electronic imprint page in a print book.[39] E-books travel with metadata including author, title, and publisher.[40] E-books also carry metadata specific to the world of DRM such as monetization, account holder information, licensing, and rights.[41] There is no one standard in place for what metadata should be included or how it should be formatted. Different venders have different requirements.

Within the world of metadata, there are identifiers to classify elements of book data.[42] An ISBN (International Standard Book Number) is an example of an identifier. When we think of metadata from the standpoint of DRM authentication, it is important to remember metadata will help us identify the correct material and in certain systems the correct price, license, and account holders.

Specific Technology

After identifying methods and their components, let's turn to some specific technologies.

E-book Technologies

To truly understand e-book authentication, we should first look at the common types of e-book technology (see table 3.1).

ePub is an XML-based specification that allows publishers to package material and metadata in a format that can be read by any ePub-compliant device. ePub is a product of the International Digital Publishing Forum, making it the only specific technology on this list not owned by a vendor.[43] It is free and open standard, making it wildly popular.[44] It is supported by a large range of readers, including Amazon Kindle and iBooks.[45] DRM is completely optional in ePub, but ePub is too prevalent in digital publishing not to be mentioned here.[46] No one system is endorsed by ePub, meaning

Table 3.1. Common E-book Technologies

Technology	Extension	DRM	Open Standard	Vendor
ePub	.epub	Optional	Yes	International Digital Publishing Forum
PDF	.pdf	Yes	Yes	Adobe
Topaz	.tpz or .azw1	Yes	No	Amazon
KF8	.azw3 or .azw	Yes	No	Amazon
Mobipocket	.prc or .mobi	Yes	No	Amazon

publishers still have to consider carefully the ultimate platform of their material when thinking of DRM.

PDF (portable document format) is Adobe Acrobat's document platform.[47] Since version 5.05, Adobe has included some digital security features, mostly allowing publishers to identify features through metadata.[48] In 2014, Adobe rolled out an entirely new DRM system relying heavily on encryption.[49] Instead of producing their own device, Adobe invites vendors to license directly with Adobe to develop DRM plugins using the Adobe platform. Almost all popular reader devices allow PDFs.[50]

Adobe's DRM scheme, ADEPT, can be applied to PDFs or ePubs. PDFs can be read on a free reader available for download, on most third-party readers, as well as with Adobe Digital Editions.[51]

Mobipocket is a complete software product including more than just a DRM solution.[52] Currently owned by Amazon, Mobipocket allows users to read e-books on many formats by allowing third-party companies to develop platforms that will display material.[53] Relying heavily on metadata, Mobipocket checks user rights and then through encryption releases the material to licensed users.[54]

Topaz, though much less used than in the past, uses its own encryption system. It is both valued and hated for its use of scans of material instead of fonts: loved because it allows content creators to specify special fonts and placements, but hated because many features (like increasing font size) do not work on Topaz documents.[55]

KF8, or **AZW3**, is a newer Kindle format. It is actually a compilation of several different components. It uses an Amazon DRM system. For backward compatibility (KF8 is supported by firmware 4.1.0 and later), a Mobi file is generally included in KF8 files, making the file size a little larger but ensuring compatibility in older Kindles.[56]

DRM Schemes

Adobe's ADEPT, mentioned above, is a DRM scheme that can be applied to PDFs or ePubs.[57] ADEPT stands for Adobe Digital Experience Protection Technology.[58] ADEPT uses keys to authenticate material. Each digital material receives a key, and each potential user has a key. Adobe encourages use of its own Adobe ID system for user keys.

When a user attempts to access content, the reader (Adobe Digital Editions software or another third-party reader) contacts the distributor's server running Adobe Content Server, which in turn contacts Adobe.[59] When all goes well, the keys presented are authenticated and the user is rewarded with licensed content. Through this communication Adobe is able to track all the purchases of each user, creating a privacy concern for users.

Apple also has a DRM scheme, named FairPlay. Based on technology from Veridisc (a now dissolved Illinois software corporation), FairPlay is applied to ePubs and can be read on Apple's iBooks platform on any iOS device (e.g., iPhones, iPads, MacBooks).[60] Every user must create an Apple ID. Since FairPlay materials only play on Apple devices, they rely on encryption keys stored in an Apple repository.

A key is created when a user creates an Apple ID. Then, every time a device is authorized with that ID, it is associated with that ID in the Apple repository. Likewise, each time content is authorized, a key is attached to the user ID. Each authorized device is sent a copy of each content key for the corresponding user. Like Adobe, Apple is able to keep track of purchases for users.

Barnes and Noble has its own DRM system, though it is implemented by Adobe. It uses ePub and some older formats. It uses encryption keys and like other services stores keys on its own server. You can read books authorized through Adobe ADEPT on your Nook device, but you must use Adobe Digital Editions to transfer the book to Nook.

Amazon also has its own DRM system that is applied to KF8, Topaz, and Mobipocket files.[61] Much like with Apple, you must use an Amazon device to view Amazon-protected materials. Since Amazon uses its own file types, this has presented problems for pass-through systems (see below).

ENTERPRISE DRM

Enterprise DRM, often called E-DRM or ERM or even IRM (information rights management), is not an authentication method but rather the process of making proprietary business documents secure using DRM methods.[62] Enterprise DRM is mentioned here to help eliminate confusion. Often the acronyms *ERM*, *E-DRM*, or *IRM* are presented with limited explanation of why they are being used.

For the librarian's purposes, E-DRM should be remembered simply as any system that protects company documents from outside distribution. For example, Samsung uses an internal system to provide E-DRM for many documents. This disallows proprietary documents from circulating outside the business in question. Consider a business like Coca-Cola. The secret recipe of Classic Coke is a highly guarded item. Enterprise DRM keeps the document safe from outside use while letting it be stored and circulated among authorized users. Again note, any of the methods above or combination thereof can be used to create an E-DRM system.

PASS-THROUGH SOLUTIONS

DRM pass-through solutions like OverDrive are very important to libraries. They provide DRM solutions that are at least in some part geared toward ease of use for patrons. When classifying these solutions in your head, think of them as sitting between the content provider and the library user. The first time a library user accesses material using OverDrive, they may be met with quite a complicated system. "I have yet to figure out how to use it! I think it is installed, but I'm not even sure of that. It is not user friendly. I have read several online help sites and nothing helps. From the sites, I'm not the only one with this problem."[63]

OverDrive was an early leader in digital content, creating interactive diskettes in the 1980s. In 2000, Content Reserve was launched as a digital e-book marketplace. Content Reserve became OverDrive, a fully automated e-book system for libraries.[64] It is currently compatible with iPad, iPhone, iPod Touch, Android phones and devices, Nook tablets, Windows and Mac computers, Chromebook, Windows phones, Kobo eReader, and Kindle.[65] It also has its own reader, OverDrive Reader. Because OverDrive provides DRM for more than just e-books, it is not simple to describe its total DRM solution. Adobe's ADEPT is one partner of OverDrive, though OverDrive has also partnered with Microsoft. OverDrive's own materials state, "OverDrive utilizes DRM through identity authentication and other industry security standards without exposing the file behind the e-book."[66]

To use OverDrive you must download the OverDrive application and create an OverDrive account.[67] You must enter your name and provide an email address, or you may sign up using Facebook if you have an account. Signing up using Facebook autopopulates the email address you used to sign up for Facebook. Then you register the libraries you are associated with. Depending on your library, you will not have to provide your library account information to OverDrive; you will sign in on your library's site instead.[68]

Owned by Bibliotheca, 3M Cloud Library licenses DRM from Adobe to create a fully automated library e-book system.[69] Much of its initial reader platform was derived from a German company named txtr.[70] 3M has been a provider of library services in the way of RFID tags and detection systems for many years. The Cloud Library allows you to browse, check out, and return library materials from participating libraries. It is currently compatible with iPad, iPhone, iPod Touch, Android phones and devices, Nook tablets, Windows and Mac computers, Kobo eReader, and Kindle Fire. It is not supported by non-Fire Amazon Kindle systems.[71] To use the system you must download the 3M Cloud Library application and enter your state, participating library, library username, and a library password if your participating library requires one.[72] This information should only be required the first time the application is used.

OverDrive is a subscription-based solution, while 3M Cloud Library is a purchase solution. Pricewise, OverDrive is more expensive. Both services work with most major publishers, including Random House, HarperCollins, and Penguin. Most other features are the same (with the notable exception of 3M being compatible with Kindle Fire devices but not other Kindle devices), but OverDrive is notably more complex to set up and use. [73]

LIBRARIAN'S ROLE

Authentication systems and requirements impact the user's ability to access material the library has specifically identified as relevant to its users. As a result, it is critical for librarians to be well versed in the types of authentication systems.

With an understanding of terminology, kinds of technologies, and the many different issues surrounding authentication, librarians are able to make the best decisions for their systems and develop the best advice for their patrons. These are important questions to consider in the authentication evaluation process:

- How many steps must a patron perform to initially use material?
- How many steps must a patron perform subsequently?
- Will the patron be asked to create a separate account?
- Will they be asked to provide an email address?
- Will they be asked to download additional software or applications?
- Will they be able to read the material on most devices?
- What file types will be available?
- What information about the patron will be stored on servers outside the library?
- What is the pay model for the library?
- Are help materials available for patrons?

CONCLUSION

While librarians will always care deeply about protecting the rights of content owners, we must carefully balance that obligation with serving our patrons. As long as DRM remains a commercially driven application, librarians must be informed and vigilant in our pursuit of balanced patron access. One way we can do so is by fully understanding DRM and its authentication systems and the manner in which they impact patrons.

NOTES

1. Dhanendran, "Digital Rights Management."
2. Bartik, "3 Different Types of User Authentication."
3. Baker, "DRM and the Challenge of Serving Users."
4. Sachan and Emmanuel, "Rights Violation Detection," 498.
5. Ibid.
6. Seattle Public Library, "Getting Started with Library Kindle eBooks."
7. The New York Public Library offers a program to help patrons choose a reader; New York Public Library, "eReader Basics."
8. *Kindled Health News*, "eReader Comparison Chart."
9. Educause, "7 Things You Should Know about E-readers."
10. King County Library has videos patrons can view to help understand e-readers; King County Library System, "eBooks & Downloads."
11. Weinraub Lajoie, Nichols, Hussong-Christian, and Bridges, "Four Librarians, Four E-readers."
12. Kent District Library, "Comparison of Popular eReaders."
13. *Kindled Health News*, "eReader Comparison Chart."
14. Microsoft TechNet, "Understanding Public Key Cryptography."
15. Maheshwari, "Secure Key Agreement," 114.
16. Johansson and Grimes, "Great Debate."
17. Microsoft Support, "Support for Microsoft Product Activation Problems."
18. Microsoft, "Packaged Software."
19. Smith, "Digital Rights Management."
20. Ibid.
21. Nuttall, "EA under Fire."
22. Apple, "View and Remove Associated Devices."
23. Apple, "Authorize Your Computer."
24. Ibid.
25. Apple, "View and Remove Associated Devices."
26. Smith, "Digital Rights Management."
27. Makuch, "Maxis."
28. Yin-Poole, "Id Software."
29. Bruno, "High Watermark."
30. Ibid.
31. Halder, Pal, and Cortesi, "Watermarking Techniques," 3165.
32. Kozlowski, "Digital Watermarks."
33. Planky, "Crypto Primer."
34. Arsenova, "Technical Aspects of Digital Rights Management."
35. Zhang, "Survey of Digital Rights Management."
36. Jorstad and Smith, "Cryptographic Algorithm Metrics."
37. Pal, "Application of Digital Rights Management," 13.
38. Microsoft, "Windows Media Player DRM."
39. Paskin, "Components of DRM Systems Identification," 26.
40. Ibid., 27.
41. Ibid., 56.
42. Ibid., 28.
43. International Digital Publishing Forum, "EPUB."
44. Book Industry Study Group, "Endorsement of EPUB 3."
45. Rothman, "At Least 16 E-reader Devices."
46. International Digital Publishing Forum, "EPUB."
47. Adobe, "What Is PDF?"
48. Planet PDF, "Adobe Systems Updates Acrobat."
49. Kozlowski, "Adobe Cracks Down."
50. *Kindled Health News*, "eReader Comparison Chart."
51. Zhang, "Survey of Digital Rights Management."

52. Mobipocket, "Introduction."
53. Acohido, "Amazon Expands."
54. Mobipocket, "Security/Encryption Options."
55. MobileRead, "Topaz."
56. Amazon, "Kindle Format 8."
57. Sfetcu, *What Is eBook?*
58. Hoepman, "Analysing ADEPT."
59. Adobe. "Adobe Content Server 4 User Manual."
60. Sfetcu, *What Is eBook?*
61. Ibid.
62. Zeng, "Quantitative Evaluation of Enterprise DRM," 160.
63. Microsoft, "Windows Media Player DRM."
64. OverDrive, "History."
65. OverDrive, "Getting Started with OverDrive."
66. OverDrive, "FAQ."
67. OverDrive, "Getting Started with Android."
68. OverDrive, "Which Sign-In Option."
69. Peet, "Bibliotheca Acquires 3M Library Systems.
70. Hellman, "3M's eBook Cloud Library."
71. 3M Cloud Library, "Overview."
72. 3M Cloud Library, "3M Cloud Library Reading Apps."
73. Colorado Library Consortium, "Libraries and eBooks."

REFERENCES

3M Cloud Library. "3M Cloud Library Reading Apps User's Guide." November, 2014. http:// www.3m.com/us/library/eBook/docs/3M%20Cloud%20Library%20Reading%20Apps% 20User%20Guide%202_9.pdf.
———. "Overview." http://www.3m.com/us/library/eBook/.
Acohido, Byron. "Amazon Expands into More Niche Markets." *USA Today Money*, April 19, 2005.
Adobe. "Adobe Content Server 4 User Manual." February 20, 2009. https:// www.assembla.com/spaces/bialec/documents/download/aKSkp41uyr35jCeJe5cbLA.
———. "What Is PDF?" https://acrobat.adobe.com/us/en/products/about-adobe-pdf.html.
Amazon. "Kindle Format 8." http://www.amazon.com/gp/feature.html?docId=1000729511.
Apple. "Authorize Your Computer in iTunes." August 31, 2015. https://support.apple.com/en-us/HT201251.
———. "View and Remove Associated Devices in iTunes." September 24, 2015. https:// support.apple.com/en-us/HT204074.
Arsenova, Emilija. "Technical Aspects of Digital Rights Management." http://wob.iai.uni-bonn.de/Wob/images/01212504.pdf.
Baker, Mitchell. "DRM and the Challenge of Serving Users." *Mozilla Blog*, May 14, 2014. https://blog.mozilla.org/blog/2014/05/14/drm-and-the-challenge-of-serving-users/.
Bartik, Christopher. "3 Different Types of User Authentication." *CloudEntr*, January 10, 2014. http://www.cloudentr.com/latest-resources/industry-news/2014/1/10/3-different-types-of-user-authentication.
Book Industry Study Group. "Endorsement of EPUB 3." August 6, 2012. https://www.bisg.org/ endorsement-epub-3.
Bruno, Anthony. "High Watermark: New DRM Technology Could Flood Consumers with Bonus Features." *Billboard*, January 19, 2008.
Colorado Library Consortium. "Libraries and eBooks." http://clicweb.org/save-money/ebooks.
Dhanendran, Anthony. "Digital Rights Management." *Computer Act!ve*, May 13, 2010. http:// bi.galegroup.com/essentials/article/GALE|A236961358/cd204e44f92b1e8d68af68ac1b6a 224d?u=tulane.

Educause. "7 Things You Should Know about E-readers." March 2010. http://net.educause.edu/ir/library/pdf/ELI7058.pdf.

Halder, Raju, Shantanu Pal, and Agostine Cortesi. "Watermarking Techniques for Relational Databases: Survey, Classification and Comparison." *Journal of Universal Computer Science* 16, no. 21 (2010): 3164–90.

Hellman, Eric. "3M's eBook Cloud Library Didn't Come out of Nowhere!" *Go to Hellman*, June 30, 2011. http://go-to-hellman.blogspot.com/2011/06/3ms-ebook-cloud-library-didnt-come-out.html.

Hoepman, Jaap-Henk. "Analysing ADEPT (Adobe Digital Experience Protection Technology)." *On Privacy, Security, and . . .*, April 12, 2012. http://blog.xot.nl/2012/04/12/analysing-adept-adobe-digital-experience-protection-technology/.

International Digital Publishing Forum. "EPUB." http://idpf.org/epub.

Kent District Library. "Comparison of Popular eReaders." October 23, 2014. http://kentisdat.pbworks.com/w/file/fetch/50998784/KDL%20Tablets%20price%20comparison.pdf.

Kindled Health News. "eReader Comparison Chart." July 6, 2010. https://kindledhealthnews.wordpress.com/2010/07/06/ereader-comparison-chart/.

King County Library System. "eBooks & Downloads." October 30, 2015. https://www.kcls.org/downloads/index.cfm?fontSize=normal.

Johansson, Jesper, and Roger Grimes. "The Great Debate: Security by Obscurity." *TechNet Magazine*, June 2008. https://technet.microsoft.com/en-us/magazine/2008.06.obscurity.aspx.

Jorstad, Norman, and Landgrave T. Smith Jr. "Cryptographic Algorithm Metrics." Institute for Defense Analyses, January 1997. http://csrc.nist.gov/nissc/1997/proceedings/128.pdf.

Kozlowski, Michael. "Adobe Cracks Down on Piracy with New ePub and PDF DRM." *Good eReader*, January 23, 2014. http://goodereader.com/blog/e-book-news/adobe-cracks-down-on-piracy-with-new-epub-drm.

———. "Digital Watermarks Take the Publishing World by Storm." *Good eReader*, November 4, 2014. http://goodereader.com/blog/e-book-news/digital-watermarks-and-social-drm-take-the-publishing-world-by-storm.

Maheshwari, B. "Secure Key Agreement and Authentication Protocols." *International Journal of Computer Science & Engineering Survey* 3, no. 1 (2012): 113–26.

Makuch, Eddie. "Maxis: SimCity's Always-On DRM for Gamers' Benefit." *GameSpot*, December 21, 2012. http://www.gamespot.com/articles/maxis-simcitys-always-on-drm-for-gamers-benefit/1100-6401896/.

Microsoft. "Packaged Software." https://www.microsoft.com/en-us/howtotell/Software.aspx#Packaging.

Microsoft. "Windows Media Player DRM: Frequently Asked Questions." http://windows.microsoft.com/en-us/windows/media-player-drm-faq#1TC=windows-7.

Microsoft Support. "Support for Microsoft Product Activation Problems." December 18, 2014. https://support.microsoft.com/en-us/gp/cu_sc_prodact_master.

Microsoft TechNet. "Understanding Public Key Cryptography." May 19, 2005. https://technet.microsoft.com/en-us/library/aa998077(v=exchg.65).aspx.

MobileRead. "Topaz." February 3, 2015. http://wiki.mobileread.com/wiki/Topaz.

Mobipocket. "Introduction." April 24, 2008. http://www.mobipocket.com/dev/article.asp?BaseFolder=prcgen&File=mobiformat.htm.

———. "Security/Encryption Options." http://www.mobipocket.com/dev/article.asp?BaseFolder=creatorpublisher&File=security.htm.

New York Public Library. "eReader Basics." April 9, 2015. http://www.nypl.org/events/programs/2015/04/09/ereader-basics.

Nuttall, Chris. "EA under Fire for Spore Piracy Measures." *Financial Times*, September 10, 2008.

OverDrive. "FAQ." http://readinfo.overdrive.com/about/faq.

———. "Getting Started with Android." April 19, 2016. http://help.overdrive.com/customer/portal/articles/1481622.

———. "Getting Started with OverDrive." April 19, 2016. http://help.overdrive.com/customer/en/portal/articles/1481729-getting-started-with-overdrive.

————. "History." http://company.overdrive.com/company/who-we-are/history/.

————. "Which Sign-In Option on My Library's New OverDrive Website Is Best for Me?" February 9, 2016. http://help.overdrive.com/customer/en/portal/articles/2319476-which-sign-in-option-in-the-overdrive-app-is-best-for-me-.

Pal, Ashish Kumar. "Application of Digital Rights Management in Library." *DESIDOC Journal of Library & Information Technology* 34, no. 1 (2014): 11–15.

Paskin, Norman. "Components of DRM Systems Identification and Metadata." *Lecture Notes in Computer Science* 2770 (2003): 26–61.

Peet, Lisa. "Bibliotheca Acquires 3M Library Systems." *Library Journal Industry News*, October 7, 2015. http://lj.libraryjournal.com/2015/10/industry-news/bibliotheca-acquires-3m-library-systems/.

Planet PDF. "Adobe Systems Updates Acrobat to v.5.0.5." December 19, 2001. http://wob.iai.uni-bonn.de/Wob/images/01212504.pdf.

Planky. "Crypto Primer: Understanding Encryption, Public/Private Key, Signatures and Certificates." *Plankytronixx*, October 22, 2010. http://blogs.msdn.com/b/plankytronixx/archive/2010/10/23/crypto-primer-understanding-encryption-public-private-key-signatures-and-certificates.aspx.

Rothman, David. "At Least 16 E-reader Devices Support or Will Support ePub via Adobe Digital Editions." *TeleRead*, August 13, 2009. http://www.teleread.com/ebooks/17-e-reader-devices-supporting-epub-via-adobe-digital-editions/.

Sachan, Amit, and Sabu Emmanuel. "Rights Violation Detection in Multi-level Digital Rights Management System." *Computers & Security* 30, no. 6 (2011): 498–513.

Seattle Public Library. "Getting Started with Library Kindle eBooks." September 2014. https://www.spl.org/Documents/collection/Getting_Started_with_Library_Kindle_eBooks.pdf.

Sfetcu, Nicolae. *What Is eBook? A Guide to Free eBook Publishing*. N.p.: Nicolae Sfetcu, 2014.

Smith, Steve. "Digital Rights Management." *TQA Weekly*, August 31, 2015. https://tqaweekly.com/episodes/season5/tqa-se5ep50.php.

Weinraub Lajoie, Evviva, Jane Nichols, Uta Hussong-Christian, and Laurie Bridges. "Four Librarians, Four E-readers, One Month." *Digital Shift*, October 11, 2011. http://www.thedigitalshift.com/2011/10/ebooks/four-librarians-four-ereaders-one-month/.

Yin-Poole, Wesley. "Id Software on Always-On Internet Debate." *Eurogamer*, October 8, 2011. http://www.eurogamer.net/articles/2011-08-10-id-software-on-always-on-internet-debate.

Zeng, Wen. "Quantitative Evaluation of Enterprise DRM Technology." *Electronic Notes in Theoretical Computer Science* 275 (2011): 159–74.

Zhang, Xiao. "A Survey of Digital Rights Management Technologies." November 28, 2011. http://www.cse.wustl.edu/~jain/cse571-11/ftp/drm/.

Chapter Four

Organizations and Workflow

Leveraging Your Library to Make the Most of DRM

Ashley Krenelka Chase

There are many complicated factors to consider when dealing with digital rights management (DRM) in libraries. So many factors are at play, in fact, that the impact on the library's organizational structure and the workflows within that structure are likely to be last-minute considerations, if considered at all. While the swift and rather unforgiving entrance of DRM into libraries has not left much room for a weighing of organizational and workflow pros and cons, it is essential to the successful administration of every library to take a step back and determine the following:

- Can the library's current organizational structure and workflows be leveraged to seamlessly incorporate DRM and its intricacies?
- Do the library's organizational structure and workflows need to be overhauled to allow DRM to be dealt with appropriately?
- Is the staff of the library adequately equipped to deal with DRM, and if not, what needs to be done to better situate the current staff members for success?
- What are the benefits and detriments of suggested strategies for dealing with DRM in your library?

Many libraries have been haphazardly responding to, working around, or ignoring DRM. With proper planning and an awareness of the organization's strengths and challenges, any library's organizational structure and workflows can be adapted or changed completely to efficiently integrate DRM and the related technologies.

BACKGROUND

It is widely known that libraries and librarians are masters of change, whether they want to be or not. The shift from print to digital has radically changed the way libraries operate—from public services to technical services—and the related technological changes often come on rapidly, leaving organizational structures and workflows steps behind and constantly striving (or struggling) to keep up. Changes of this nature affect all kinds of libraries, and both libraries and librarians need to understand and realize the benefit arising from these changes instead of merely being forced to deal with their side effects.[1] As change occurs, library departments tend to merge (or divide) and individuals are asked to work together in new and unexpected ways.[2] For example, technical services staff may now need to train or explain to frontline circulation staff how to help library users struggling with e-book access. Concepts such as authentication protocols and limits on use, once the purview of technical services, are now front-and-center access service issues. It is no surprise, then, that the introduction of DRM into ongoing library operations may have as much impact as joining forces with another department or setting up a second reference desk. Organizational change, whether in the structure of the library or in workflows, impacts everyone in the library and everyone the library serves, from the most forward thinking to the most resistant. And, as we know, change is never easy.

DRM: How Did We Get Here?

The introduction of DRM into a library will likely mean something different depending on the type of library discussed. At public libraries, DRM's impact may be felt most significantly by a patron who can't play a DVD on her personal laptop or another whose text-to-voice software won't play an e-book because the product can't be "read."[3] In an academic library, the impact of DRM may be felt when the library is asked to add streaming video services; when it must explain on-campus and other access requirements to students; when faculty refuse to use a publication due to restrictions on use;[4] or when institutions implement DRM for born-digital works created in-house. All of these DRM scenarios are frustrating for the patron, and none is easy to deal with or explain to patrons challenged by DRM limitations, particularly for a library that is ill-prepared to handle challenges of this nature.

In identifying many of the DRM-related issues that plague libraries, Russell detailed those related to copyright law and fair use and what those mean for both libraries and end users.[5] The issues outlined range from CDs being produced and sold as "copy proof," which eliminates any and all fair or educational uses, to e-books that are unable to be copied or loaned, including e-books that are in the public domain. Without an attorney on call, libraries have been left to wade through these complicated, often convoluted issues with little guidance. Additionally, many of the conversations around DRM and its various and sundry issues involve the back end: how does the technology make the resources usable (or not), and what are the barriers for access that don't exist with traditional print resources or electronic resources with unrestricted access? Issues related to DRM are not this simple, however, and librarians are in a unique position with regard to DRM not only because they understand the need for meaningful access and user privacy, but because they also have a greater understanding of the fine line between being a body that creates information and one that uses information.[6] A "good" DRM system would, Russell argued, provide ample rights to both copyright holders and users, while allowing for all fair uses.[7]

The issues Russell identified over a decade ago continue to resonate today. What is the one change in the DRM of today from the DRM of yore? Today users are so acclimated to accepting terms of service for everything that they rarely blink an eye at a DRM contract that pops up on a DVD or e-book without necessarily understanding to what they are agreeing. Librarians without training are equally guilty of this level of resigned, well-intentioned compliance, and where there is poor communication about DRM in the workplace, the intersection of public and technical services in dealing with DRM causes additional issues. In public services, communication with patrons about DRM, and the materials that it affects, can cause frustration. In technical services, a lack of understanding about how patrons are using items affected by DRM may cause similar frustrations. For these reasons, organizational structures and workflows must be adjusted—and the related training must be provided—to ensure that the library is acting as an appropriate liaison between provider and end user. For example, in order to properly educate users, the frontline staff must rely on training and information from the technical services department, and the technical services staff must listen to patron feedback (provided through public services staff) when purchasing and implementing new electronic resources.

Organizational Evolution

Much like DRM has changed since it first came on the scene, libraries have undergone an advancement and evolution unlike almost any other industry. This can be most obviously seen in the shift from collections being primarily print to including a substantial amount of electronic resources, but it also can be seen in other shifts—for example, from serving as access points for information to also being creators of information. Libraries are in a constant evolutionary process, and library literature reflects this shift. Between 1965 and 2005, literature in the field of library and information science went from primarily investigating individual library systems and institutions to looking at how individual libraries provide services to end users, how individuals use the library, and how people behave within and use the library.[8] One thing has remained constant despite this shift: library changes are driven by technology.[9]

Previously, much of the changes to library technology involved how materials were processed by technical services departments, as opposed to how materials were used by patrons. Instead of changing the workflows to react to the changes in technology, Breeding indicates that these changing technologies were, historically, applied to improve the workflows, which tended to remain constant.[10] Because technology was being used to make libraries more efficient, workflows were simply being tweaked for improvement without being changed. As libraries waded through the print-to-digital revolution, Breeding found that libraries needed not only to keep up with the shift in materials but to constantly evaluate the library's organization and workflows, allowing libraries to utilize more staff and cross-train in a more effective manner. Fortunately, the changes some library organizations underwent in the original shift from print to digital collections may make them more adaptable to the continued changes that will likely be essential in effectively implementing increasingly complicated DRM programs and related technologies. In order to do this effectively, a library must look at workflows and the organizational structure to determine strengths and weaknesses; this internal examination and assessment is essential to any organizational change.[11]

The Evolution of Librarian Skills

In line with the need for libraries to be adaptable and constantly ready for change, librarians must be similarly forward thinking. Fifty years ago, it was unfathomable that a librarian would need to catalog digital materials or advise walk-in patrons on what could or could not be accessed on the Internet. Today, along with reader's advisory, reference, and traditional cataloging, librarians are expected to understand complicated integrated library systems, the intricacies of Internet privacy, the ins and outs of electronic media, and more. No longer considered a fringe skill, the ability to use technology efficiently and effectively is now a core competency of librarianship. Core competencies are "knowledge or abilities related to a specific subject area or skill set."[12] When discussing core competencies, it is important to remember that they will vary given the type of position (paraprofessional versus professional) and the position itself (systems librarian versus reference librarian), as well as the way these types of positions intersect. Some hard and soft skills, however, are essential for every librarian.

In 2009 the Library and Technology Association (LITA) identified sets of required hard and soft skills for every librarian charged with understanding and working with library technology.[13] These skills include the ability to understand computers, their functions, and operating systems and basic troubleshooting; the capacity to learn and adapt quickly; and the ability to embrace change and manage projects. In the time since LITA published the *Core Technology Competencies for Librarians and Library Staff,* the North American Serials Interest Group (NASIG) published the "NASIG Core Competencies for Electronic Resources Librarians."[14] While it is obvious, based on job descriptions alone, that not all librarians are electronic resources librarians, NASIG's core competencies are particularly relevant for all librarians in the age of DRM, regardless of whether the words *electronic resources*, *web*, or *technology* appear in their position description.

Among the many core competencies outlined by NASIG, there are several standouts. The first is that librarians must understand the life cycle of electronic resources. This includes understanding the basics of electronic acquisitions, access, administration, and support of the electronic resources.[15] There are a variety of ways to ensure that all librarians understand this cycle, from additional, informal training to more formal professional development opportunities, and the use of resources such as charts or checklists, created specifically with an individual library's needs in mind, may be helpful.[16] In addition to encouraging an understanding of the electronic resources life cycle by all paraprofessionals and librarians, any member of the library staff dealing with electronic resources must have effective communication skills, flexibility, and a high tolerance for complexity. These skills are also valuable for all librarians, and not just those who work with electronic resources regularly. Each of these skills, individually, is arguably preferred in any librarian, but when dealing with DRM and the associated technologies, the ability to use these skills is more important than ever. As librarians continue to learn to work with a wide variety of technological systems, these skills should continue to evolve.

ORGANIZATIONAL STRUCTURES

Even the smallest libraries have added digital resources to their collections and, along with these resources, have the responsibility of effectively and efficiently navigating and managing the related DRM. What is a library to do to best deal with the challenges and opportunities presented by the DRM integrated into its collections? Would it be in the best interests of the library to restructure, or can the current organizational structure and workflows be leveraged for success? There are many factors to consider with both of these options.

Restructuring

The first question to ask when determining how best to implement DRM in a library is whether or not the organizational structure of the library and, logically, the workflows need to be restructured to accommodate the technologies.

Determining whether or not to revamp and restructure the library requires consideration of a number of factors. Are the library employees entrenched in their current positions and unwilling or unable to learn new skills, particularly those skills related to technology? Restructuring may be beneficial in that instance, as a total overhaul is sometimes needed to reframe perceptions about the work that needs to be done and how it can be done. Are there staff in the library who don't work particularly well together? DRM involves constant interplay between technical services and public services. While technical services staff are more likely to understand the nuts and bolts of DRM, public services staff may be more likely to understand why a type of DRM will or won't work for the library's patrons. The public services staff is also going to be on the front line explaining DRM's restrictions and limits to frustrated patrons. These groups are going to have to work together to successfully implement DRM, and combining departments or shifting responsibilities may be the only way to facilitate those changes.

Asking these difficult (or perhaps not so difficult) questions about the reality of a library's current organizational structure is an essential starting point to making any organizational change, but it is particularly pertinent when the changes involve cross-departmental workflows. The practical realities of DRM mean a constant interpretation and evaluation of library patrons' needs while simultaneously maintaining technology (that the library may not own or control) that may prevent this access or make it significantly more difficult. It may be beneficial to pull staff members in from both sides, public and technical services, to form a new electronic services staff that deals primarily with electronic materials. If the library is like most in the twenty-first century, however, "technical services" already has much more to do with digital than print, so an entirely new department may not be what is needed.

Renaming a technical services department or realigning it with circulation (including a merger or reorganization of workspaces) can yield interesting results for dealing with DRM, as well as a variety of other issues, including acquisitions problems, customer service disruptions, or a staff shortage. [17] Combining two departments allows paraprofessional staff with a variety of different workflows to work together, and the internal brainstorming of a new department may lead to new ways to deal with DRM. On the other hand, this alternative leaves professional librarians who may not, formally, be considered a part of either technical services or circulation—often the first responders to access issues related to DRM—out in the proverbial cold. There are many ways to prevent this, the most successful being to include librarians in meetings where workflows and issues are being discussed, and to make sure that librarian job descriptions include time spent with the circulation and technical services teams, working through these issues. Increasing communication between paraprofessionals and librarians, regardless of whether these individuals fall within technical services or circulation, will ensure that each member of the library staff is on the same page when dealing with DRM.

Because of the challenges associated with reorganizing and renaming departments, an entire reorganization of the library may not be a viable option to use to incorporate the new needed workflows involving disparate staff groups. A team-based approach to a DRM-focused library reorganization is likely to work best. Each and every reference librarian is likely to be asked questions about access to electronic resources: *Why can't I use this on my Windows Phone? How come I can't print this document from my iPad? Why won't my Nook load this e-book? Why can't I access this database outside the library? Why can't I access this e-book when it is in the main university catalog but not my campus catalog?* Providing the folks who answer these questions, the DRM first responders, with a team member from technical services may allow for a more seamless experience for the patron. This, of course, requires each first responder to understand that a DRM-related question will undoubtedly be asked by a patron and each technical services partner to be prepared to help with delivering an answer the patron can understand and implement. Because staff don't all work identical schedules, a full-scale explanation of DRM and related training sessions will likely be required to pull everyone on board.

After training, applying an organizational "team" approach will allow for open communication between the front and back ends of the DRM process. Ensuring that any first responder has quick, convenient access to another, possibly more tech- or DRM-savvy person in the library guarantees that user questions will be answered in a timely fashion and any DRM-related issues that may crop up, whether they involve access on the front or back end, will be addressed quickly. This approach will allow additional opportunities for everyone in the library to learn about, and hopefully understand, DRM while ensuring the best possible service to patrons. Additionally, this team approach will highlight those with a better understanding of DRM and the technologies and challenges, or those interested in stepping up and learning more or managing a team, which could lead to additional role shifting within the organization in the future.

The benefits of implementing organizational change with this level of cross-training and departmental involvement may not seem obvious, but when dealing with new technologies such as DRM, staff often have a better ability to cope with the changes in workflows when other changes, such as changes to departments or physical space, occur simultaneously.[18] Asking every professional and paraprofessional staff member in the library to take on responsibility for understanding a new technology and associated workflow is likely to be met with a lot of resistance, particularly by those who are resistant to change. But implementing a DRM workflow as part of a greater library reorganization may cushion the blow, make new opportunities for those willing to step up, and make all parties more open-minded about embracing new things that can only raise the value of the library in the eyes of patrons.

Utilizing Current Structures

It is clear in many libraries that the type of physical, organizational, and cultural upheaval encouraged by Cohen might not work for everyone or every situation. In situations where factors make a large-scale reorganization, retraining, or rebranding impossible, current organizational structures should be leveraged to best implement DRM and its related workflows. Some libraries may even benefit from maintaining the organization's structural status quo as it relates to DRM.

As there are many benefits to reorganization, there are, alternatively, many benefits to utilizing the library's current organizational structure to more formally implement DRM and the related technologies. DRM issues will vary widely depending on the type of library, the library's patron base, and the extent to which the library finds itself dealing with electronic resources. In addition, some DRM issues affecting patrons are outside the library's scope. A library's staff is, arguably, its greatest resource in responding to these varied DRM issues: they know the patron base, they know the collection, and they know how these two things come together to make the library a uniquely useful and wonderful place to be. Utilizing this built-in panel of experts may better inform the library's response to DRM. Librarians and staff who regularly work with patrons will likely be able to quickly identify if the issue is truly one related to the library's DRM technology, such as licensing limitations, or simple patron error.

As an example, at the Dolly & Homer Hand Law Library at Stetson University College of Law, the collection does not currently include traditional e-book packages. The e-books that are currently a part of the collection are not separately cataloged or managed and are only discoverable through vendor discovery systems (namely, LexisNexis and Westlaw). While this is a unique situation, it means that a laundry list of DRM considerations, such as ensuring that the books can be read on multiple devices or that talk-to-text will work on a given patron's computer, do not apply. Similarly, a bookmobile that does not provide access to electronic resources, other than on an internal, single shared computer, will not have to worry about operating system issues that may come from patrons trying to access those resources from their home computers, laptops, or tablets. In order to best determine if a library's current organizational structure can be used to implement DRM, the starting point is identifying which resources are affected by DRM and how patrons use these resources. Once known, factors such as these should be considered, with the consultation of the entire library staff, in developing a response to DRM.

In gathering together this panel of experts, patterns may start to emerge. One or two librarians or staff may express an interest in DRM, while others will likely say they do not know much about it and are not interested in learning more. From that conversation, a task force to deal with and implement DRM may be born. Allow the members of the library with interest to take the lead, and encourage (or require, depending on how the library functions) others to participate. It is likely that a lack of interest in DRM is born out of fear of the unknown or because they feel they are locked into a particular position due to library policies. Educating members of the library staff on DRM can negate some of these fears, as can inviting every member of the staff to participate in DRM-related workflows, with the understanding that it is a learning experience, mistakes will happen, but the library's patrons will be better served if every member of the team becomes comfortable working with the technology. In the end, requiring individuals from each department of the library with varying levels of interest to participate in a task force will be to everyone's advantage.

With guidance from a systems librarian or particularly tech-savvy member of the library administration, this task force should be allowed to meet regularly to work out best practices for DRM implementation, as well as deal with the challenges brought to light internally or by patrons struggling to access resources. This task force should provide regular updates to the entire library staff on the current state of the library's electronic resources and formulate a list of frequently asked questions that would allow all staff members to answer patron questions. Keeping every member of the library staff informed, without requiring them to learn new skills or workflows, allows for a less disruptive implementation of DRM that is still likely to provide all of the benefits of a restructuring.

SKILLS AND EXPERTISE

Much like the decision to change a library's organizational structure or workflows to accommodate the use of DRM, the implementation of DRM may also require some consideration of the library's current talent pool to determine whether or not the library can achieve success with its current staff. It is highly likely, of course, that a library's budget will not allow for the hiring of new talent. In that instance, it is essential to identify talented, interested staff members within the library and implement DRM training to use the current talent to meet the needs of today's library.

Bringing in New Talent

In a perfect world, each member of the library staff would have expertise in an area (or two) and new staff members with new expertise would be hired to meet new needs as they arise. Unfortunately, libraries don't exist in a perfect world. For those libraries fortunate enough to be able to hire when needs arise, there are many benefits to fresh talent, particularly with regard to DRM.

As much as there has been a shift in library collections in recent years, there has also been a significant shift in the field of library science and what is being taught in graduate programs all over the United States (and the world). Courses that previously were not considered to provide a core competency are now commonly integrated into graduate curricula (e.g., web design). In addition, course content now typically includes information and course work on topics such as digital libraries, information technology, information governance, library networks, and database management and creation.[19]

The benefit of hiring a newly minted librarian seems obvious in light of the curriculum changes in graduate programs. Due to the expanded availability of tech-centric courses, it is hoped that librarians fresh out of a graduate school understand what DRM is and why it is important for libraries to effectively manage it. In addition to having a basic understanding of DRM upon entering the profession, these new librarians are likely to be more familiar with the patron-side technologies related to DRM, as most of them will be digital natives, familiar with technology, such as e-books, to a degree previously unheard of in the field of information science.

In addition to the change in course work that librarians who are new to the profession will have experienced, they are also more likely to join a library staff with less preconceived notions about what a library's organizational structure or workflows should look like. Adding a new librarian with an understanding of DRM and a flexible approach to organizational structure can provide a breath of fresh air and allow DRM to be implemented more easily, even without other changes to the library's organizational structure or workflows.

Conversely, some current library staff may resent the introduction of not only a new member of the team but one with an entirely new set of responsibilities in an area that current staff have not previously handled in a formal way. Communication needs to remain a constant. As previously indicated, large-scale conversations across the library about what DRM is, how it is going to be employed in the library, what the impact will be on the library, and who is going to bear the brunt of the work related to (internal and external) DRM need to begin as soon as the library starts to consider formal plans for implementation, as opposed to mere case-by-case management or on-the-spot troubleshooting.

Utilizing Who (and What) You Have

In uncertain economic times, libraries all over the country are cutting budgets or reallocating funds, and these funds are not always put toward staff or professional development. The economic climate surrounding libraries is likely to mean that a library implementing DRM won't have the luxury of bringing in new talent to manage the process.

As referenced in the previous sections, an essential first step in formally implementing DRM within a library's current organizational structure and workflows will be identifying the people who are interested in DRM and who have the skill set to work with DRM effectively. This will likely be a cross-section of library staff; individuals from both public and technical services and from the paraprofessional and professional groups will need to be involved to make formal implementation successful. After identifying the groups of individuals who are best suited to work with DRM, training becomes the next step in ensuring success.

Training for DRM in libraries is scarce. A quick Google search for DRM training available online reveals a multitude of courses aimed at professionals working with data relationship management but very few related to DRM. This scarcity of training resources may make the implementation of DRM with current staff seem daunting, but steps can be taken to ensure a relatively seamless beginning and success in the long term.

Initially, a meeting of the library staff who will be involved in the formal DRM implementation process will be helpful in identifying potential issues, not only within the team but with the workflows created to manage this new type of resource management. The team should brainstorm the following questions:

- What are the resources involved?
- Is each resource being created within the library, and if so, what kind of DRM is needed (if any)?
- On what platform are the resources available?
- Are there any operating system or device limitations?
- Will the resources be accessible to those with disabilities?
- Will the resources be available to all of the library's patrons?
- How many users will the resources accommodate?
- Is the location of the user relevant to use of the resources?

- How will the library communicate DRM issues with its patrons?
- Should a ticketing or other system be used to track DRM issues? Should the system be only for library-created content or for all resources?

These questions do not, of course, touch on everything that must be discussed related to DRM and its implementation. Additional conversations will likely flow from these questions, and library staff from both public and technical services backgrounds are likely to have differing opinions on these issues and how they impact the library, if at all.

Using these questions to start the DRM implementation conversation with existing staff will allow for logical discussions about the next questions: Who in the library feels most comfortable answering or resolving most (or any) of these questions? Should more individuals be involved? When these questions come up in the future, who needs to be involved in answering them? What can be done to ensure that every member of the library feels comfortable, to some degree, answering basic questions about DRM? Is there anyone on the team who would feel comfortable taking the lead on training initiatives for the entire library? It's important to remember that, while a core team is essential for DRM implementation, it will take all members of the library staff to truly make DRM functional, especially in a situation in which a new librarian with the requisite expertise cannot be hired to assist with the process.

If an individual can be identified to spearhead the training process, it may make the implementation of DRM easier on the entire library team. The individual chosen to lead training should have the qualities identified by NASIG in the core competencies for electronic resources librarians, as well as an in-depth knowledge of the library's patrons and patron use of the library. This understanding should be of not only what patrons are using in the collection but also how they are using the collection, where they use it, and any changes patrons would like to see to the library's resources. Finding a librarian or paraprofessional with all of these skills may sound like finding a unicorn—remember, this combination of talents can be developed or identified in more than one person. It is important that whoever is chosen to lead DRM training understands the politics of incorporating change in libraries and the impact that new organizations, processes, and workflows can have on staff who have worked in the library for any length of time.

It is important to remember that DRM can be a difficult concept to understand, the technologies may be unfamiliar, and people may be reluctant to learn. Patience is essential, as well as a desire by the person doing the training to accept feedback and tailor training to meet the needs of library staff and patrons and incorporate necessary changes discovered throughout the process.

TYING IT ALL TOGETHER

There is nothing easy about DRM. It is a hard concept for most to understand (and to translate for the patron), even at the most basic level, and becomes more challenging in libraries where the DRM issues are so vast and the technologies so disparate. There is no surefire way to know what will work best in any individual library. Some libraries will benefit from maintaining the status quo and formally implementing DRM into existing organizational structures and workflows, while others may need to reorganize teams or departments or hire new staff to accommodate the change in responsibilities.

One thing remains constant regardless of the type of library, the structure of the organization, or the current or anticipated workflows: shifting from a haphazard, shotgun approach to DRM to a more formal implementation is a trial-and-error process. A library may hire a new librarian to assist with the process and find that the person is better suited to traditional reference work and need to start from scratch with current staff to move forward. There is no perfect way to go about integrating an entirely new set of knowledge and understanding, as well as the associated challenges and confusion, into an already well-functioning library.

Libraries seeking to properly implement DRM are likely to experience growing pains. The patrons will be confused about usage terms for resources that they believe to be limitless. Staff will be confused about what to tell patrons or where to look for the answer. These problems should be anticipated and accepted without resistance. Answering questions as they come up after implementation allows the entire library to continue to evolve and become better equipped to deal with DRM. Sit down and think about how the library wants to use DRM and how that will impact the library's unique organizational structure and workflows. Every library can (and should) prepare to deal with DRM in a more formal, efficient, and effective way; as collections become increasingly electronic, DRM will impact all of our workflows and organizations—whether we're ready or not.

NOTES

1. Brunelle, "New Learning."
2. Glazier and Glazier, "Merging Departments," 263.
3. Russell, "Fair Use under Fire."
4. Albanese, "MIT Faculty Say No."
5. Russell, "Fair Use under Fire."
6. Ibid.
7. Ibid.
8. Tuomaala, Jrvelin, and Vakkari, "Evolution of Library and Information Science."
9. Saracevic, "Information Science."
10. Breeding, "New Library Collections."
11. Chase, "Watch Out for the Bus."

78   *Ashley Krenelka Chase*

12. Thompson, *Core Technology Competencies*.
13. Ibid.
14. Sutton et al., "NASIG Core Competencies."
15. Ibid.
16. Chase, "How to Manage Electronic Resources."
17. Chase and Barnes, "Road Oft Traveled."
18. Cohen, "How Physical Space Can Drive Cultural Change."
19. Noh, Sang-Ki, and In-Ja, "Study on Developing Library and Information Science."

REFERENCES

Albanese, Andrew. "MIT Faculty Say No to Restrictive DRM." *Library Journal* 132, no. 8 (2007): 20
Breeding, Marshall. "New Library Collections, New Technologies: New Workflows." *Computers in Libraries*, June 2012, 23–25.
Brunelle, Eugene. "New Learning, New Libraries, New Librarians." *Journal of Academic Librarianship* 1, no. 5 (1975): 20–24.
Chase, Ashley Krenelka. "How to Manage Electronic Resources." In *The Small Library Manager's Handbook*, edited by Alice Graves, 127–38. Lanham, MD: Rowman & Littlefield, 2014.
———. "Watch Out for the Bus: Tales of Cross-Training, Teams, and Rotating Duties in an Academic Law Library." In *Partnerships and New Roles in the 21st-Century Academic Library: Collaborating, Embedding, and Cross-Training for the Future*, edited by Bradford Lee Eden, 149–58. Lanham, MD: Rowman & Littlefield, 2015.
Chase, Ashley Krenelka, and Elizabeth C. Barnes. "The Road Oft Traveled: Collection Analysis and Development in a Modern Academic Law Library." *Collection Management* 39, no. 2/3 (2014): 196–210.
Cohen, Richard J. "How Physical Space Can Drive Cultural Change." *Philadelphia Business Journal*, December 1, 2014. http://www.bizjournals.com/philadelphia/blog/guest-comment/2014/12/how-physical-office-space-can-drive-cultural.html.
Glazier, Rhonda R., and Jack D. Glazier. "Merging Departments in a Small Academic Library." In *Innovative Redesign and Reorganization of Library Technical Services: Paths for the Future and Case Studies*, edited by Bradford Lee Eden, 263–73. Westport, CT: Libraries Unlimited, 2004.
Noh, Younghee, Sang-Ki Choi, and In-Ja Ahn. "A Study on Developing Library and Information Science Core Course Syllabi." *Canadian Journal of Information & Library Sciences* 38, no. 3 (2014): 145–87.
Russell, Carrie. "Fair Use under Fire." *Library Journal* 128, no. 13 (2003): 32–33.
Saracevic, Tefko. "Information Science." *Journal of the American Society for Information Science* 50, no. 12 (1999): 1051–63.
Sutton, Sara, Eugenia Beh, Steve Black, Clint Chamberlain, Susan Davis, Katy Ginanni, Selden Lamoureux, Sanjeet Mann, Cynthia Porter, and Taryn Resnick. "NASIG Core Competencies for Electronic Resources Librarians." North American Serials Interest Group, July 22, 2013. http://www.nasig.org/Uploaded_files/92/Files/CoreComp/CompetenciesforERLibrarians_final_ver_2013-7-22.Pdf.
Thomspon, Susan M., ed. *Core Technology Competencies for Librarians and Library Staff*. Library and Information Technology Association Guide 15. New York: Neal-Schuman, 2009.
Tuomaala, Otto, Kalervo Jrvelin, and Pertti Vakkari. "Evolution of Library and Information Science, 1965–2005: Content Analysis of Journal Articles." *Journal of the Association for Information Science & Technology* 65, no. 7 (2014): 1446–62.

Chapter Five

Provisions for Digital Collections and Sample Language

Brian R. Huffman and Victoria J. Szymczak

Digital acquisition constitutes a game changer for all types of libraries. It affects space, usage, preservation, and, ultimately, collection policies. Availability of materials in digital form has many advantages over print material, but it comes with a cost.[1] Unlike with traditional print materials, digital providers make their product available through the lens of contract law rather than copyright law. The guidelines and policies that guided U.S. libraries for decades have been replaced by contract provisions we collectively refer to as digital rights management (DRM). It should not be surprising that this material type requires rethinking our classic collection development plans. Here we will look at the background of DRM and how it affects library operations, contract negotiation, and developing and managing collections that are increasingly digital. We focus on e-book selections; however, our review and examples of collection development plan (CDP) e-book provisions are relevant across all types of digital content.

CONTRACT MODELS FOR LIBRARY ACQUISITIONS AND BEST PRACTICES

Our discussion of digital collections starts with a review of the licensing and contract models available to libraries. Typically, digital content is licensed rather than owned outright. Libraries encounter two types of license agreements: end use agreement (EUA) and site license. An EUA involves CD-ROMS, email, blogs, iTunes, smart phone apps, and other general software programs. Site licenses involve databases, e-journals, and other continuing electronic resources. Historically, contracts for digital content offer less favorable terms than those for print: they commonly have embargo periods for newer content, limit circulation, and may provide for in-library access only. Other DRM obstacles include restrictions on who can access the material and for what purposes, printing or downloading, frequency and length of time users can view the content, the number and type of devices where the content can be viewed, and how it can be shared.[2] Digital licensing contract models are in flux and continue to evolve. No single business model will offer ideal terms for all libraries, nor will all models be adopted by every publisher. The following discussion outlines five factors to consider when reviewing digital content contracts.

Five Factors to Consider When Reviewing Digital Content Contract Models

Restrictions and Enforcement. Significant attention should be paid to DRM restrictions or important factors that are absent, vague, undefined, or given limited treatment in the licensing contract. Enforcing contract terms through DRM software allows vendors to respond unilaterally to perceived breaches, without giving libraries recourse to disagree with the vendors' interpretation or an opportunity to confirm facts.[3] This results in blocked access to collections or new fee structures to maintain access to collections. DRM restrictions often supplement those found in the license. If important "use" considerations are missing from the contract, it is imperative for the library to track them down, clarify, and negotiate them before signing a contract. Make sure you test and fully understand DRM restrictions before signing a contract.

Term and Pricing. The term of the license can be either perpetual or of limited time and may or may not have a cap on annual price increases. When libraries choose an ownership model, there are two choices for data storage: the library owns and maintains perpetual access on its own servers, or the library purchases the content and pays an annual platform maintenance fee to support ongoing hosting. If negotiating for perptual access, a cap on annual price increases is recommended.

Content. Content may be bundled or come alone. If it is bundled, you may be receiving material of little or no interest to your patrons, or you may be receiving copies of titles that you already own in print. Understand that the stability of content is typically not promised, especially with journal aggregators. Unilateral business decisions by the vendor may result in the disappearance of certain years of a journal or the entire title. Be conscious of this before you discard your print collection.

Vendor. The relationship of the vendor to the content will often dictate the type of business model being utilized.[4] Vendors are suppliers who act as intermediaries between libraries and publishers. They can offer a variety of books, serials, and services that make them attractive to libraries. Publishers offer their own journals and books. Theresa Arndt suggests that one advantage to working with publishers directly is most do not impose DRM restrictions on their content.[5] However, there are disadvantages. Working with just one publisher limits the breadth of your collection. Yet working with multiple publishers can result in confusion for patrons if it means learning how to use multiple user platforms. Agents are another type of intermediary that facilitate a working relationship with libraries and publishers (commonly as subscription agents or book vendors). Aggregators are third-party providers that assemble various books or articles from serials on certain topics or academic fields of study and offer a search engine for locating full text and abstracts. Nonowner providers are also subject to contract renewals with the content owners, and this may cause a disruption in the library's access. Be sure to understand *who* you are entering into the contract with and their relationship to the content in order to best protect your investment.

Models. The final factor is the type of access model. There is currently no ideal business model, and each library has to investigate and chose what works best at the particular moment in time for its patrons. The goal of any model is to be attractive to libraries while generating income for the content provider or owner. Many librarians find these models confusing and complain that they lack transparency. These misgivings lead to a lack of confidence when it comes to making purchasing decisions. Understanding business models and finding an ideal fit is crucial to the successful management of the library's digital collections. Six business models are outlined in this section:

Subscription Model. Some vendors have made available large lists of e-books that can be subscribed to on an annual basis, much like electronic journals. The subscriptions usually offer unlimited simultaneous access to a defined set of e-books for a single year for a flat fee. The advantage of this model is the ability to rely on publishers to update and refresh their titles annually. This eliminates the need for library staff to weed the digital collection. The obvious disadvantages are paying for something you do not own, uncontrolled price increases, and losing access to the content when you stop paying the subscription fee.

Unlimited Simultaneous Access. This model is the most common for e-books in primary and secondary school libraries. Compatibility with various reading devices is typical, as is permitting remote access to users working outside the library. The license is usually priced per site (usually a building). The pricing structure can lead to inequality as a smaller institution pays the same as a larger institution with more students.

One-to-One License. Unlike unlimited simultaneous access, this model replicates print by only allowing single-user access to an e-book. When in use, the e-book is checked out and unavailable to other users until it is returned. Libraries may purchase additional copies to provide greater access. This is the typical model when items are provided through an aggregator service like OverDrive.

Purchase or Perpetual Access. Under the perpetual access model, the library purchases and owns the digital material, much like a print book. Issues of storage, preservation, and access are the considerations at the forefront of this model. The library either needs to store the content on a local server or pay a maintenance fee to a vendor to have the item stored and made accessible off-site. Preservation and access concerns relate to the ability to access the material in the future should the medium no longer be accessible due to format or software changes.

Rental or Pay-per-View. With a rental model, a library can establish an account that is debited a set monetary amount every time a patron accesses and uses an e-book. Patrons can be limited to a set number of simultaneous checkouts and may be restricted to an annual checkout limit to control costs. Some licenses allow a purchase to be triggered at a certain use plateau. This model can help keep costs down compared to the high prices of purchasing e-books outright. Limits may be set that require a certain portion of the book be read before a rental charge is imposed (i.e., readers are allowed to read up to 25 percent of a book before a paid checkout is charged), thus eliminating cost during mere browsing or inactivity.

Patron-driven acquisition (PDA) is a creative method of implementing a pay-per-view model. Acquisition librarians may find PDA attractive as it presents an opportunity to develop the collection in a manner that aligns with a user's research needs. PDA also ensures that only items that get used are purchased for the collection. This model takes some control of collection development out of librarian hands and makes budget accounting more challenging. One must also exercise caution when developing a PDA selection pool. The titles in the pool should fit the library's selection standards and not duplicate titles that are already available on the shelves.

Open Access. An alternative to conventional publishing business models, open access (OA) encourages the sharing of academic content free of charge and is growing as a distribution channel for digital materials. This model requires storage space, the application of quality digitization standards, a discovery tool to locate and search the material, and metadata. Some notable OA publishers include BioMed Central, PLOS (Public Library of Science), and SciELO, in addition to institutional repositories using software such as DSpace.

SELECTION CRITERIA UNIQUE TO E-RESOURCES

E-books are becoming more acceptable in academic libraries, but usage rates among patrons remain lower than anticipated.[6] Van Arnhem and Barnett contend DRM itself has negatively impacted user adoption of e-books by hindering the discovery of digital content. Users have found it difficult to locate a library's holdings and licensed material on the Internet. A starting point for libraries committed to growing digital collections is a CDP. Although digital content and DRM require additional considerations, Diane Kovacs, among others, suggests adopting the same basic collection policies for digital materials as those articulated for print reserves.[7] When editing your CDP, consider amending existing language for selecting print materials with terms and procedures that reflect subscription to or acquisition of digital content. Common crossover considerations include critical reviews,[8] institutional relevance,[9] duplication of titles,[10] quality of material,[11] and availability of review periods.[12] There are also considerations unique to digital acquisition. The following discusses these unique considerations as well as noting some advantages and disadvantages to be mindful of when acquiring e-books for the library.

ADA Accessibility. Ask yourself if the electronic resource requires special software or adaptive technology to allow access for the disabled. Is it provided as part of the purchased content, or has the vendor provided a solution for this in their proprietary platform or via a universal format? Concerns of accessibility for disabled patrons must be considered. Ideal media formats should allow large print and make use of screen readers that narrate the text.

Compatible with Multiple Web Browsers. While testing an electronic resource, it is wise to make sure it works fully in the major web browsers or those recommended and supported by your local IT office. At a minimum, it should perform in the latest version of Safari, Firefox, and Chrome.[13]

Cost and Learning Curve. The ongoing cost of maintaining and updating technology must be considered when budgeting and planning for digital items. Additional costs include ongoing expenditures such as hosting and licensing fees. During times of budget crisis, libraries must evaluate whether digital formats and their associated technologies are worth the staff training time and budgetary resources expended in purchasing, managing, training, and delivering e-books.

Currency. A great advantage to electronic materials is the speed and ease with which they can be updated and revised. Time spent waiting for mail deliveries and updating material manually can now be reassigned to other tasks. However, update costs may not be included as part of the original contract fee. Libraries need to balance contractual maintenance fees against the cost of staff time.

DRM Restrictions. Inclusion of DRM in this list serves as a reminder that libraries must take into consideration the restrictions DRM can place on using and accessing electronic materials when making collection decisions. This includes printing, copying, saving, annotating, and sharing (via ILL) materials. Selection factors should weigh these restrictions as well when considering digital content. The important role DRM plays in a library collection is more fully considered in the next section.

Format and Interoperability. There are many formats for digital content: PDF (portable document format), Mobi, and ePub are just a few. Most are proprietary, and a few are open source. PDF is reportedly the preferred format for libraries because of its ease of use, compatibility, search capabilities, and text linking. The lack of format standards for e-books presents an uncertainty within e-book collection development when considering what format to purchase for the future. Format is also connected to the preservation of e-books. A future change in format might impact access to older titles published in an obsolete format.

The ability to use the file on different devices (laptops, smart phones, e-readers) and operating systems (Android, Apple, Windows, Amazon) speaks to the interoperability. There are applications and software solutions that let you read your file formats across different operating systems and electronic reading devices.

MARC Record Availability. In order to fully integrate electronic resources into library collections, MARC records for these resources must be created and loaded into online catalogs and discovery tools. However, there is no standard for MARC records for e-resources. Some vendors provide low-quality records or make the process prohibitive by outsourcing it to third-party providers who charge a fee for this service. Setting e-book cataloguing standards should be an industry priority. As noted earlier, the ability to locate an item impacts user adoption of e-books.

Navigation. User experience is an important consideration. If possible, conduct a trial of the resource and ask users if they find it easy to use. The ideal format should load seamlessly on a reading device and be responsive. Preferred features include a table of contents, index, and full-text search capability. Annotation tools, as well as capability to save for review, are also important.

Ownership versus Subscription. The issue of ownership versus subscription was raised earlier in this chapter. Which business model the provider uses may make this issue a nonnegotiable point, but libraries should still take this factor into consideration when developing collections and providing the most ideal method of access and use for patrons.

Privacy Concerns. There remains uncertainty regarding the privacy of patrons when e-books are added to collections since electronic activity can be tracked. In 2014, Adobe's Digital Editions e-book and PDF reader tracked reading experience data and transmitted it to Adobe via an unsecured channel.[14] Additionally, attention should be paid to patron privacy when considering what information the integrated library system and DRM captures during the circulation process.

Remote Access—IP or Password. Understanding the access parameters to digital materials is important. Can the resource be accessed only when at the library or by a select few patrons via username and password? When possible, making the resource available via IP access through a proxy server is preferred so your patrons can have access anywhere they have an Internet connection.

Space. Deciding to collect digital materials can free up physical space if you are purchasing digital to replace out-of-date or even current print materials. Beware, though, that the space once used for bookshelves may now need to be repurposed for computer stations or workspace for laptops and other electronic devices necessary to access the digital materials.

Usability. DRM restricts the accessibility of e-books and often confuses or frustrates users. A 2010 survey of 364 U.S. academic libraries showed that restrictive licensing clauses are among the most serious problems patrons encounter when trying to use e-books.[15] The library must also be sensitive to patrons who are less experienced or confident in accessing digital materials.

Vendor Provides Support through Tutorials. Beyond the usual help screens and textual assistance, an improved support suite involves live chat, phone support, recorded webinars, and screen-cast tutorials. Be sure to ask to see and test these support features. In addition, ask for customer reviews, referrals, and feedback from the vendor.

Vendor Provides User Statistics (COUNTER Compliant). Another important selection consideration involves user statistics. Libraries gather statistics to inform them of collection use in order to assess resources for cost-effectiveness and patron utilization. An ideal vendor provides an interactive web service that lets you create custom reports showing use over time. The library industry recommends COUNTER (Counting Online Usage of Networked Electronic Resources) compliant statistics. It is crucial to have a reliable, consistent way of comparing the usage of various electronic resources.

Web Links Are Accurate and Not Broken. The quality and upkeep of a digital resource is important. It should be available when needed and not suffer from inordinate downtime, inaccurate web links, or link rot. It is time consuming to check links manually. Superior vendor services include link checking on a periodic basis without library involvement.

USING YOUR CDP TO GUIDE LICENSING NEGOTIATIONS

The library's CDP policies guide selection of items in terms of subject and format. Traditionally, the CDP focused on the acquisition and deselection of physical items in library collections. Library directors, acquisitions librarians, and subject selectors rely on these policies for appropriate resource allocation and to ensure that the library meets its mission and strategic plans within the boundaries of an established budget. An estimated 94 to 97 percent of U.S. academic libraries own access to e-books.[16] E-books account for nearly 9 percent of the academic book market and 7 percent of academic library budgets.[17] In a growing digital environment where subscription services consume more of a library budget with each year, licensing criteria should be considered a critical element of a library's CDP.[18]

In the above section on e-book business models, we identified the types of contracts used in digital licensing arrangements. Some characteristics of e-book business models include single-user access or loan, limits on the numbers of loans, restrictions on interlibrary loans, delayed sales for current titles, and requiring use of materials in the brick-and-mortar library.[19] There are no standardized or emerging trends among vendors regarding these provisions, although there are several projects that propose best practices and present model agreements.[20] Lack of standardization results in longer negotiating time and requires more staff time to keep track of institutional obligations under the various DRM restrictions. Contract terms can also alter central services, such as circulation, course reserves, and interlibrary loan.[21] Creating a core set of principles in your CDP establishes uniform negotiation terms, streamlines workflows for negotiation and collection practices, and stabilizes access to digital collections. In this section we identify some of the common clauses found in licensing agreements and illustrate how they affect use of a collection and recommend CDP language to address restrictions.[22] Librarians should review their licensing agreements carefully to consider how vendor restrictions on digital assets affect their collection decisions. These are unique decisions for each library and should be made with knowledge about how these terms work and impact on both the library and the user.[23]

Licensing Terms and Collection Policies

An assessment of patron needs and the mission of the library inform the library's CDP and will help determine what is important for you to stand firm on during negotiations or alternatively accept even if the terms are less than ideal. For example, many academic collection policies lay out the intensity of a collection organized by subject. Collection depth indicators typically range from 0 through 5, with 5 being the most comprehensive.[24] When evaluating a database that focuses on a subject with a level 5 collection designation, you may be willing to work with a more restrictive contract than you would if considering a resource that was more general or focused on a level 1 subject area. Similarly, if you know a resource is being considered for use by a small subset of your user population, limits on the number of users who can access the material at any time is of less concern than a resource that might be tapped by faculty for e-course reserves.

The controversies surrounding patron services and collection policies center around the following common concepts:

- Who is an authorized user?
- What are the authorized or permissible uses?
- What limits are placed on authorized or permissible uses?
- What monitoring obligations are placed on the library?

Authorized User

The definition of the term *authorized user* in a license agreement can severely affect the mission of a library. Libraries should ask themselves if the definition of *authorized user* provides access for all possible patrons who would use the resource on-site or remotely for the duration of the contract. Consider a library that wants to take advantage of current technologies and relies on a licensed database for all or part of its core collection. Generous access rights must come with that purchasing decision or the library will fail to meet its mission. Which of these two authorized user clauses would be more amenable?

> 1. "Authorized Users are those individuals officially affiliated or registered with the Licensee."
> 2. "Authorized Users are those individuals affiliated with the Licensee, for example, full- and part-time students, faculty and staff of Licensee and Walk-In Users who are not affiliated with Licensee but are physically present at Licensee's site(s)."

Clearly, the second clause is broader, yet it still lacks important details. Does it cover permanent and temporary employees, visiting scholars or faculty, consultants or alumni? Does it include access at the institution and remotely? When evaluating contract clauses and developing selection criteria for inclusion in your CDP, it is imperative that you consider all possibilities and take the opportunity to define terms in a light most favorable to your situation.

If a digital resource will serve a broad function, a standardized definition that accommodates the complete patron group should be included as a threshold for acquisition in the library's CDP. Highly specialized resources, such as data sets for certain researchers or technical subject-oriented databases, will not require that same standard. In that case, a more restrictive definition could be acceptable. Libraries may prefer to bargain for a broad, uniform understanding of an authorized user for all resources, but this may affect the cost of the license. Vendors frequently tie licensing fees to the number of potential users.

Consider the following two sample collection policy clauses to help guide licensing decisions:

> Broad Provision. When selecting digital resources that provide access to core collection materials as defined in this policy, contracts will define authorized users to include all full-time, part-time, temporary, and permanent students, faculty, staff, visitors, and consultants who are affiliated with [insert name of institution], whether physically present on the premises of [insert name of institution], satellite offices or campuses, or other remote locations. Licenses will also provide for on-site access to materials for public patrons (usually defined as walk-in patrons in license agreements).

> Restrictive Provision. Digital resources that provide access to specialized materials needed by a select group of library users are not required to be made available to all patron groups. Contracts should provide on-site and remote access for a specified number of end users regardless of geographic location. Acquisitions should adopt a one-user license for end users unless the vendor offers flat pricing for one to x number of users.

Authorized or Permissible Uses

Vendors try to control access to licensed materials by prescribing uses. Licensors who employ DRM software can monitor their product for violations and control the consequences, often without input from the library. Vague terms should be avoided, especially if vendors are employing software controls on length of sessions or limits on extraction. Use violations can automatically trigger a new fee structure or completely cut off access without additional notice to the library.

Single or Multiple Users

It is not in the best fiscal interests of a vendor to provide unlimited access to titles. When determining whether a resource will be available as unlimited or as a charge per title, publishers apply a cost analysis, arriving at a monetary cap. A price per e-title is calculated as the cost of a print title plus a certain percentage for its digital counterpart to arrive at a final cost per book. This cost is multiplied by the number of users who can access an item in any single session. When the monograph is part of a series, costs can be calculated for each title in the series or for the entire series. Access policies vary from single user regardless of publication date to unlimited access to older titles with highly restrictive access for current titles. Where practical, libraries may want to include language in their contracts that allow them to purchase access for additional users on an as-needed basis. This would allow libraries to take advantage of a lower-cost single user license for newer and older titles but purchase additional user licenses if needed. For example, a book written by a popular faculty member who is also teaching on the subject is often a popular student resource. Titles being used for course reserves would also benefit from an expanded user license. Your CDP can present a flexible approach for the number of users using this type of clause.

For a single/multiple/unlimited use license, preference will be given to single-use licenses provided that the library can purchase additional access without penalty during the life of the contract. Additional usage can be purchased if a title needs to be placed on course reserve or is in great demand. Policies concerning the number of users allowed will follow the policy guidelines concerning paper course reserves or exceptions to single-copy purchases as appropriate.

Extraction Clauses

Extraction clauses limit printing or downloading to a certain number of pages, chapters, or articles. This is also the section that permits copying of print materials for course packages, which, in a digital world, is replaced by placing text of articles and books on a course management platform. Aside from normal circulation concerns for academic libraries, limits on usage can effectually remove the licensed material from serving as a viable course reserve item even if the licensing agreement provides for access through course management or course reserve platforms. Examples of these types of licensing restrictions may be vaguely worded with stipulations like the following:

> 1. "Authorized Users may print or download a *reasonable* portion of the Licensed Materials."
> 2. "Authorized Users may not print or download a *substantial* portion of digital resources."

Vague licensing terms such as these should be avoided by libraries.[25] Presumably, vendors may be placing restrictions on a complete reprint of an item that would render their product less useful, or they may be simply protecting their copyright interests. CDP provisions can be made for resources that are meant to support a broad spectrum of your patron group as opposed to highly specialized material that will not experience as much traffic. Since licensing is removed from the copyright law framework, this frees the library to negotiate broader usage terms than might otherwise be allowed. A more restrictive policy guideline might tie extraction limits to fair use provisions in 17 U.S.C. § 107 (2012).[26] Consider the following sample language that handles extraction limits on standard services:

> Extraction/Broad Provision. E-book, e-journal, or other digital collections that are expected to provide broad support for educational programming and research needs will be free of extraction or use limits placed on the library and its authorized users.
>
> Extraction/Restrictive Provision. E-book, e-journal, or other digital collections that are expected to provide broad support for educational programming and research needs will not be licensed if use limits exceed those already incumbent on the library and its authorized users via the copyright laws of the United States.

Specified Uses

Vendors may also attempt to limit use of the resource for specific purposes. Many publishers and aggregators prohibit the use of e-books in course packs or as reserve readings for courses. These clauses may simply state that licensed materials may not be used in the preparation of course packs or educational materials. Licensing language may even be broader in scope. For example, the contract might state something like this:

> Licensed materials may only be accessed by authorized users for noncommercial research purposes and class preparation directly connected with the [name of institution].

This type of clause may create problems for legitimate university research endeavors that are funded by commercial enterprises (for example, the local copy store that prepares course packets), or it may limit access for institutional employees or faculty who work off-site in community centers or other not-for-profit organizations affiliated with an institution. An even less generous interpretation might prohibit using licensed materials in the growing field of online education.

A CDP provision can offer a range of permissible restrictions. E-books, e-journals, or other digital collections that are expected to be included as part of course reserves or support for education programming on-site or remotely must be made accessible through course management/reserve software or distance education platforms. Materials must be available for multiple courses and multiple semesters without limitation on printing, downloading, transference, or length of time that an authorized user can view the material. If restrictions must be imposed to secure licensing for a resource, they will be limited to those provided for under the fair use provisions and the TEACH Act as codified in Title 17 of the United States Code.

If a resource is licensed for specific projects funded through grants, commercial, government, or other third-party entities, the library can arrange subscription to materials and provide administrative support but will require backing from those third-party funds.

Interlibrary Loan Services

Interlibrary loan (ILL) services supplement a library's home collection by borrowing materials from other libraries. The practice of ILL is rarely discussed in relation to collection development. In a recent survey of two hundred academic libraries, only five had specific CDP provisions related to ILL services for e-books.[27] With the ability to control use, vendors can indirectly affect collections by monitoring or building triggers into a license agreement that mirror a patron-driven collection model. For example, multiple loans of a particular title or chapter downloads can trigger additional fees or block access completely.

Historically, use of databases to fulfill ILL services has been problematic for publishers. A license agreement may outright prohibit ILL fulfillment. Some contracts may not address the issue at all, leaving a lending library in the difficult position of interpreting the legality of using the digital resource in its interlibrary loan service. Some contracts include provisions for ILL services that alert a library that they need to negotiate separate terms for that contractual right. Librarians should take advantage of that opportunity and negotiate the best terms possible relative to their mission and collection.

New partnerships between publishers and libraries are paving the path toward a workable solution. Academic institutions are thinking outside the box and helping shape the future of digital lending. The University of Hawai'i at Mānoa, Texas Tech University, and the Greater Western Library Alliance partnered with Springer in 2015 to develop a software program that piggybacks on the Illiad platform and enables interlibrary loaning of e-books between the three institutions. This type of venture requires the agreement of the publishing house. In the Manoa-Texas project, Springer was a full and willing participant. These visionary partnerships are, unfortunately, still exceptions to the general state of affairs.[28]

Lending services for physical items such as print monographs, CDs or DVDs, manuscripts, journals, and so on are protected under 17 U.S.C. § 108 and made possible under the first sale doctrine codified at 17 U.S.C. § 109. Libraries are further advised by the *Final Report* of the National Commission on New Technological Uses of Copyrighted Works (CONTU). Specifically, chapter 4 of the CONTU report applies to machine reproduction of materials distributed through ILL practices. The report, issued in 1978, tackles the new technology of that era: photocopying. Among the recommendations, CONTU advises libraries that making more than five copies of articles from a single title runs afoul of the library exception for interlibrary loan services allowed by 17 U.S.C. 108(g)(2). This is generally known as the "Rule of 5."[29]

License agreements that do not outright prohibit ILL fulfillment may alternatively place limitations on how requests may be filled. For example, the vendor may require that only "print" ILL is allowed, which forces the library to print out material and hand it or mail it to the intended recipient. Another variant allows digital distribution but requires a library to print and then scan the material. Presumably, the vendor is capturing usage statistics for licenses that have extraction limits. These types of clauses may go on to specify that retrieval of books or articles that are published in multiple journals but accessed from a single aggregator count toward the Rule of 5. In addition to mangling the intent behind the Rule of 5, these types of arrangements burden the lending library's ILL processes and place strains on staffing, office supplies, and postal fees. You also run the risk of violating your contract terms and losing access to your collection because of the difficulty in monitoring ILL use.

A lending library with a strong commitment to ILL services should refuse a contract that prohibits using the resource to fulfill interlibrary loan requests; however, if the resource covers a subject that is of paramount importance to the library end users, it would be foolish to avoid the contract completely. Consider the following selection criteria that take ILL services into account:

> The library will license digital resources for its core patron group if the license agreement (a) provides for similar lending rights as those provided by 17 U.S.C. 108, (b) allows direct lending of material in digital form using [insert preferred service, i.e., ILLIAD] or another network service that deletes the electronic copy once it is downloaded by the receiving library, and (c) does not count extractions from different titles within its library toward the Rule of 5 provided for in clause 4 of CONTU.
>
> The library will license specialized digital resources that support the mission of the institution and the research and scholarship of its primary patron groups. It is not of primary importance to the library to make these resources available to third parties for ILL or otherwise. ILL clauses for these licensing contracts will be negotiated individually depending on the need and importance of the resource to the library's core constituency. The stronger preference is to negotiate for terms outlined in the sample clause above.
>
> The library will not execute contracts that require the library staff to reformat requested ILL materials if it would create a staffing or cost burden too great for the library to incorporate into its standard ILL procedures.

CONTENT

Access to the most current titles in e-book collections or to prepublished editions of journal articles may not be possible at all or alternatively require premium fees. Intuitively, one would assume that digital versions of titles would be available more quickly than their print counterparts; however, this is not always true. Frequently, e-books are purchased in prearranged packages, and these packages do not always contain the most current titles. They may also contain titles that the library has already purchased in print, and the library may not need or want a second copy in a digital format.[30]

Journal articles seem to behave in the opposite way. Even when a library owns an online subscription to a journal, prepublished editions of articles are publicized and accessible for an additional fee. Further restrictions are typically placed on these versions of the article. You may be purchasing access for a twenty-four- or forty-eight-hour period, the article may only be viewed on the computer where you purchased it, and you will not be able to download or print it.

Realizing that there are always exceptions to CDP policies, libraries may want to establish ground rules for packaged collections or short-term purchases. For example:

> Bundled Digital Packages. The library will consider bundled packages to meet the core collection needs of its primary patron groups provided that at least 33 percent [insert percentages that are comfortable for your library] of the titles are published within the last three years, and of that 33 percent, 15 percent have been published in the last eighteen months. The library will not acquire bundled packages if it already owns at least 20 percent of the titles in print or the cost of already-owned titles exceeds 20 percent of the full annual subscription fee, whichever is less.
>
> Short-Term Article Purchases. The library will not fund temporary, short-term access to prepublished versions of articles unless these can be downloaded and transferred to the requesting patron. These requests will only be fulfilled for full-time faculty members who need such an article for publication or speaking deadlines. If full-time faculty members request purchases, they will be informed that the cost will be debited from their faculty publication stipends.

Resources that serve as aggregators present another issue for collection management. These issues involve revolving database content and notification to the licensee. At a minimum, a list of titles should be appended to a licensing contract. Often MARC records for cataloging are provided free or for an additional fee. Changes in content should also trigger an update of MARC records, and the library should be notified separately of any changes. As part of the CDP, a percentage of change over a period of time should be identified as an action point for termination or refund.

The following language can guide planning for adding and removing content as it addresses changes in the licensed material:

> Content Change. For digital resource acquisition, the publisher/vendor/ aggregator will undertake to provide an initial schedule of titles included in the license and update it as changes are made to the resource. In addition to updating the schedule of titles, the publisher/vendor/aggregator will need to notify the acquisitions department via email within thirty calendar days regarding any deletions or substitutions. A change of more than 15 percent [insert the percentage you are comfortable with] of the original title list should be flagged as a material breach where the library will have the option to cancel with a refund for the balance of the contract. The library will allow the vendor to reinstate the original titles within fourteen business days of the removal in order to cure the deficiency.
>
> MARC Records for Digital Resources. The library will import MARC records for digital resources if they are provided by the publisher/vendor/ aggregator at no cost or a nominal cost (no more than 5 percent [insert the percentage you are comfortable with] of the total annual fee). MARC records will be updated as needed to reflect content changes. No additional charges should be incurred for records. The cataloging department will be directly responsible for managing the MARC records and edits. The cataloging department will close the records if the subscription is canceled and the collection is archived. The head of cataloging will be the main contact person for this process.
>
> Other possibilities to consider for purchasing MARC records include making purchases only for perpetual access licenses or only for e-books and e-journals that are not made available through an aggregator.

MONITORING THE RESOURCE

Libraries must also be concerned with the monitoring and reporting obligations imposed on them under the contract. Again, this may be couched in vague language:

> The Licensee will make *reasonable* efforts to ensure that only Authorized Users are accessing the Licensed Resources.

Licensors may also require a library to establish policies to enforce contract terms and imply that the library or institution will be liable for any violations by its end users.

Although monitoring use does not directly affect collection decisions, it is similar to purchasing a resource that is cumbersome to update or occupies staff time with repeatedly late updates. At some point, these resources become too labor intensive to justify their place in the library collection. Libraries should avoid undertaking any monitoring activities as a condition of licensing.

Difficult titles might already be addressed in your library guidelines for deselection or weeding. Workflow parameters for digital monitoring can be added to those guidelines or as criteria for selection. The following CDP language sets up a workflow to add use restrictions into the library's outreach material. Since the information concerning use will be collected as a matter of contract formation, it will not be difficult to disseminate and can easily be updated as resources come and go. As a side note, the publisher may not want its restrictions revealed to your user population, in which case you should identify their reluctance in your contract. These concerns can be addressed in a CDP provision that includes best practices and workflows:

> Informing Patrons about Authorized Users and Uses. The library will not monitor use of digital materials. The acquisitions department will inform library patrons about e-resource restrictions through its "Guide to Digital Resources" (or Library Guide) provided to all students, faculty, and staff upon joining the institution and available on the institutional intranet. Restrictions are also advertised when the new acquisition is announced to library patrons.
>
> Enforcement of Licensing Terms. The electronic resource librarian will be the primary contact person for notices regarding license violations. The library will intervene within seven business days of learning about inappropriate use of digital materials by the vendor. The vendor must provide specific information about the infraction, including the date, time, resource used, and type of infraction. If the library learns of inappropriate use of licensed materials, we will address the infraction within seven business days. Steps taken to address infractions will be consistent with institutional policies and procedures. The library will not undertake to inform vendors of an infraction. The library will not refuse access to a patron for an infraction unless there are three infractions of the same type within six months of each other.

ARCHIVES

Including digital resources in a collection plan necessarily involves deciding whether to lease information as opposed to adopting an ownership model. Ownership models have their own challenges for access and retrieval; however, leasing data presents the possibility of losing access to books and journals if the vendor goes out of business, a journal is transferred to a new publisher, or a contract is terminated.[31] Alternatively, a library might decide to terminate a contract if it becomes too expensive, the database has low usage, or a change in direction for the library warrants a cancellation.[32] Decisions to acquire dependable access to materials may hinge on costs. For example, if you are at a public institution with unpredictable annual funding, your library may decide that it will only purchase digital resources for core collections on an ownership model, or if you are negotiating a license for materials that serve a short-term purpose, a license that frees you from long-term commitments will be a preferable option. The connection to collection development seems obvious.

Contracts for digital resources should address archival status for digital resources posttermination regardless of the type of contract. Although the majority of licensing agreements contain "perpetual license" clauses, the language is frequently vague or may place additional burdens on the library. For example, archival access may be defined as access "similar to the current means of providing access," or the library "may make necessary back-up copies." Another common issue for library collections is the format for archival access. Rather than providing access through a searchable database structure, a publisher may provide content through unsearchable DVDs, CDs, PDFs, or hard drives or require libraries to host the data on their own servers.[33] Perpetual license clauses also fail to provide for terms on interlibrary loan use postcancellation, which again leaves the library in a quandary about data usage.

Most libraries do not provide a workflow for archival access, retrieval, or use.[34] Adding these parameters into the CDP will assist libraries when negotiating terms that present workable solutions. A central part of the discussion will focus on the use of third-party content archivers such as Portico or LOCKSS (Lots of Copies Keep Stuff Safe).[35] These services provide access to postcancellation licensed materials for a fee if the provider or publisher has agreed to cooperate with the service. This has proven to be a viable solution for many libraries, but due to the third-party fees involved, libraries with smaller budgets or unpredictable funding may shy away from yet another fee. And not all publishers cooperate with content providers. This example provision anticipates these many challenges:

> Acquisition of digital resources through permanent or leased access rights will provide for perpetual access to all materials that were accessible during the term of agreement. Access to and content of archived material must be "substantially" similar to access and content that was available during live access. The data must be searchable, available for print or download, and eligible to be used for interlibrary loans. Preferably, access will be in the same manner and form that it would be under the licensed agreement. Before entering a contract for digital resources, the acquisitions department will determine if the provider cooperates with a third-party content provider and will contact that provider to determine what fees may be involved for the resource should we choose to terminate the relationship. If content through a third-party provider is unavailable or not feasible, the library will accept hosting on an internal server. Archival access will not be accepted in the form of CDs or DVDs. If content is to be stored on internal servers, the acquisitions department will consult with the information technology department to determine feasibility and any additional institutional fees. Agreements should also provide for notice and access to a journal upon transference to a new publisher postcancellation.

CONCLUSION

This chapter introduced unique issues that arise in digital collection planning. We began by identifying the growth of digital resources in libraries and how it affects core services. Access to these materials are provided under different and evolving business models that use DRM to limit or remove the traditional copyright exceptions and protections that libraries rely on to provide core services to their users.

When determining the degree to which use terms proposed by model licenses have become institutionalized across different publishers' licenses, one study concluded

> the majority of final licenses in this study deviated from library model license best practices by not including fair use clauses, by including print requirements for ILL, by not permitting ILL for commercial users and by not permitting e-reserves hyperlinks. Examining use terms over time, our data show statistically significant increases in the percent of licenses recognizing scholarly sharing, permitting e-reserves, and permitting hyperlinks in e-reserves. [36]

Publishers shape use limits and parameters through standard licenses. Those negotiating contracts must be aware of this end goal of publishers. Think outside the box and push for contract terms that are more ideal for library stakeholders. Attempts should be made to negotiate contracts that serve your constituency best and provide the best value for your money.

In response to DRM licensing restrictions, the American Library Association recommends that libraries recognize their obligation to make use of public-domain works and open license e-books if these materials meet the needs of patrons. [37] The ALA also advises creative solutions and aggressive negotiating that include discounted prices for delayed e-books, possible revenue sharing of books purchased through a library's website, and limited free access to selected titles. When considering e-books, three attributes are essential to libraries under any business model: inclusion of all titles, enduring rights, and full integration into the library catalog with metadata and management tools to enhance discovery. [38]

When selecting electronic resources to add to your collection, there are many parallels to the print material selection process, but there are also many unique considerations. We recommend that provisions affecting a library's core functions be addressed in a collection development policy, and we have provided a number of examples for policy provisions. Officially adopting standards into your collection policy creates common negotiating goals, provides uniformity in workflows, and creates more stability in the overall collection.

NOTES

1. Walters, "Sharing and Use," 87, table 1.
2. Eschenfelder, "Every Library's Nightmare?," 208, table 1.
3. Walters, "Sharing and Use," 89.
4. Johnson, *Developing and Managing Electronic Collections*, 23.
5. Arndt, *Getting Started with Demand-Driven Acquisitions*, 11.
6. Van Arnhem and Barnett, "Is Digital Rights Management (DRM) Impacting," 63.
7. Kovacs and Robinson, *Kovacs Guide to Electronic Library Collection*, 4.
8. Libraries might list specific sources to obtain critical reviews of databases or e-book platforms from different publications or organizations. For example, selectors could routinely review *Library Journal, Information Today*, and *ALA Library Technology Reports* to obtain unbiased reviews.
9. This idea in relation to digital collections is more fully explored under "Licensing Terms and Collection Policies."
10. Pay attention to what percentage of the electronic resource is duplicative of your print collection. This can be a challenge with aggregators if they change the years of coverage or drop or add titles with little notice. Some aggregators provide a comparison chart between your print collection and their online offering. Librarians should ask if that service is available during negotiations.
11. The metrics of quality are similar as those for print collections: accuracy, currency, authority, credibility, lack of bias, and organization. Publisher embargoes are also a factor to consider when assessing the quality of a digital resource. This category also involves reproduction quality and additional content associated with some electronic formats (i.e., live links and features such as book marking, notes, etc.).
12. Can you return a title without penalty within a certain number of days if it fails to meet expectations? For digital materials, review periods are often called "trials." You should consider the length of time for the trial as well as access to the appropriate patron groups. When setting up the review period for digital materials, librarians may want to consult a focus group to be sure they are available and willing to participate in the trial.
13. This is particularly important for those using Internet Explorer since it is no longer supported and may not be updated or compatible with a proprietary platform.
14. Gallagher, "Adobe's E-Book Reader." Adobe did not directly address reports that previous versions of the platform were not subject to data gathering, but it claims that the user agreements governing versions 3 and 4 do not differ with respect to user data. An Adobe spokesperson said, "While additional product capabilities were added in version 4 to facilitate additional publisher requirements and business models, the end user license agreement and privacy policy did not require changes. The information collected from the user in version 3 *and* version 4 is collected solely for purposes such as license validation and to facilitate the implementation of different licensing models by publishers." See DBW, "Adobe Confirms It's Gathering Ebook Readers' Data," Digital Book World, October 7, 2014. http://www.digitalbookworld.com/2014/adobe-confirms-its-gathering-ebook-readers-data/.
15. *Library Journal*, "Survey of E-book Penetration," 57.
16. Ibid., 9.
17. See Sharp and Thompson, "'Just in Case.'" One of the main obstacles to continued growth of e-book collection in academic libraries is poor content from the publishers. This might take the form of embargoes on current titles in bundled packages, reproductive quality, or lack of features end users typically expect in digital materials, such as live links, book marking, and so on. See also Kahn and Underwood, "Issues Related to the Adoption of E-Books," 12.
18. McGinnis, "Selling Our Collective Souls."
19. Brennan, "EBook Business Models."
20. Walters, "Acquisition and Collection Management," 194.
21. Walters, "Sharing and Use," 85.
22. The terms and clauses used in the examples are composites created by the authors based on examples provided in the literature cited here. Resemblance to specific contracts or exam-

ples provided in the reviewed literature is purely coincidental. These examples represent the repeated concerns raised by libraries and publishers in relation to DRM and acquisition policies. Individual publishers' contracts can be reviewed at the Center for Research Libraries LIBLICENSE Project, http://liblicense.crl.edu/licensing-information/publishers-licenses.

23. Librarians can inform themselves about licensing terms by consulting the LIBLICENSE Project; Lipinski, *Librarians Legal Companion*; NorthEast Research Libraries Consortium, "Generic License Agreement"; Alford, "Negotiating and Analyzing"; among others.

24. This qualitative method of collection building is referred to as the Conspectus Model; Johnson, *Fundamentals of Collection Development*, 234.

25. Lipinski, *Librarians Legal Companion*, 640.

26. Ibid., 391.

27. Zhu and Chen, "Survey of E-book Interlibrary Loan Policy."

28. Springer, "Occam's Reader Project."

29. National Commission on New Technological Uses of Copyrighted Works, *Final Report*, 54.

30. Walters, "Acquisition and Collection Management," 197.

31. Bulock, "Tracking Perpetual Access."

32. Evans, "From Here to There."

33. Beh and Smith, "Preserving the Scholarly Collection."

34. Bulock, "Techniques for Tracking Perpetual Access."

35. For Portico, see http://www.portico.org/digital-preservation; for LOCKSS, see http://www.lockss.org. JSTOR has been a long-standing provider of back issue access of journals for institutional subscribers; see http://www.jstor.org.

36. Eschenfelder, Tsai, Zhu, and Stewart, "How Institutionalized Are Model License Use Terms?," 329.

37. Brennan, "Scorecard for Public Libraries."

38. Brennan, "Ebook Business Models."

REFERENCES

Adams, Jennifer. "Digital Divide: Tips for Developing a Digital Collection Development Policy." *AALL Spectrum* 15, no. 1 (September–October 2010): 36–37.

Alford, Duncan E. "Negotiating and Analyzing Electronic License Agreements." *Law Library Journal* 94, no. 4 (2002): 621–44.

Arndt, Theresa S. *Getting Started with Demand-Driven Acquisitions for E-Books: A LITA Guide*. Chicago: ALA TechSource, 2015.

Ashmore, Beth, Jill E. Grogg, and Jeff Weddle. *The Librarian's Guide to Negotiation: Winning Strategies for the Digital Age*, Medford, NJ: Information Today, 2012.

Barribeau, Susan, and Jim Stemper. "Perpetual Access to Electronic Journals: A Survey of One Academic Research Library's Licenses." *Library Resources & Technical Services* 50, no. 2 (2006): 91–109.

Beh, Eugenia, and Jane Smith. "Preserving the Scholarly Collection: An Examination of the Perpetual Access Clauses in the Texas A & M University Libraries' Major E-journal Licenses." *Serials Review* 38 (December 2012): 235–42.

Bielefield, Arlene, and Lawrence Cheeseman. *Interpreting and Negotiating Licensing Agreements: A Guidebook for the Library, Research, and Teaching Professions*. New York: Neal-Schuman, 1999.

Bluh, Pamela, and Cindy Hepfer. *Managing Electronic Resources: Contemporary Problems and Emerging Issues*. ALCTS Papers on Library Technical Services and Collections 13. Chicago: Association for Library Collections & Technical Services, American Library Association, 2006.

Bulock, Chris. "Techniques for Tracking Perpetual Access." *Serials Librarian* 68 (2015): 290–98.

———. "Tracking Perpetual Access: A Survey of Librarian Practices." *Serials Review* 40, no. 2 (2014): 97–104.

"Ebook Business Models for Public Libraries." American Library Association, August 8, 2012. http://connect.ala.org/files/80755/EbookBusinessModelsPublicLibs.pdf.

Eschenfelder, Kristin R. "Every Library's Nightmare? Digital Rights Management, Use Restrictions, and Licensed Scholarly Digital Resources." *College & Research Libraries* 69, no. 3 (May 2008): 205–26. doi:10.5860/crl.69.3.205.

Eschenfelder, Kristin R., Tien-I. Tsai, Xiaohua Zhu, and Brenton Stewart. "How Institutionalized Are Model License Use Terms? An Analysis of E-journal License Use Rights Clauses from 2000 to 2009." *College & Research Libraries* 74, no. 4 (July 2013): 326–55. doi:10.5860/crl-289.

Evans, Wendy. "From Here to There: Library Content in the Digital Age." Biomedical & Life Sciences Collection, Henry Stewart Talks, December 30, 2012. http://hstalks.com/?t=BL1523387.

Fieldhouse, Maggie, and Audrey Marshall, eds. *Collection Development in the Digital Age.* London: Facet Publishing, 2011.

Frederiksen, Linda, Joel Cummings, Lara Cummings, and Diane Carroll. "Ebooks and Interlibrary Loan: Licensed to Fill?" *Journal of Interlibrary Loan, Document Delivery & Electronic Reserve* 21, no. 3 (July–August 2013): 117–31.

Gallagher, Sean. "Adobe's E-book Reader Sends Your Reading Logs Back to Adobe—in Plain Text." *Ars Technica*, October 7, 2014. http://arstechnica.com/security/2014/10/adobes-e-book-reader-sends-your-reading-logs-back-to-adobe-in-plain-text/.

Gasaway, Laura N. *Copyright Questions and Answers for Information Professionals: From the Columns of Against the Grain.* Charleston Insights in Library, Archival, and Information Sciences. West Lafayette, IN: Purdue University Press, 2013.

Harris, Christopher, Ric Hasenyager, and Carrie Russell. "School Library Ebook Business Models." *American Libraries Magazine*, June 10, 2014. http://americanlibrariesmagazine.org/2014/06/10/school-library-ebook-business-models/.

Holleman, Curt. "Electronic Resources: Are Basic Criteria for the Selection of Materials Changing?" *Library Trends* 48, no. 4 (2000): 694–710.

Johnson, Peggy. *Developing and Managing Electronic Collections: The Essentials.* Chicago: ALA Editions, 2013.

———. *Fundamentals of Collection Development and Management.* Chicago: ALA Editions, 2009.

Kahn, Michelle, and Peter Underwood. "Issues Related to the Adoption of E-Books in Academic Libraries: A Literature Review." *South African Journal of Libraries and Information Science* 79, no. 2 (2013): 10–17.

Kaplan, Richard. *Building and Managing E-Book Collections a How-to-Do-It Manual for Librarians.* How-to-Do-It Manuals for Libraries 184. Chicago: Neal-Schuman, 2012.

Kovacs, Diane K., and Kara L. Robinson. *The Kovacs Guide to Electronic Library Collection Development: Essential Core Subject Collections, Selection Criteria, and Guidelines.* New York: Neal-Schuman, 2004.

Lee, Stuart. *Electronic Collection Development: A Practical Guide.* New York: Neal-Schuman, 2002.

Library Journal. "Survey of Ebook Penetration and Use in U.S. Academic Libraries." November 2010. http://c0003264.cdn2.cloudfiles.rackspacecloud.com/Academic%20Library%20Ebook%20Report_2.pdf.

Lipinski, Tomas A. *The Librarian's Legal Companion for Licensing Information Resources and Services.* Chicago: Neal-Schuman, 2013.

McGinnis, Suzan D. "Selling Our Collective Souls: How License Agreements Are Controlling Collection Management." *Journal of Library Administration* 31, no. 2 (2000): 63–76.

National Commission on New Technological Uses of Copyrighted Works. *Final Report.* Washington, DC: Library of Congress, 1978. http://digital-law-online.info/CONTU/contu1.html.

NorthEast Research Libraries Consortium. "Generic License Agreement for Electronic Resources." http://nerl.org/nerl-documents/nerl-model-license.

Polanka, Sue. *No Shelf Required 2: Use and Management of Electronic Books.* Chicago: American Library Association, 2012.

Primary Research Group. *Library Use of Ebooks, 2013 Edition.* New York: Primary Research Group, 2013.

Rogers, Sam. "Survey and Analysis of Electronic Journal Licenses for Long-Term Access Provisions in Tertiary New Zealand Academic Libraries." *Serials Review* 35, no. 1 (2009): 3–15.

"A Scorecard for Public Libraries: Ebook Business Models." American Library Association, January 25, 2013. http://www.districtdispatch.org/wp-content/uploads/2013/02/Ebook_scorecard.pdf.

Sharp, Steve, and Sarah Thompson. "'Just in Case' vs. 'Just in Time': E-book Purchasing Models." *Serials* 23, no. 3 (2010): 201–6.

Springer. "The Occam's Reader Project Is a Partnership between Texas Tech, the University of Hawaii at Manoa and GWLA." Press Release, January 31, 2014. https://www.springer.com/gp/about-springer/media/press-releases/corporate/occam-s-reader-project/23776.

Todorova, Tania, Ivan Trenchev, and Tereza Trencheva. "Digital Right Management (DRM) and Library Copyright Policy." *Digital Presentation and Preservation of Cultural and Scientific Heritage* 2 (2012): 123–31.

Van Arnhem, Jolanda-Pieta, and Lindsay Barnett. "Is Digital Rights Management (DRM) Impacting E-Book Adoption in Academic Libraries?" *Charleston Advisor* 15, no. 1 (January 2014): 63–65. http://www.ingentaconnect.com/content/charleston/chadv/2014/00000015/00000003/art00020.

Walters, William H. "E-books in Academic Libraries: Challenges for Acquisition and Collection Management." *Libraries and the Academy* 13, no. 2 (2013): 187–211.

———. "E-books in Academic Libraries: Challenges for Sharing an Use." *Journal of Librarianship and Information Science* 46, no. 2 (2014): 85–95.

Weir, Ryan O. *Managing Electronic Resources.* Chicago: ALA TechSource, 2012.

Wikoff, Karin. *Electronics Resources Management in the Academic Library: A Professional Guide.* Santa Barbara, CA: Libraries Unlimited, 2012.

Zheng, Mai, and Kristin Eschenfelder. "License Analysis on E-journal Perpetual Access of Library." *Proceedings of the American Society of Information Science and Technology* 49 no. 1 (January 2013): 1–4.

Zhu, Xiaohua, and Lan Chen. "A Survey of E-book Interlibrary Loan Policy in U.S. Academic Libraries." *Interlending & Document Supply* 42, no. 2/3 (2014): 57–63.

Chapter Six

Managing Digital Rights in Open Access Works

Benjamin J. Keele and Jere D. Odell

Librarians, researchers using scholarly works, and consumers using popular media generally think of digital rights management (DRM) as only a limitation on their access and use of digital resources. DRM and open access (OA) works would strike one as a very unlikely combination.

In almost all cases, we would agree; however, we note two instances in which DRM and OA may be compatible. The first case is DRM used to enable more accessible and durable rights information and proper attribution for a work. The second case is DRM that limits some uses as an appropriate part of a compromise to make works OA that would not otherwise be so.

This overlap between DRM and OA is narrow compared to the set of non-OA works equipped with DRM, but understanding this overlap is useful for at least three reasons. First, librarians may use DRM to better manage rights in OA works; second, librarians may persuade a reluctant author or publisher to make a work OA with appropriate DRM; and, third, librarians may recognize when DRM negates access to an ostensibly OA work.

This chapter will review OA and discuss cases in which DRM can complement OA objectives. We organize these cases by two roles played by many academic librarians: collectors and publishers. By considering the relationship between DRM and OA, one may better recognize when DRM should be adopted or resisted in projects involving OA materials.

OPEN ACCESS

Once thought to be an experiment, OA scholarly literature is now produced by large, mainstream academic publishers—including Elsevier, Taylor &

Francis, Wiley, Springer, Sage, and many more. In fact, OA is the fastest growing segment of the academic publishing market.[1] OA publishing options are now available in some form to creators of any educational, scholarly, cultural, or professional work—including textbooks, monographs, classroom materials, models and diagrams, images, tests and measures, tutorials, data sets, and journal articles. If a work can be made available in digital form, it can be published as an OA resource.

Given the rise of OA, most readers will already be familiar with the idea. Nonetheless, when thinking about the role of DRM in OA publishing and dissemination, it is useful to reflect on the origins of the OA movement and the many routes to OA that are now available.

At the end of the twentieth century, the Internet became a common feature in academic and medical libraries in the United States and other developed countries. This changed how librarians accessed information and provided services to their patrons. For example, the MEDLINE database was launched in 1964.[2] For many years it was accessible only to those with specialized searching skills, typically medical librarians, but in 1997 it was made available for free to any Internet user through the PubMed website.[3] A database that was once available to only a few was now available to the many at no cost to its users. While PubMed was providing free access to bibliographic information, others were also providing free access to the scholarly literature. The OA repository arXiv (http://arxiv.org) began in 1991 and showed that scholars in mathematics and physics were willing to share their research and writings at no cost to their readers.

Following arXiv's model, Harold Varmus and others in the National Institutes of Health (NIH) proposed a similar OA repository for the health and life sciences.[4] This repository launched in 2000 as PubMed Central and now provides free access to more than 3.6 million articles (http://www.ncbi.nlm.nih.gov/pmc/).[5] At roughly the same time, large and ultimately successful OA journal initiatives were created, most notably BioMed Central in 1998 and the Public Library of Science in 2000.

These OA archiving and publishing efforts developed in parallel with an advocacy movement. In 2001, with the support of the Open Society Institute, a group of prominent OA advocates met in Budapest to write the Budapest Open Access Initiative (BOAI).[6] The declaration not only gave momentum to those who saw OA as a social value, but also helped define self-archiving and OA publishing. In the same year, Lawrence Lessig and others established the Creative Commons organization, which encourages the adoption of licenses to facilitate open sharing and permission for reuse of digital works by their copyright holders.[7]

In the decade and a half that followed, the OA principles envisioned by the BOAI and Creative Commons were promoted by the adoption of institutional policies. The NIH and other research-funding entities adopted public access policies that mandated, at the very least, self-archiving in an OA repository, such as PubMed Central. Similarly, many universities adopted OA policies to require or to encourage their faculties to self-archive works in OA institutional repositories. As authors began to realize the benefits of OA distribution, libraries launched OA repositories and publishing systems and educational programming to support copyright practices that are friendly to authors and readers.

As this short history is meant to illustrate, OA is both pervasive and multifaceted. When thinking about DRM, it is best to keep in mind the ways authors, publishers, libraries, and readers participate in OA. Peter Suber has articulated OA as "digital, online, free of charge, and free of most copyright and licensing restrictions."[8] To provide a structure for understanding both the rights and the models of open access distribution, we rely on Suber's terminology of green and gold OA and, more to our point, gratis and libre OA.

Green and Gold OA

OA resources are often categorized as either green or gold. This vocabulary, used by Suber and attributed to Stevan Harnad,[9] is widely used by OA advocates and librarians. Green OA refers to the practice of self-archiving— uploading a work to an open website. The work may or may not have already been published elsewhere, and as a result the copyright holder may have placed limitations on its use beyond the author's initial act of self-archiving. In Harnad's vocabulary, this is green OA because the publishers have given the author the "green light" to post the work on an OA website. Typically, green OA works are uploaded to an institutional repository or a disciplinary repository.

On the other hand, gold OA refers to the practice of publishing a work in an OA venue, such as a journal. In gold OA, the work is free to all readers at the point of publication. To recover their costs, some gold OA publishers require processing charges from the authors or their institutions. The gold in gold OA is often presumed to be associated with the exchange of funds, but most OA journals require no fees for publication.[10] Because gold OA works are published with the original intention to never require payment for access, gold OA copyright holders are more likely to permit others to redistribute and reuse the work through an open license.

Gratis and Libre OA

Free is an ambiguous word in the English language. Struggling with this ambiguity, Richard Stallman, a founder of the free software movement, insisted that he meant "'free' as in 'free speech,' not as in 'free beer.'"[11] The former is a liberty to be exercised, the latter a gift to be consumed. Although a memorable analogy, it's not without its own complicated interpretations. Thus, to bring some clarity to the meaning of "free," the words *gratis* and *libre* were used to describe varieties of free software. The OA movement adopted these terms—with, one might argue, fewer complications. Suber describes gratis OA as "free of charge, but not more free than that."[12] In essence, one may have access to read or view an item at no cost, but she may not be free to do much of anything else with the work. For any use that exceeds fair use, one must seek permission from the copyright holder. Thus, as Suber writes, "Gratis OA removes price barriers but not permission barriers."[13] By this definition, most of the manuscripts available to readers in PubMed Central are gratis OA. Readers may read them at no cost, but they do not have permission to reproduce, redistribute, adapt, or repurpose. Such uses, when beyond fair use, require additional permissions from the copyright holders.

In contrast, Suber describes libre OA as "free of charge and also free of some copyright and licensing restrictions."[14] Libre OA gives the user permission to move beyond the limits of fair use in one or more ways. This permission is granted prior to and without any written exchange between the user and the copyright holder. Thus a libre OA work might be available for reposting to a public website or for modifications or for repurposed reuse or for all of the above. Varieties of libre OA permit text mining and mashups in ways that gratis OA does not. While libre OA offers more freedoms to the user, it is less common than gratis OA and, given that there will be fewer prior copyright issues to accommodate, more likely to be a feature of gold OA publishing.

CREATIVE COMMONS

For libre OA to work, the user must know the permissions that have been granted. This is usually accomplished with a license, most commonly a Creative Commons license. Creative Commons licenses may be assigned by the copyright holder to an OA work to permit others to use the work beyond the usual constraints of copyright and without having to receive individual permission from the copyright holder. Meant to enable reuse for works found online, the licenses include three layers: a Legal Code, a "human readable" Commons Deed, and a "machine readable" Rights Expression Language (REL).[15]

Creative Commons licenses give rights holders a prepackaged assortment of permissions that they can grant to others. This takes some of the burden of permissions development away from the copyright holder and also alleviates confusion about the terms of reuse for users. Most Creative Commons licenses have an attribution (BY) requirement to ensure the creator is appropriately credited. Creators can also add a combination of a noncommercial (NC) requirement to prevent commercial uses and no derivatives (ND) requirement to specify that derivative works cannot be made under the license. Finally, the share-alike (SA) condition requires that works incorporating content under a SA license also have the same license. (This is the license favored by Wikipedia.) One can also waive all intellectual property rights with a Creative Commons Zero (CC0) Public Domain Declaration. CC0 is most open, while the Creative Commons BY-NC-ND is most restrictive. Because this license allows unlimited copying as long as attribution is given, no derivative works are made, and the purpose is noncommercial, it is only slightly less restrictive than mere gratis open access, which would not authorize unlimited copying.

Creative Commons licenses help implement libre OA by clearly stating permissions granted by the author. Keeping these licenses attached to digital copies of works can be accomplished by DRM.

DRM FOR ATTRIBUTION AND USAGE LIMITS

We take a more expansive view of DRM, in which any technological measure that indicates or enforces intellectual property rights and licenses counts as DRM. Some of these devices have also been called technological protection measures (TPMs).[16] Generally, TPM refers to relatively strong access and usage restrictions on digital works applied to non-OA works. In this chapter we will use DRM as a broader umbrella under which TPMs fit.

Other chapters discuss the wide variety of types of DRM. We focus on DRM options that are compatible with OA, so the range of possibilities is smaller. For instance, we consider neither DRM that limits accessing a work on computers registered in particular countries or institutions nor DRM that prevents accessing more than a sample of the work until a fee is paid. Applying such DRM to a work makes that work non-OA.

Attribution

While open licenses like Creative Commons are not necessary for a work to be gratis OA, many authors and publishers apply open licenses to their works, making them libre OA. A crucial part of properly using libre OA works is attribution, which is giving appropriate credit to the work's creator. Digital copies of a work may circulate, and new copies may be posted in places beyond the original publication site. The work may be translated, reformatted, or mashed up with other content. If metadata is lost in any way, future users may not know what rights have been granted or how attribution should be made. For instance, suppose an article is published in an OA journal with a Creative Commons Attribution license. A professor downloads the article and emails it to a fellow professor. The second professor wants to add the article to a digital packet of readings she is assembling for a course. This use is permitted by the license, but unless the file sent by the first professor contained all necessary information about the license and article citation, it may be difficult for the second professor to follow the license through appropriate attribution.

DRM can reduce these difficulties by embedding rights information into the digital work, making it less likely that this information would be lost as the work is copied or reused. One option is applying watermarks to the digital files. One often sees visible watermarks on PDF files downloaded from licensed databases; the watermarks generally indicate the licensing institution and time of download. This is an example of using a watermark to monitor and enforce license terms, but watermarks can display rights or attribution information instead.[17] For OA works using Creative Commons licenses, the watermark could list the license URL and preferred citation. The watermark could be placed in an unobtrusive spot in the margins on each page so that if the file is broken up, the rights information will still be visible on each part.

Watermarks can also be invisible. This type of watermark is generally used for enforcing rights in non-OA works, but if a visible watermark seems unattractive or otherwise undesirable, an invisible watermark may be suitable. The attribution information would have to be readable by software, such as a citation management program, or have a visible notice telling users how to view the rights watermark when needed. Some watermarks are easier to remove than others without disrupting the file contents, but for OA works, there is not much incentive to wipe off information that helps one use the work appropriately (assuming the watermark does not hinder reading the work).

Another option is embedding rights information in the file metadata. Creative Commons has proposed the Creative Commons Rights Expression Language (CC REL),[18] a standard for a rights expression language that enables computers to detect what license or rights apply to a digital object. CC REL can be embedded in most files, including PDF and image formats, using the Extensible Metadata Platform (XMP) standard. The metadata embedded in the file is invisible to a human reader unless she looks for it in the metadata, but computers can read the CC REL data when needed. Examples of software using such rights data are a search program looking for works with a given license or a citation management application creating citations to quoted works.

A relatively new option is registering rights in digital work on a public blockchain. The blockchain is a public register that is maintained, updated, and verified by a distributed network on computers performing complex cryptographic calculations. Blockchains are most well known for the role they play in the Bitcoin payment system. Some benefits of a public distributed ledger are that anyone can verify a transaction and the ledger does not depend on a central server. The Bitcoin system uses a blockchain to record transfers of bitcoin units from one user to another, but the same technology can be used to record rights claims in a digital file.

This has been done by an organization called ascribe (https://www.ascribe.io/). Using ascribe's system, a rights holder uploads a digital file and enters their intellectual property claim. The system creates a hash (essentially, a digital fingerprint) for the file and enters the hash and rights information onto a public blockchain. The rights holder now has a public, time-stamped claim on a digital work.

This service was initially designed for creators wishing to sell digital works of art,[19] but Creative Commons France and ascribe have adapted the system to also register Creative Commons licenses.[20] Authors and publishers can register the rights information in OA works, whether most rights are reserved or granted through a Creative Commons license, in a verifiable way. This option does not embed the rights information in the file, but one can link to a page for each work that displays the rights registration in the ascribe system.

Each of these options can be used singly or in combination. The author of a work published OA could select a Creative Commons license, register that license in ascribe's blockchain, embed rights information in the file's metadata, and apply a watermark with rights information or a link to that information. Through these uses, DRM is furthering OA and open licenses by making rights information about OA works more available and facilitating proper use and attribution.

Use Limits

Perhaps a publisher is interested in making a publication gratis OA, but with some limitations on how the files are used. DRM can make a work freely readable but prevent uses like downloading, copying and pasting text, or breaking the work into pieces for reuse. For some OA advocates, this approach may seem an unacceptable compromise. This reaction is understandable, but our view is that gratis OA is often better than no OA, and some forms of DRM applied to gratis OA works are acceptable.

The set of DRM that can be used to limit some uses of OA works is fairly small. First, PDF files can be locked to prevent copying and pasting text, editing, or printing.[21] Second, works could be displayed in Flash or HTML5, a format that permits readers to access and read a work in a web browser but prevents downloading or copying and pasting. This option could be used to control uses of an entire work or, for works published in HTML, to control copying of figures or images. For audio and video works, streaming provides access but prevents users from keeping a copy or editing it.

To further OA goals, these technologies should be deployed only if an author or publisher is unwilling to publish their works OA without DRM. Some readers may expect to be able to make certain uses of OA works, so libraries or publishers should include appropriate notices of the DRM restrictions and means for contacting the rights holders to request permission and more usable copies.[22] To the extent possible, librarians should seek to set expiration dates on DRM restrictions or try to revisit the issue with authors or publishers in the event their experience with OA publishing has reduced their concerns.

Having reviewed OA and how DRM can be used to further OA objectives, let us now consider how librarians can apply this information when building library collections and publishing works of authorship.

LIBRARIANS AS COLLECTORS

All budgets have limits, but the gap between available funds and the rising expense of subscription-based library resources continues to grow. The cost of subscribing to health science journals has increased by 7 percent annually,[23] and library expenditures on subscription resources have more than quadrupled in the last three decades.[24] At the same time, library shares of institutional budgets are shrinking,[25] and a growing number of medical libraries have shut their doors.[26] While OA resources are not an immediate solution to this problem, they are the fastest growing segment of the scholarly publishing market and a welcome respite from the budget crunch.

Furthermore, OA resources are, by nature, readily available and often easy to use. They can be particularly useful when serving visitors and other patrons without institutional credentials, especially when these patrons need ongoing access to a source. OA resources are often a better source for these patrons and may be the preferred tool even when subscription-based alternatives are available. For example, MedlinePlus, a free online consumer health reference tool, is preferred for patient use in the medical library over any number of subscription-based databases that might be available on-site.

Given these factors, from budgets to usability and patron needs, libraries of all sizes add OA resources (in one way or another) to their digital collections. In some cases, OA resources are merely listed on a web page or included with other works in a topical guide to library resources. In other cases, OA resources are supplemented with bibliographic description and added to the library's online catalog. In either case, there are at least three DRM-related issues that librarians should consider while collecting or linking to OA resources: metadata, usability, and preservation.

Metadata

When adding an OA resource to an online finding guide or catalog, the library will want to investigate the resource's DRM characteristics. How are the rights managed? What are the rights available to the user? If some form of libre OA is provided, what rights are restricted or what conditions are imposed on reuse? Communicating these rights in an item's metadata record or in the finding aid will help readers identify works that fit their needs. It will also assist the library in efforts to maintain reliable access to the works. This may be as simple as adding a work's Creative Commons license to a metadata field. In addition, rights information may have been directly embedded (by watermarking or other technologies) in the work itself. These DRM features can be communicated to the user to assist with efforts to select works available, for example, for educational reuse or data mining.

Usability

Some DRM technologies limit a user's ability to work with a text, image, or other digital resource. As with subscription-based electronic books, DRM can provide access to the item but prevent file downloads, copying blocks of text, or printing a high-resolution image file. Although, read-only, gratis OA may be better than no access, there may be some circumstances in which the usability barriers are such that including the work in a finding aid is not advisable. The library will want to weigh these usability problems against the value of using the resource as a supplement to its holdings on a given topic.

Preservation

Some OA resources will prove to be core items regularly used by a library's patrons. In these cases, an OA resource has the potential to outlive its original publisher and online provider. The library may want to include a copy of the work in its own digital archives or download a backup for offline use or preservation. Unfortunately, many OA resources (as with the majority of PubMed Central's articles) have gratis OA licenses that prohibit these practices. As with the potential usability barriers of DRM, licenses or technologies that restrict the ability to preserve access to a work should be weighed against the value of adding an OA item to a library's holdings.

LIBRARIES AS PUBLISHERS

Many libraries now recognize that they serve a role identical or similar to that of a publisher for their constituents. Libraries are publishers in that they participate in a "set of activities . . . to support the creation, dissemination, and curation of scholarly, creative, and/or educational works."[27] While some libraries may have participated in print-based publishing in one form or another for their organizations in the past, many now host or build digital collections that would not otherwise be available to users. In their most common forms, these publishing activities take place in library-facilitated digital collections, institutional repositories, and other online publishing platforms, such as Open Journal Systems (OJS).

Using these tools, a library may find that it is the first and only provider of digital access to materials about its community or organization; previously unpublished scholarly works by its patrons; or entire peer-reviewed journals, monographs, thesis collections, or conference proceedings. In all these cases and others, the library is effectively the publisher of record—participating in the "production process . . . and apply[ing] a level of certification to the content published, whether through peer review or extension of the institutional brand."[28] Most of these library publishing services seek a broad audience and aim to be as openly accessible as possible.

In whatever way libraries participate in publishing activities, copyright concerns and approaches to managing these concerns will be common. At the very least, the library will want to ensure that it has sufficient rights to distribute the work. At the same time, the publishing collaborator (an author, creator, editor, or organization) may have a strong interest in retaining selected rights. These details are typically communicated in copyright agreements and nonexclusive permissions to distribute. DRM also can be used to reiterate and clearly communicate the rights status of a library-published OA work and, as described above, restrict use to read-only gratis OA.

OA Library Publishing and DRM for Rights Expression

CC REL, a widely used rights expression language, is currently integrated in the submissions systems for many library publishing tools, including DSpace, DigitalCommons, and OJS. In these publishing systems, the information about the rights status of an OA work is included in a published item's metadata and displayed on the landing page describing the item. In turn, when coupled with a metadata exchange standard, such as the Open Archives Initiative Protocol for Metadata Harvesting (OAI-PMH), this practice permits other search tools to identify OA works and to display them with reference to the Creative Commons license. This communication of rights reduces uncertainty about the exact rights of an OA work, enabling reuse when it is permitted and discouraging uses that overstep the limits of the license.

Although this expression of rights in library publishing systems is useful, it does not ensure that all users will see these communications. When a user downloads and saves a file to their personal collection, it is likely that it will be separated from the original metadata. Furthermore, even if the file includes a statement and icon displaying the terms of the license, it is possible that these may be removed during reuse. The DRM tools mentioned above, including watermarking, embedding rights information in file metadata, and registering rights information in ascribe's blockchain ledger, all make rights information visible and more persistent and should be considered alongside rights information displayed in library publishing systems.

OA Library Publishing and DRM for Reuse Restrictions

While Creative Commons is a method for expressing the rights associated with an OA object published by a library, it does not enforce those terms. It is difficult to imagine how DRM technologies could be used to enforce the exact terms of a Creative Commons or other OA license on reuse. The terms might be fully embedded and watermarked in the file in a way that enables others to quickly identify a use that oversteps the limits of the license—for example, the rights holder might be notified when their work was uploaded to another site or to a selected list of sites prohibited by the license. This notification, however, would occur after the fact and would not have prohibited the initial violation of the terms.

Given the difficulty of enforcing the exact terms of a reuse license, it is more likely that library publishers would use DRM to provide read-only gratis OA to a work. Libraries and their patrons are already familiar with this approach to DRM of electronic resources, particularly in e-book platforms and other page-turning display programs. Likewise, many digital image collections hosted by libraries provide free access to a low-resolution image file but do not permit users to download high-resolution images for easy reuse. It is also possible for authors or editors, prior to uploading a work to an OA repository or journal, to use common document creation software to protect the file from modifications without a password.

These and other enforced restrictions on reuse will frustrate readers and, potentially, the library that offers the publishing service. Therefore, as with collecting OA works with DRM restrictions, the library will want to carefully consider the costs and benefits of using DRM technologies in OA library publishing. Key factors for a library to consider prior to adopting a DRM for OA works should include honoring the mission of the library OA publishing program, reducing barriers to persistent access and resource preservation, and promoting the adoption of OA publishing.

Does the DRM approach under consideration align with the mission of the library as an OA publisher? Many library publishing efforts began with the expressed intention of providing OA to the works that they distribute. A DRM approach that overly limits reuse or dramatically reduces readability may compromise the original intentions of many library publishers of OA works.

Does the DRM introduce barriers to persistent access and resource preservation? In order to provide persistent access to a published work, libraries will need to make digital copies. A DRM technology that interferes with this process would reduce the ability of the library to serve as a reliable publisher of OA works. In such cases, at the very least, the library should ensure that the rights agreement between the library and the publishing partner permits the library to keep a DRM-free version of the work in a dark archive.

Does the DRM increase the adoption of OA publishing? Even if DRM introduces features that restrict reuse of an otherwise OA work, there may be times when a library is willing to accept the restrictions. For some collaborators, providing gratis OA to a published work is a first step toward increasing access. Others may be transitioning from a subscription to a fee-based OA or another nonsubscription-based business model. Some authors may balk at the notion that others could adapt or redistribute their work without seeking direct permission. Likewise, the organizations that sponsor an OA publication may be interested in tracking and maximizing usage metrics at one Internet location. These limits to access and reuse are less than ideal for most OA advocates and publishers, and in fact some prominent OA publishing organizations have begun to adopt policies that encourage fewer restrictions on reuse.[29] Even so, gratis OA is better than no access at all—particularly when the former means that the library is serving the needs of one of its constituents or developing a relationship with a new publishing partner. Thus, despite the complications for users and for the library as a publisher, some DRM technologies that enable read-only gratis OA may warrant careful consideration.

CONCLUSION

DRM, narrowly defined as an intervening technology that limits access and use of a digital publication, runs counter to the purpose of most OA publishing and against the better interests of the authors that chose an OA dissemination route. However, DRM, broadly defined as approaches to managing and communicating the rights associated with a digital publication, is a desired and necessary feature of all OA publishing activities. When the digital rights associated with an OA work are not fully communicated, libraries and users have to seek clarification from the rights holder or risk misjudging the limits to use. The most widely used DRM (broadly defined) approach in OA publishing is the Creative Commons license. Many OA publishing platforms currently embed Creative Commons licenses in web pages and communicate them in their metadata protocols; however, these managed rights are often separate from the digital object that they describe.

Therefore, DRM technologies that watermark or integrate a Creative Commons license or other rights information across all aspects of a digital work may be a welcome addition to the OA publishing toolkit. Users and developers of these DRM technologies for OA works will want to weigh the benefits against any barriers to usability, preservation, and access. Even so, while collecting or publishing OA works, a library may have good reasons for applying DRM restrictions to OA works. A library that must choose between pointing to a DRM-restricted, gratis OA digital resource for its patrons and providing no access to the digital resource may decide that read-only access is worth the price of some frustration and limited utility. Likewise, an OA library publishing service may decide to accommodate the interests of authors and editors that are unfamiliar with OA and its benefits to rights holders; some of these potential partners may be more comfortable with DRM that limits reuse, perhaps even to read-only gratis OA. Finally, while DRM technologies are unlikely to be the primary focus of a library-supported OA initiative, those that collect or publish OA works will want to watch developments in DRM technologies, particularly those that facilitate open licenses without reducing the digital integrity of OA work.

NOTES

1. Ricci and Kreisman, *Open Access*, 8.
2. Dee, "Development of the Medical Literature."
3. U.S. National Library of Medicine, "Free Web-Based Access."
4. Kling, Spector, and Fortuna, "Real Stakes of Virtual Publishing."
5. National Center for Biotechnology Information, "Home."
6. Budapest Open Access Initiative, "Budapest Open Access Initiative."
7. Creative Commons, "History."
8. Suber, *Open Access*, 4.
9. Harnad et al., "Green and the Gold Roads."
10. Peterson, Emmett, and Greenberg, "Open Access and the Author-Pays Problem."
11. Free Software Foundation, "What Is Free Software?"
12. Suber, *Open Access*, 66.
13. Ibid.
14. Ibid.
15. Creative Commons, "About the Licenses."
16. Samuelson and Schultz, "Should Copyright Owners."
17. Fitzgerald and Reid, "Digital Rights Management."
18. Abelson et al., "CC REL."
19. Pearson, "This Digital Art Gallery."
20. Klein, "Creative Commons France Experiments."
21. Adobe, "Protect Your PDF File."
22. Samuelson and Schultz, "Should Copyright Owners."
23. Bosch and Henderson, "Whole Lotta Shakin'."
24. Association of Research Libraries, "Monograph & Serial Costs."
25. Association of Research Libraries, "Library Expenditures."
26. Thibodeau and Funk, "Trends in Hospital Librarianship."

27. Skinner et al., "Library-as-Publisher."
28. Lippincot and Skinner, "Building a Community-Driven Organization."
29. Directory of Open Access Journals, "DOAJ Seal Is Now Live."

REFERENCES

Abelson, Hal, et al. "CC REL: The Creative Commons Rights Expression Language." In *The Digital Public Domain: Foundations for an Open Culture*, edited by Melanie Dulong de Rosnay and Juan Carlos De Martin, 149–87. Cambridge: OpenBook, 2012. http://www.communia-association.org/wp-content/uploads/the_digital_public_domain.pdf.

Adobe. "Protect Your PDF File with Permissions Using Adobe Acrobat XI." July 2012. http://www.adobe.com/content/dam/Adobe/en/products/acrobat/pdfs/adobe-acrobat-xi-protect-pdf-file-with-permissions-tutorial-ue.pdf. Archived at http://perma.cc/VJ75-FEPY.

Association of Research Libraries. "Library Expenditure as % of Total University Expenditure, 1982–2011." 2012. http://www.libqual.org/documents/admin/EG_2.pdf. Archived at http://perma.cc/4HMG-2ETY.

———. "Monograph & Serial Costs in ARL Libraries, 1986–2011." 2011. http://www.arl.org/storage/documents/monograph-serial-costs.pdf. Archived at http://perma.cc/C7RE-AYM7.

Bosch, Stephen, and Kittie Henderson. "Whole Lotta Shakin' Goin' On: Periodicals Price Survey 2015." *Library Journal*, April 23, 2015. http://lj.libraryjournal.com/2015/04/publishing/whole-lotta-shakin-goin-on-periodicals-price-survey-2015/. Archived at http://perma.cc/Q8ZH-HZZP.

Budapest Open Access Initiative. "Budapest Open Access Initiative." http://www.budapestopenaccessinitiative.org/. Archived at http://perma.cc/RZA6-QZVW.

Creative Commons. "About the Licenses." http://creativecommons.org/licenses/. Archived at http://perma.cc/W2T8-SM4U.

———. "History." https://creativecommons.org/about/history. Archived at http://perma.cc/6YLY-3JTC.

Dee, Cheryl Rae. "The Development of the Medical Literature Analysis and Retrieval System (MEDLARS)." *Journal of the Medical Library Association* 95, no. 4 (2007): 416–25. doi:10.3163/1536-5050.95.4.416.

Directory of Open Access Journals. "DOAJ Seal Is Now Live on the Site." June 11, 2015. https://doajournals.wordpress.com/2015/06/11/doaj-seal-is-now-live-on-the-site/. Archived at http://perma.cc/6KVR-W9ZM.

Fitzgerald, Brian, and Jason Reid. "Digital Rights Management (DRM): Managing Digital Rights for Open Access." In *Handbook on the Knowledge Economy*, edited by David Rooney, Greg Hearn, and Abraham Ninan, 268–77. Northampton, MA: Edward Elgar, 2005.

Free Software Foundation. "What Is Free Software?" http://www.gnu.org/philosophy/free-sw.en.html. Archived at http://perma.cc/VW9S-HNL5.

Harnad, Stevan, et al. "The Green and the Gold Roads to Open Access." *Nature Web Focus*, 2004. http://www.nature.com/nature/focus/accessdebate/21.html. Archived at http://perma.cc/JB38-SEYS.

Klein, Mike. "Creative Commons France Experiments with Ascribe to Support Copyleft through the Blockchain." Ascribe, May 28, 2015. http://blog.ascribe.io/creative-commons-and-ascribe-enable-copyleft-on-the-bitcoin-blockchain/. Archived at http://perma.cc/JC2G-7FA4.

Kling, Rob, Lisa B. Spector, and Joanna Fortuna. "The Real Stakes of Virtual Publishing: The Transformation of E-Biomed into PubMed Central." *Journal of the Association for Information Science and Technology* 55, no. 2 (2004): 127–48. doi:10.1002/asi.10352.

Lippincot, Sarah, and Katherine Skinner. "Building a Community-Driven Organization to Advance Library Publishing." In *Library Publishing Toolkit*, edited by Allison P. Brown et al., 367–73. Geneseo, NY: IDS Project Press, 2014. http://opensuny.org/omp/index.php/IDSProject/catalog/book/25.

National Center for Biotechnology Information, U.S. National Library of Medicine. "Home." http://www.ncbi.nlm.nih.gov/pmc/. Archived at http://perma.cc/7MKE-VUE8.

Pearson, Jordan. "This Digital Art Gallery Immortalizes Your Patronage in the Blockchain." *Motherboard*, June 19, 2015. http://motherboard.vice.com/read/this-digital-art-gallery-immortalizes-your-patronage-in-the-blockchain. Archived at http://perma.cc/K33B-YEAG.

Peterson, A. Townsend, Ada Emmett, and Marc L. Greenberg. "Open Access and the Author-Pays Problem: Assuring Access for Readers and Authors in a Global Community of Scholars." *Journal of Librarianship and Scholarly Communication* 1, no. 3 (2013): eP1064(3). doi:10.7710/2162-3309.1064.

Ricci, Laura, and Rich Kreisman. *Open Access: Market Size, Share, Forecast, and Trends.* Burlingame, CA: Outsell, 2013. http://img.en25.com/Web/CopyrightClearanceCenterInc/%7B1eced16c-2f3a-47de-9ffd-f6a659abdb2a%7D_Outsell_Open_Access_Report_01312013.pdf. Archived at https://perma.cc/4X48-G89A.

Samuelson, Pamela, and Jason Schultz. "Should Copyright Owners Have to Give Notice of Their Use of Technical Protection Measures?" *Journal on Telecommunications and High Technology Law* 6, no. 1 (2007): 41–75.

Skinner, Katherine, et al. "Library-as-Publisher: Capacity Building for the Library Publishing Subfield." *Journal of Electronic Publishing* 17, no. 2 (2014). doi:10.3998/3336451.0017.207.

Suber, Peter. *Open Access.* Cambridge, MA: MIT Press, 2012.

Thibodeau, Patricia L., and Carla J. Funk. "Trends in Hospital Librarianship and Hospital Library Services: 1989 to 2006." *Journal of the Medical Library Association* 97, no 4 (2007): 273–79. doi:10.3163/1536-5050.97.4.011.

U.S. National Library of Medicine. "Free Web-Based Access to NLM Databases." *NLM Technical Bulletin*, May–June 1997. https://www.nlm.nih.gov/pubs/techbull/mj97/mj97_web.html. Archived at http://perma.cc/D24C-84YR.

Chapter Seven

The Quandary of Digital Rights and Information Privacy

Roberta F. Studwell and Jordan A. Jefferson

You enter the library building to open it for the day, and like many employees in similar settings, you swipe an identification card near the strike plate to record information about who you are. The security credentials entered into the database of authorized building users lets you enter the building. Once you enter the library, the lights automatically come on because your employer chose Smart Grid technology to automatically turn the lights on and off when it recognizes you as a unique user of the system in place in your library.

You walk through the building, and your movement activates the motion detector for the security camera located at the front of the library. It records your location, time of entry, and other information to the security media device capturing your movement. Those devices are refreshed every forty-eight hours, the time frame set by your building manager.

You go to your desk and put down your things. Before you begin the day, you check your smart phone or another device supplied with geolocation technology to look on a map for an address, and it tracks your present location for use with your automobile later. You turn on your desktop computer or dock your computer into your docking station so that you can begin working. You then turn on the library's systems on a separate computer so that you can help patrons with their early morning requests. You enter two sets of passwords, each of which is set to a unique profile about you that either you or a system administrator created for you.

You've just verified at least five personal information identifiers unique to you in five unconnected databases. In most instances those disparate pieces of information about you would not be of interest to anyone in particular, but what if they were? What if the information that verified your identity and credentials when you swiped your ID not only turned on your computer and logged you into your most used databases, but also had a great cup of coffee flavored the way you like it waiting in the staff lounge. Could all of these passwords and interactions be connected? Welcome to the Internet of Things (IoT).

Coined as a term in the late 1990s, the idea of the IoT is to create a network of individual databases and computer systems that are able to operate by commingling within existing Internet protocols and structures.[1] In brief, the IoT refers to "things" such as devices, smart chips, smart phones, or Fitbits that contain electronics, software, sensors, or other types of connectivity tools intended to relay personal information that they've collected about a person to those other connected devices. IoT is the concept, and perhaps the ideal situation, of being able to connect any device that has an on/off switch to other devices with similar connectivity capabilities or to the Internet. The IoT allows the companies running the software behind the devices to collect information about the person using them, ultimately to inform her about the lack of a food item in her house and her need to go to the store, the good or bad lifestyle choices she is making that could affect her health, or safety risks present in the location she finds herself in. The convenience of the IoT is the lure of ways to make people's lives easier, more efficient, and safer.

Libraries are not immune to the IoT. The interplay of libraries providing digital users with access to digital information resources such as e-books and digital articles through the library's LMS potentially adds interoperability and connections to other devices, some of which are not yet imagined. Take, for example, a user's search for Greek food ingredients for a special dish or two she wants to prepare for dinner that evening. Once she inputs that search, it could easily command a device she owns to give her directions to locations offering to sell her those ingredients, something most of us already see when we do a Google search.

Most important from a privacy perspective is that those databases are connected to each other and will add to the digital stores of information already collected about a user. Note the number of passwords and potential profile information that the employee in the first scenario was required to enter. Use of Internet resources generally means that someone has been required to input certain pieces of information about herself. Some of that information will be personal information. Personally identifiable information (PII) is a type of information that can be used on its own or aggregated with other data to identify a person or an individual in a certain context. For our library employee, this is the point at which privacy intrusions could take place.

As society becomes increasingly digital, libraries are doing their best to meet the needs (and wants) of their users. This includes providing as many digital resources as possible. Internet access, DVDs, CDs, e-books, streaming music services, e-magazines, electronic journals, and online databases are just a piece of the digital content available to patrons today.

The sheer number of e-books and copyrighted online information available to users increases the chance that numerous invasions of privacy will occur. The collection, use, and possible disclosure of reader information will be explored later in this chapter. But first, an introduction to the broad area of privacy is necessary to put potential privacy intrusions into perspective.

INFORMATION PRIVACY AND INFORMATION PRIVACY RIGHTS

Many authors offer a more thorough discussion of basic concepts of information privacy than the brief and targeted overview set out here.[2] However, a basic understanding of information privacy is needed in order to put the IoT, library privacy rationales, reader privacy, and the Digital Millennium Copyright Act (DMCA) into perspective. The notion of privacy and concepts of information privacy and other rights that spring from it go well beyond the collection of personal information that might place an individual's privacy at risk. Privacy rights are complex, and offshoots such as Internet privacy, information privacy, reader privacy, and intellectual privacy[3] take up multiple chapters of explanatory text in treatises and other library resources.

Almost all of the information that a person retrieves by using an Internet source can be traced back to that individual in a variety of ways. Blog posts, articles sought for research, or even a short book review about a research resource the library holds are immediately identified with that individual and that institution. Once a person accesses a particular digital resource of interest to him, his personally identifiable information collected as part of a profile or registration process lurks in the background waiting for verification. Although no clear meaning is ascribed to the term *personally identifiable information* under U.S. law, data elements such as name, postal address, email address, social security number, and driver's license number are typically thought of as PII. Once a profile is created, that person's digital footprint potentially increases.[4] In the paper-based analog world, information about a person was difficult to collect and combine in any meaningful way to draw conclusions about that person or her tendencies. That is no longer true in the digital world.

The central issues in most privacy disputes revolve around business practices affecting the growth of a user's digital footprint, examples of which were catalogued by Daniel Solove in his bestselling book *The Digital Person*.[5] In *Privacy Law*, Brownlee and Waleski[6] discuss the effects that commercial PII practices present to that person's privacy preferences—known or unknown to that person. Privacy problems occur when data is combined with other data, making it more likely that a person is no longer anonymous. In the paper age, the collection of personal information was difficult. In the cyber age, secondary usages of legally collected PII have become very common. "Legally-collected personal information is now in the hands (or in the cloud) of third parties. Those parties' secondary usages determine how much privacy we still have since at any point since those businesses may legally collect information about their customers, and sell it to others, perhaps even to the government."[7]

Individuals have a right to keep PII private when its use extends beyond primary collection for a specific, agreed-to use.[8] However, most online privacy policies about third-party data sharing are difficult to understand, and consumers short on time and attention may discover that their information has been used in a way they never intended. "As downstream sharing of PII becomes more widespread, the likelihood of preserving the original wishes of the user in the data sharing chain erodes."[9]

Sensitivity of information and sheer volume were issues in the paper age because storage and retrieval constrained the number of privacy violations. In the digital age, processing and secondary uses of personal information present privacy concerns that were inconceivable in the paper age. Today, the privacy issue is not collection; it is privacy violations caused by secondary data uses. One author describes it as "cybernation," which includes storing, collating (including building dossiers), analyzing, accessing, and distributing discrete items of information in concert with each other.[10]

Consumers have an interest in understanding what information is collected about them and how it is used or stored. While some consumers view sharing their information as a quid pro quo for many of the free services available to them online, others would prefer to jealously protect their information. Although the confidentiality of most information lies somewhere between public and private, users need to be notified when the privacy of their PII might be breached.[11] Because of the diversity of potential practices and consumer preferences, U.S. data privacy law has evolved based on principles of "notice and choice."[12]

Privacy is better protected if PII is not *stored*. Data banks collect records about which magazines a person reads or which restaurants a person frequents and therefore pose a high risk to reader privacy and to individual privacy. If that same information can be instantly erased, then many secondary privacy concerns disappear.[13]

With the rise of the Internet and use of email in the twentieth century, new challenges confront people who want to protect digital information privacy.[14] In the twenty-first century, information privacy is nearly impossible to protect. The history of information privacy helps explain many of the key reasons that libraries and users will want to maintain privacy when they use digital collections.

Historical Underpinnings

Basic concepts of privacy are rooted in societal norms and values such as reputation and the protection of a person. Privacy concepts have been protected by the Supreme Court under the Constitution since the early 1900s. Although the right of privacy is not an explicit part of the Constitution's Bill of Rights, privacy is considered an element of the other explicit rights set out in the Constitution and has been defended as a necessary component of that set of documents in a variety of cases. Examples include *Griswold v. Connecticut*, which recognized an independent right of privacy within the penumbra of the Bill of Rights, and *Roe v. Wade*, which established a right of privacy under the Due Process Clause of the Fourteenth Amendment.[15]

In the nineteenth century, privacy rights were not considered elements of property, tort, or contract rights. The concept of privacy came to light when, in the wake of technological change—the introduction of cameras—Justices Warren and Brandeis wrote an article about a general "right of the individual to be left alone."[16] A series of surveillance cases and state statutory enactments took place after their article appeared, and cases concerning telephonic communications, including wiretapping of telephone transmissions, were litigated.[17]

In 1928, the Supreme Court in *Olmstead v. United States*[18] decided the issue of whether a search warrant was required before the government could engage in wiretapping, which Olmstead considered an invasion of his privacy.[19] Justice Louis Brandeis dissented and stated that the right to privacy in one's home is "the right most valued by civilized people."[20] He recognized that a privacy intrusion occurred even when a physical search had not occurred.

The Warren and Brandeis privacy concepts took root in two early twentieth-century state tort law cases: *Roberson v. Rochester Folding Box Co.*[21] and *Pavesich v. New England Life Insurance Company.*[22] These cases gave rise to the notion of a common-law right of privacy.

Only a short six years after the *Olmstead* decision, Congress enacted §605 of the Federal Communications Act of 1934 in order to curtail wiretapping.[23] Wiretapping was forbidden under the act, but governmental wiretapping continued. Limits to government wiretapping were again questioned in the 1960s when the Supreme Court overruled the *Olmstead* decision in *Katz v. United States*.[24] The "reasonable expectation of privacy test" resulted from this decision. That test consists of two factors set out in Justice Harlan's concurrence: (1) does a person exhibit an "actual or subjective expectation of privacy," and (2) is "the expectation one that society is prepared to recognize as 'reasonable'"?[25]

Information privacy rights, which includes notions of reader privacy, came to be acknowledged a decade later. In 1977, in *Whalen v. Roe*[26] the Supreme Court extended the right to privacy to include a right against the disclosure of personal information. This was interpreted as the first declaration of a "constitutional right to informational privacy."[27]

The rapid and overwhelming proliferation of computers and computer applications that followed these historic legal cases gave rise to the need for lawmakers and others to put legal protections in place. An information privacy statute was not enacted after the *Whalen v. Roe* decision. However, the U.S. Deptartment of Health, Education, and Welfare published its Fair Information Practice Principles (FIPPs) in 1973 as these series of privacy cases were making their way through the court system. The FIPPs, along with laws and regulatory schemes that protect privacy and ownership of types of information, are covered in sections that follow.

Piracy, the DMCA Copyright Owner Protections, and Their Implications

As digital works began to multiply exponentially on the Internet, they replaced many analog forms that were difficult to copy and reproduce. Authors and vendors wanted to protect their works from blatant piracy. As a result, the Information Infrastructure Taskforce was convened and conducted multiple public hearings over several years to gather information to amend the copyright law.[28] Lost profits and loss of control over works found on the Internet led authors and vendors to lobby Congress to enact strict controls. The DMCA passed in 1998.[29]

Section 1201 of the DMCA is the anticircumvention provision, and it is the section that most affects digital users' privacy. It makes breaking digital locks, primarily digital rights management (DRM) systems, on digital content illegal for any purpose, including fair use, first sale, or to extract the "ideas" from the "expression."[30] The DMCA can be viewed as a "patch" to protect new technology developments where the law lagged behind the values owners and compilers thought the law should protect or where the scope of protection appeared to be lacking.[31]

In effect, the privacy section of the DMCA imposes solutions where commercial practices and judicial interpretation have not yet been given a full opportunity to respond.[32] In layman's terms, the DMCA prohibits bypassing DRM technologies (e.g., cracking copy protection on a software program, bypassing DRM on a digital music file, or reformatting Kindle e-book files).[33] The DMCA works in tandem with technological protections like encryption by providing a layered method of protection from a system breach at the outer ring and the right of the copyright holder in her work at the core.[34] To the extent that databases or collections of information qualify for copyright protection, the DMCA provides an underlying legal basis to support their protection. Users who attempt to circumvent the technology that is in place will be identified, their PII will be collected in order for the author to issue a cease-and-desist notice, and they could be prosecuted.

The DMCA goes much further than protecting the level of control an owner has over her own work and adds a significant threat of privacy intrusion when a user is merely thought to have pirated a work.[35] Some argue that the law permits copyright owners to use technological controls to deny access to information even though it qualifies as a fair use or when use of public domain information, like ideas or facts, are incorporated into protected works.[36]

The success of the DMCA can be characterized as mixed. The statute's privacy protection scheme offers few protections to users, and its content controls may have had a chilling effect on users who do not want their PII to be discovered and therefore use digital resources sparingly. During the congressional debates, DMCA opponents raised concerns about the reach of tools a copyright owner could use that might chill legitimate competition and a reader's right to academic inquiry.[37]

Databases and Protection of Works: Owners' Legal Rights

Owners nearly always prevail in the privacy battles over print content and information privacy. PII was difficult to obtain when print content alone was available to a reader. In most cases, only libraries or bookstores could provide specific information about a reader when an infringement claim was raised, and both entities have diligently protected their users' rights for decades.[38] The digital world, however, greatly enhances a copyright owner's chance of discovering who a user might be. It appears logical that the user's rights should therefore be protected by federal law since copyright law is primarily federal. However, except for what may be characterized as *sensitive personal information*, U.S. data privacy law generally is not governed by federal statutes. Instead, federal law has created a patchwork of remedies tied to very specific circumstances.[39]

The need to protect owner/compiler/distributor rights from others who might take an author's works and use them without permission is perhaps more important now than it was when most works were issued only in paper-based analog formats. However, the need to protect users, who must give away some of their privacy rights in order to gain access to digital resources, also exists. The law has been slow to catch up to technology improvements and methods that authors, owners, and compilers use to collect personal information that directly impacts user privacy.

Digital content is jealously guarded by content owners, who need to make a profit in order to stay in business. As information owners, vendors, and database compilers' PII collection practices have become more sophisticated, the scope of PII protection mandated by guidelines, regulations, or laws has increased generally, but not uniformly. Businesses aim for the bottom line when pressed to follow the law. Information owners tend to prevail in information privacy lawsuits because privacy laws typically protect only very specific forms of *sensitive* data (such as patient billing, motor vehicle records, education and financial records, video rental records, and information collected from children), usually in response to particular perceived problems. [40]

Content owners may bring an infringement lawsuit under a variety of causes of action and will usually win because of the cost of litigation and the small potential recovery by either party. Several federal and state statutes, such as the Computer Fraud and Abuse Act (CFAA), [41] the No Electronic Theft Act (Net Act), [42] and the DMCA, specifically protect an owner's digital rights in their content.

One set of state laws also protects copyright owner's rights. The Uniform Computer Information Transactions Act (UCITA) is a model law that states are encouraged to pass, originally proposed as Article 2B of the Uniform Commercial Code. [43] Although adopted in only two state jurisdictions, UCITA codifies the view that traditional software distributions are licenses, not sales. [44] It tends to favor information providers and vendors and provides another avenue for the collection of PII about users through licensing protocols.

Beyond the laws mentioned above, publishers and vendors have brought claims under a variety of other legal theories to protect their ideas or works. Idea misappropriation is a court-created concept that permits an author who pitches an idea or story to bring a claim for damages if their idea is appropriated or used without permission. Unfair competition is a common law tort fostering fairness and honesty in business dealings that occur when another author or compiler does not give appropriate credit to the work of another author from which they have drawn. Trespass to chattels involves an intentional interference in the possession of personal property that causes an owner injury. An example of this type of litigation occurred in *eBay, Inc. v. Bidder's Edge, Inc.* [45] eBay successfully used the doctrine to prevent the defendant's computer bots from crawling eBay's auction website in order to use not only eBay's data but data from other auction websites in an attempt to yield a larger aggregate auction website. [46]

Copyright Protection: Consumer's and Users' Legal Rights

Digital content is also important to content consumers such as researchers or students who need the history and background about a concept or idea that has already been preserved in a tangible form and is therefore copyrighted by someone else. These consumers seek protection under federal copyright laws in their pursuit of these important information building blocks so that they can create new knowledge and useful works, a countervailing goal of copyright law.

The digital and print worlds of copyright protections vary widely. In the print world, information seekers use their libraries to access information in print formats, and although PII about their circulation transactions is captured by their library, that information is also protected from privacy intrusions and lawsuits and often discarded as soon as it is no longer needed. In the digital world, information consumers tend not to succeed in information privacy lawsuits because in order to access digital information, information consumers often sign away many of their privacy rights under a licensing agreement. Given the popularity of digital formats, users' information privacy protections are dwindling, if a recent survey is correct in tallying more than 120 million e-book and audiobook circulations from libraries in the first nine months of 2015, representing year-over-year growth of almost 20 percent.[47]

Content consumers may bring an invasion-of-privacy lawsuit under a variety of causes of action, but they rarely prevail. The particulars of the privacy invasion, the cost of litigation, and the potential recovery under the laws they choose determine how or whether a content consumer proceeds with a lawsuit. Several laws protect that consumer's rights.

In suits brought by online consumers and privacy groups, a claim of invasion of privacy is often raised but is normally not successful based on the historical underpinnings of U.S. privacy law described above. For most digital invasion-of-privacy cases, the claims are content based, and a plaintiff generally must prove that the content at issue, including PII, is sufficiently "private" to give rise to a traditional invasion-of-privacy claim. This is rarely true for privacy lawsuits because, when plaintiffs attempt to prove harm, courts find that the information at issue is "personal" but not private.[48]

Congress has enacted legislation seeking to govern the treatment of personal information, as noted in the previous section, for *sensitive types of information* such as financial information. The Children's Online Privacy Protection Act (COPPA), the Fair Credit Reporting Act (FCRA),[49] and the Fair and Accurate Credit Transaction Act (FACTA), which added new sections to the original act, are designed primarily to help consumers fight the growing crime of identity theft along with ensuring accuracy, privacy, limits on information sharing, and new consumer rights regarding information disclosure.[50] The Gramm-Leach-Bliley Act (GLBA) prohibits financial institutions from sharing consumer financial information with nonaffiliates without first allowing the consumer to opt out.[51] These laws provide a statutory framework to strike a balance between providing citizens affordable financial services while protecting them against invasions of privacy and the misuse of personal information. They do not, however, address information privacy concerns in a pervasive fashion.

Because most reader privacy and PII privacy claims will not succeed under federal laws, some states now protect a variety of right to privacy claims. California leads the way in passing privacy laws and in following the dictates of its constitutional mandate concerning privacy. Other recent state laws regarding the right to privacy are covered in the sections that follow.

The most ambitious state enactment concerning reader privacy occurred on October 3, 2011, when California Governor Jerry Brown signed the Reader Privacy Act[52] into law. It dictates that book service providers in California are prohibited from disclosing personal information related to their users to third parties, including information that "identifies, relates to, describes, or is associated with a particular user";[53] a "unique identifier or Internet Protocol Address";[54] and information that shows a "user's access to or use of a book service or a book, in whole or in partial form."[55] The act seeks to specifically protect all book formats, including electronic formats.[56] The act may signal a wave of new state laws aimed at creating legal barriers to protect personal information related to digital books.[57]

Finally, consumers may also raise complementary causes of action for invasion of privacy under a theory of misuse. The theory could be raised when or if their shared information is stolen or misused, as it could be in an identity theft situation. The copyright misuse doctrine, however, has very limited application in the privacy context because when copyright holders attempt to use their copyright in impermissible ways, the courts have decided that antitrust law or public policy applies and not misuse of copyright.[58] Although the legal schemes between federal and state jurisdictions vary, some case law is instructive and is included below.

CASE LAW

Privacy litigation that has resulted directly from the DMCA is limited but generally centers on violations of the circumvention measures of the act. When an ISP is required to turn over personal information about an illegal use to the copyright owners so that a demand letter and other notice can be sent, privacy violations are triggered. Some of the more public lawsuits have involved DVDs. *321 Studios v. Metro Goldwyn Mayer Studios, Inc.*[59] involved users who were openly selling products used to circumvent copy protection mechanisms in DVDs. *Paramount Pictures Corp. v. 321 Studios*[60] also concerned sale of products used to circumvent copy protection mechanisms in DVDs. A more unique case, *Craigslist Inc. v. Kerbel*[61] concerned a defendant who sold a service designed to automatically post to Craigslist and circumvent its CAPTCHA restrictions, violating Craigslist terms. Most recently, in *United States v. Reichert*, the Sixth Circuit upheld Jeffrey Reichert's criminal conviction for willfully trafficking in video game modification chips.[62] *Reichert* highlights efforts to bring about criminal prosecution under the DMCA.[63]

Circumstances that were not originally intended to be covered under the DMCA have also gone to trial. In the *Chamberlain*[64] and *Lexmark*[65] cases, DRM systems were used to restrict consumer choice of goods such as a garage door opener. The copyright protection was only secondary. Both decisions expose the vulnerability of information consumers to the threat of being labeled a system code cracker in instances not targeted for DMCA protection.[66]

Online privacy policy cases that reach the courts have been limited in both scope and number. Most claims now are handled under regulatory schemes discussed in the next section.

REGULATORY SCHEMES

The lack of a comprehensive federal legal scheme dealing with privacy information disclosures and the scarcity of case law defining owners' and users' rights leaves much of the heavy lifting for defining, administering, and enforcing privacy in personal information to the Federal Trade Commission (FTC). FTC regulatory enactments, such as guidelines and enforcement actions (as well as litigation), have begun to push the boundaries of what information may be considered private when it is collected, stored, used, or transferred to third parties.[67] At the center of the FTC's enforcement authority stands the Fair Information Practice Principles (FIPPs).[68]

Evolution of the Fair Information Practices Principles

The FIPPs have been described as the gold standard for protecting personal information.[69] The FIPPs are widely accepted principles that have been adopted internationally to facilitate both individual privacy and the promise of information flows as the use of technology increases. The original Advisory Committee that drafted the 1973 U.S. Department of Health, Education, and Welfare Report discovered that "a person's privacy is poorly protected against arbitrary or abusive record-keeping practices."[70] At the core of the FIPPs is the idea of consumers' rights to notice, consent, choice, and security.[71]

As the FIPPs have evolved, so has the notion of scope, procedure, and substance encapsulated within the principles. The FTC has taken an increasingly proactive, aggressive approach to protecting consumer privacy rights. Since 1998, it has issued three reports examining the practices of leading and random Internet websites in adhering to the core "fair information practices" of notice, consent, choice, and security.[72] Each report found that self-regulation had not succeeded in protecting consumer privacy.[73]

On March 26, 2012, the FTC issued a final privacy report calling on Congress to "consider baseline privacy legislation while industry implements the final privacy framework through individual company initiatives and through strong and enforceable self-regulatory initiatives."[74] The 2012 FTC report called for all companies to implement "do not track" technology and recommended that mobile telephone service providers improve privacy protections and that data brokers create a centralized website where identities and collection-and-use practices are clearly communicated to consumers, and urged the development of sector-specific industry codes of conduct.[75] These proposals focus on transparency, individual control, respect for context, security, access and accuracy, focused collection, and accountability, the original precepts of the FIPPs.

Only in the last few years have federal policy makers started to create updated privacy best practices based largely on the FIPPs. A type of privacy framework to protect users and owners alike has started to emerge. The White House's Consumer Privacy Bill of Rights, the beginning steps of which are set out in its "Consumer Data Privacy in a Networked World: A Framework for Protecting Privacy and Promoting Innovation in the Global Economy,"[76] and the FTC's Privacy Framework in its 2012 report do not establish new FIPPs, but they do create a framework for privacy protection and a blueprint for privacy in the information age. The reports emphasize and focus on the "context of the transaction" or the "sensitivity" of the data in order to create more flexible practices for companies in determining what data can be collected, how it can be used, and how long it can be retained.[77]

In addition to creating guidelines, regulatory actions protecting privacy, or potential legislation, the FTC can also initiate enforcement actions. Actions are initiated based on alleged unfair or deceptive online consumer privacy violations of section 5 of the Federal Trade Commission Act (FTCA).[78]

FTC Enforcement Actions

The capture of personally identifiable information by social media sites is perhaps the most vexing enforcement matter for the FTC today. Cases such as *In the Matter of Twitter, Inc.*[79] signal the FTC's desire to hold social media sites accountable for privacy violations. The FTC alleged that Twitter had deceived consumers and put their privacy at risk by failing to safeguard their personal information using its administrative control systems. Pursuant to the terms of an agreed-upon settlement, Twitter was barred for twenty years from misleading consumers about the extent to which it protects the security, privacy, and confidentiality of nonpublic consumer information. [80]

Most recently, the FTC has brought enforcement actions for alleged deviation from stated privacy policies against MySpace, [81] Facebook, [82] TRENDnet, [83] and Snapchat, [84] all of which agreed to settle PII-related issues with the FTC. These cases make it clear that the FTC believes that storing of PII raises privacy concerns.

The FTC has not yet focused attention on third-party information storing and sharing enforcement actions. However, its new role outlined below may now permit it to focus more on information storing and sharing.

ANTICIPATED PRIVACY PROTECTION CHANGES

New FTC Role

The White House Consumer Bill of Rights holds promise for change in the protection of personal information and its use by businesses. [85] The Bill of Rights emphasizes that companies should offer consumers clear choices, presented at times and in ways that enable consumers to make informed decisions about what information will be collected. Additionally, the report strongly recommends that companies should offer ways for consumers to limit or withdraw consent after it is given, and that they should create do-not-track mechanisms so that consumers may exercise control over how or if third parties receive their personal information. The report also suggests placing reasonable limits on personal data that companies could collect and retain along with the strong recommendation that companies should securely dispose of or de-identify data they have collected once they no longer need it.

The report calls on Congress to codify the Bill of Rights and to grant the FTC the authority to enforce it. Additionally, the report suggests that the FTC provide assistance and advice regarding the development of company policies and promote "Privacy by Design" concepts. Privacy by Design is an approach to protecting privacy that aims to foster context-based rights for individuals by incorporating privacy "at all stages of the design and development of products and services," including expanding choices to include whether data collected may be shared with third parties. [86]

Facebook's new "Privacy Checkup" feature is a good example of a privacy-enhancing tool that is situation specific (appearing to those who have not changed their settings in some time and are posting publicly) and just-in-time (appearing when the user is typing a post). A good design should also address third-party sharing, which Facebook has yet to do. The major stumbling block to Privacy by Design is the design part—how to provide useful, just-in-

time information to let consumers make informed decisions and not be pater-
nalistic or disruptive.[87]

Center for Copyright Information

The new kid on the block in terms of enforcement mechanisms is private, not
a governmental organization. The Center for Copyright Information (CCI)
was established in 2011 and on February 2013 implemented the Copyright
Alert System (CAS), also known as the "Six Strikes" program, to combat
online piracy.[88] The CAS was designed with an educational purpose in mind:
to create awareness of illegal file sharing by motivating individuals to legally
exchange copyrighted works. Once copyright owners monitor and later notify ISPs about possible copyright infringement, the ISP then independently
issues a maximum of six escalating alerts. These are sent to Internet subscribers thought to be infringers, and each level carries harsher consequences.
Although this is not the United States' first attempt to quell online file sharing piracy, it is the country's first attempt at a "graduated response" scheme.
Other rights management schemes are likely to follow.

Other options should be explored in order to enhance reader privacy
protections to add to those already mentioned above: legislation by a handful
of states, the anticipated passage of laws to accompany the Consumer Bill of
Rights, or work by other watchdog entities. One answer may be to push for
intellectual privacy interests important to the rights of readers—as opposed
to information privacy, which appears to be a nonstarter with the courts—by
modifying DRM technologies to provide the elements necessary to best protect readers from unwanted privacy intrusions.[89]

READER PRIVACY, THE LIBRARY, AND DIGITAL MEDIA

With the introduction of digital media came the fear of copyright infringement and later the advent of DRM. At its most basic, DRM is a collection of
technologies that "prevent you from using a copyrighted digital work beyond
the degree to which the copyright owner (or a publisher . . .) wishes to allow
you to use it."[90] The purpose of DRM is to "control access to, track, and limit
uses of digital works."[91] While librarians are rightly concerned about each of
these components, the focus of this chapter is the ability of the technology to
track the behavior of a patron using DRM-enabled digital media. Librarians
are not strangers to maintaining records on patrons; collecting information on
patrons has been a practice since libraries began. Basic patron information
such as name and address is routinely collected, while status, privileges, and
borrowing record are attached to the patron's personal information. As a
matter of professional policy, most librarians are accustomed to generating
these records and then destroying them as soon as practical or as soon as the

records have been scrubbed of identifying information and used to create statistical analyses of services and patron behavior.

However, maintaining patron records and protecting patron privacy were simpler endeavors in the era before the Internet of Things and the move to digital media. Protecting patrons' privacy and confidentiality has always been a key tenant of the profession, and until recently libraries have been guarding the patron records they created. Now libraries must be concerned with what information vendors and third parties are collecting about patrons' reading, listening, and viewing habits. The library's role in safeguarding user privacy as its readers utilize these technologies seems to present a logical template that can be the model for other third parties who are now in control of digital media.

The challenges of reader privacy in the digital age cannot be answered with solutions developed for a prenetworked, paper-based world because nonlibrary intermediaries now facilitate much of the digital reading taking place both inside and outside the library.[92] Because libraries have designed their administrative and technical infrastructures to safeguard patrons' records and to facilitate patrons' anonymous browsing of third-party resources, their policies may provide a template that third parties could adopt in order to avoid disclosure of a patron's reading history.

Nondisclosure of protected records is the minimum requirement of such a simple solution and is compatible with information-age companies' business interests. The goodwill associated with protecting privacy remains important to most companies; therefore, in order to protect reading records, businesses should permit users to opt in to a company's use of their data and explain to consumers *why* they should agree to give up their privacy.[93] Even if consumers opt in to receive customized, personalized recommendations or the ability to review their research histories, they should still be allowed to set an "expiration date" for their data at the time they complete a transaction or request deletion of certain records on an ad hoc basis after their transactions.

THE IMPORTANCE OF PRIVATE READING

While humans are born with the capacity for speech and thought, reading requires years of learning and practice to achieve mastery. As such, the act of reading rewires our brains, making humans, quite literally, shaped by what we read.[94] Reading is a fundamental way that we as a society engage with information—how we develop, learn, and share thoughts and ideas. Private reading allows us to grapple with unpopular, frightening, or even dangerous concepts in the relative comfort of our anonymity. Because of its importance, the act of private reading implicates the civil liberties of a free society. It is fundamentally important because private reading allows people to "engage with controversial ideas, develop intellectually, and formulate speech they intend to share with others."[95] In a library or at home, while reading a physical book or digital resource, a reader has the right to seek and find information anonymously. When that anonymity is compromised, there is a chilling effect on the reader's potential for free thought, free speech, and free exercise.

Private, anonymous reading done in solitude in the confines of a library or bookstore may soon be a thing of the past. This is due in part to a shift toward research and reading facilitated by private entities with an interest in gaining access to readers' data, instead of by trusted institutions, like libraries, which espouse legal commitments to privacy. Services such as Amazon facilitate e-book borrowing for the Kindle e-reader as a service to library patrons. It also collects detailed reading records from these patrons and uses the records for marketing purposes. In late 2014 users learned that Adobe's Digital Editions e-book and PDF reader, a trusted software used in thousands of libraries worldwide, "actively logs and reports every document readers add to their local 'library' along with what users do with those files."[96] Because third parties like Amazon and Adobe are not libraries, confidentiality rules do not restrict their collection of the very sorts of data that library confidentiality policies are meant to protect.[97]

Third-party intermediaries such as Internet service providers, advertising partners, or content providers are not compelled to protect information that they receive from Internet users. Because so many digital users search in solitude, they may believe that they must give up some privacy protections in order to gain access to information they find on the Internet that they want to use. The extent to which intellectual privacy is protected (or not) in our reading future is a choice that we will have to make as a society. If we don't have the conversation about why reading and reader privacy matter, the choice will still be made, but it will be made only by companies interacting with the market.[98]

HISTORY OF LEGAL PROTECTIONS FOR READERS

The United States has a long legal tradition of protecting reader privacy. In *Griswold v. Connecticut*,[99] mentioned above, the Supreme Court indicated that the right to receive speech is a critical component of the First Amendment. "The right to freedom of speech and press includes not only the right to utter or to print, but the right to distribute, the right to receive, the right to read."[100]

Federal courts have indirectly supported the notion that the right to receive speech, embodied in the First Amendment, incorporates a right to reader privacy.[101] During the McCarthy era, the United States Supreme

Court found that a bookseller cannot be convicted for refusing to give the government a list of customers who purchased certain political books.[102] A decade later, the Supreme Court reaffirmed its stance on reader privacy by invalidating a requirement that individuals submit a written request to the postal service in order to receive communist political mailings.[103] In both cases, the chilling effect of monitoring readers was cited as a determining factor. In 1969 the Supreme Court explicitly confirmed support of the freedom to read in an obscenity case in which Justice Marshall stated, "a State has no business telling a man, sitting alone in his own house, what books he may read."[104] But we should not think that reader privacy is not a timely issue. In the late 1990s and early 2000s, booksellers in both Washington, DC,[105] and Colorado[106] brought suits to protect their customers' reading proclivities from government intrusion. In 2007 reader privacy protections made its way into the digital realm when the Western District of Wisconsin quashed a government subpoena seeking the identities of over twenty-thousand Amazon customers who purchased books from one seller.[107] Once again, the potential chilling effect of allowing the government to review the reading habits of citizens was a primary factor for the court, which stated, "well-founded or not, rumors of an Orwellian federal criminal investigation into the reading habits of Amazon's customers could frighten countless potential customers into canceling planned online book purchases, now and perhaps forever."[108]

In addition to judicial recognition of reader privacy, federal and state legislation has been enacted to address the privacy concerns of American readers. At the federal level, the Privacy Act of 1974,[109] Family Educational Rights and Privacy Act (FERPA),[110] and COPPA[111] all work to protect citizens from various privacy intrusions by the federal government and private actors. At the state level, forty-eight states and Washington, DC, have laws protecting the confidentiality of library patron records.[112] The protections afforded by these laws vary depending on the state, but many include requirements for the confidentiality of library records, restrict libraries from disclosing records to third parties without subpoena or warrant, and require notice be given to the library patron being investigated. Some statutes specifically address records of library materials viewed electronically.[113]

As noted above, California became the first state to address the multifaceted issue of reader privacy in an online environment. The California Reader Privacy Act of 2011[114] focuses on books users browse, read, or purchase from online booksellers and electronic services. The law requires the government and third parties to "demonstrate a compelling interest in obtaining reader records [and] show that the information contained in those records cannot be obtained by less intrusive means."[115] This heightened requirement acts as a deterrent to third parties seeking personal records as part of routine investigations.[116] While not implicating libraries directly, the California

Reader Privacy Act highlights the need for privacy laws to address the realities of reading in a digital environment. Record and reader privacy laws provide legal support for librarians to stand up for their patrons' privacy and confidentiality as part of their ethical obligation as information professionals.[117]

In the past decade, two states passed laws that prohibit private booksellers from disclosing information about reader purchases.[118] Although many states have dealt with privacy issues related to online activities, only four state legislatures, with California in the lead, have adopted reader privacy statutes that apply to private e-book sellers. The others include Arizona, Delaware, and Missouri.[119]

LIBRARY PRIVACY PRINCIPLES, POLICIES, AND NORMS

Librarians have a set of principles and norms that act as a guide for the profession. In 1939 the American Library Association adopted the Library Bill of Rights.[120] While protection of privacy was not specifically mentioned, the Code of Ethics, adopted shortly after the Bill of Rights, explicitly states that libraries must "protect each library user's right to privacy and confidentiality with respect to information sought or received and resources consulted, borrowed, acquired or transmitted."[121] Subsequent interpretations of the initial document have found privacy implications on both intellectual freedom and privacy grounds. Noting that "the privacy of library users is and must be inviolable,"[122] the Library Bill of Rights recognizes that "when users recognize or fear that their privacy or confidentiality is compromised, true freedom of inquiry no longer exists."[123]

The ALA interpretation of privacy establishes the following rights and responsibilities of libraries and patrons to safeguard the privacy of library users:

- To the greatest extent possible, the user should be in control of as many choices as possible, including decisions about selection, access, and use of information and resources.
- The library must inform users of any policies or procedures that govern the amount and retention of personal information, why it is being collected, and whether the library patron can opt in or out of the collection of such information.
- Safeguarding user privacy is the duty of all librarians, staff, and patrons. Libraries should maintain an "environment respectful and protective of all users."
- Data collection should only be done when it is necessary to the operation of the library.

- Libraries should not share user information with vendors or third parties without the permission of the user.[124]

In addition, the ALA recommends the following guidelines when establishing privacy policies:

- Limit the degree to which personally identifiable information is monitored, collected, disclosed, and distributed.
- Avoid creating unnecessary records.
- Avoid retaining records that are not needed for efficient operation of the library, including data-related logs, digital records, vendor-collected data, and system backups.
- Avoid library practices and procedures that place personally identifiable information on public view.[125]

Privacy is an essential element to intellectual freedom and enterprise. In libraries, privacy is "the right to open inquiry without having the subject of one's interest examined or scrutinized by others."[126] When that freedom is compromised, whether it is by the library, other users, or third parties, users' trust in the library as an institution is damaged and their intellectual endeavors may be in danger.

DRM AND THE THREAT TO PRIVACY

Knowing what we do about the history of reader protection in the United States and the commitment of libraries to safeguarding patron privacy, why is DRM an issue? The crux of DRM is at odds with much of what libraries as institutions stand for: use, access, intellectual freedom, and privacy. Of the general functions of DRM technologies, the two of the most interest to libraries are constraint and monitoring.[127]

Constraint

DRM technologies are designed to "set and automatically enforce limits on user behavior,"[128] such as controlling how users can interact with the resource by limiting access and preventing users from sharing, copying, printing, or saving the content.

Monitoring/Tracking

DRM is implemented to protect the rights of copyright holders. As a consequence, DRM allows copyright holders and publishers to monitor the private use of that content by individuals, whether they purchase the digital media or access it through a library. Monitoring is done for a variety for reasons. Protection of the initial copyright is one, but another, far more lucrative reason to monitor a user's digital media consumption is to turn a profit on the user's preferences. Such monitoring turns the reading and research endeavors of a user into a commodity, allowing vendors and third parties to identify and market other goods and services to the user.[129]

What Can DRM Track?

"The level of detail that these services can collect would require an offline library or bookstore to hire an agent to follow each individual patron around the stacks, throughout their day, and finally into their homes."[130] While this statement is flippant, it does have some truth. DRM systems can track a number of private transactions during the use of the work. For instance, some vendors require user authentication prior to reading, listening to, or watching the digital media. In that case, the user's media consumption is linked to their personal information (think logging into Amazon prior to checking out a book from OverDrive). In the case of e-books (in libraries or purchased) a nonexhaustive list of the information DRM technologies can track includes name, email address, physical address, location, IP address, any other personally identifiable information provided when setting up an account, browsing (or other online) activity, history of book read through the technology, pages read, time/date of reading, annotations/highlights made by the user, and text searches.

BEST PRACTICES FOR PROTECTING PATRON PRIVACY

A 2014 survey of over 1,200 library professions found that there is a "high level of concern . . . over information privacy and a desire to control access and use of personal information."[131] Of the respondents, 90 to 95 percent agreed or strongly agreed that (1) individuals should have control over who accesses their personal information, (2) companies collect too much personal data, and (3) personal information shared with a company by an individual should only be used for the purpose it was given.[132] On a library-specific level, 97 percent of respondents believe that libraries should never share "personal information and circulation or Internet records without [the user's] authorization or court order," and 75 percent believe the library should play a role in educating the public on privacy matters.[133] Despite the perceived concern with privacy, less than 60 percent of libraries surveyed communicate their privacy policies to users, and only 13 percent engage in community education on privacy issues.[134]

What can libraries do to protect the privacy of their users given the proliferation of digital media with DRM restrictions that can track a user's personal information? On a normative level, current privacy protection measures undertaken in many libraries include "engaging in limited tracking of user activities, instituting short term retention policies, and generally enabling anonymous browsing of materials,"[135] but more can be done. Below you'll find a set of suggestions and best practices to implement in your own library.

Communication

One of the most basic ways a library can protect patron privacy is to articulate to its users the types of tracking/monitoring that occur in the library (whether by the library or by third parties). A library's privacy policy is one of the most effective ways to communicate the following to users:

• What personally identifiable data will be collected while the patron is using the library
• How that data will be collected and used
• How long patron information will be retained
• Who will have access to the patron's personal information (library and/or third parties)[136]
• Any actions the user can take to opt in or out of the collection of that data

ALA/FTC Privacy Principles for Library Privacy Policies

The American Library Association has promulgated the Privacy Toolkit[137] to help libraries draft effective privacy policies and create workable privacy and confidentiality mechanisms for library staff. The core components are the following:[138]

Notice and Openness. This section should notify users of their right to confidentiality and privacy as well as articulate the library policies governing these rights. Included in this section should be the type of data collected, why it is collected, how it is being stored, and what parties have access to it and for what purposes.

Choice and Consent. Users should be given the option to either opt in or opt out of how their private information is used. When a user opts out, any privately identifying information is not automatically included in the data collection—the user must take affirmative steps to allow it. When a user opts in, the personal information is automatically included in collection efforts and the user must take affirmative steps to exclude it.

Access by Users. Users have a right to access the personal information gathered about their use of the library and its resources. Privacy policies should clearly articulate this right and highlight the user's right to verify the accuracy and status of their information.

Data Integrity and Security. Integrity requires that the library ensure the accuracy of the information collected, using only reputable sources. ALA further recommends "providing library users access to their personal data, updating information regularly, destroying untimely data or converting it to anonymous form, and stripping PII from aggregated, summary data."[139] Further, libraries have an obligation to protect patron data from loss, unauthorized access/use/disclosure, or destruction. All efforts should be taken to ensure that the security of patron data is "integrated into the design, implementation, and day-to-day practices of the library's entire operating environment."[140]

Enforcement and Redress. Where there is a privacy policy, there must be a means of enforcement, including privacy audits and reporting and investigative mechanisms. If a user believes their privacy has been violated, there must be a corresponding remedy for the violation.

An additional consideration is the library's reliance on emerging technologies and third-party vendors that may collect user data outside of official library channels. In cases where a user may have to provide personally identifying information to a third-party vendor, the library must make that fact explicitly clear: a statement posted near computer workstations where patrons access e-resources and pop-up text prior to redirecting the patron to the vendor's website. Such text should state the following:

- The library does not share users' personal information with external sources.
- Third-party vendors may request personally identifying information in exchange for access to resources.
- Third-party vendors may track the patron's use of resources, including what was searched/read/accessed.
- Third-party vendors may or may not follow the same privacy guidelines as the library.

Notice of this type gives patrons an opportunity to determine whether they would like to share their personal data in exchange for access to a particular e-resource.

Licensing

Libraries have control over what data they collect and how that data is used, stored, and disposed of. And library norms dictate that librarians have an obligation to protect user-specific information about the use of library materials. However, librarians are not always in control of that data due to the growing reliance on emerging technologies that include DRM software. Library patrons not only believe that libraries protect their confidentiality, they expect it. In order to best protect the sanctity of patron privacy, libraries must work to ensure that all contracts with vendors comply with the heightened standards for privacy that libraries aspire to.

The current library acquisition model requires libraries to enter into contracts with commercial vendors to provide patrons with access to digital resources from electronic and audiobooks to e-journals and databases. These vendors often collect user data for a variety of purposes—DRM (to ensure copyright is being protected), analytics (to determine who is using the resources and how), and personalization (giving the patron a customized user experience).[141] Libraries should advocate for their patrons by vigorously negotiating the terms of e-resources licenses.

The Center for Research Libraries is home to LIBLICENSE, which provides model licensing terms to aid libraries negotiating for digital content. Of particular interest to libraries negotiating DRM and privacy terms are the following sections:

Usage Statistics. "Licensor shall provide to Licensee [monthly] usage statistics for the Licensed Materials. Statistics shall meet or exceed the most recent project Counting Online Usage of NeTworked Electronic Resources (COUNTER) Code of Practice Release, including but not limited to its provisions on customer confidentiality. . . . *Licensor shall not provide Licensee's usage statistics in any form to any third party without the Licensee's written authorization*, unless the third party owns rights in the Licensed Materials. In all cases, the disclosure of such data shall *fully protect the anonymity of individual users and the confidentiality of their searches, and will comply with all applicable privacy laws.* The Licensor shall not disclose or sell to other parties usage data or information about the Licensee or its Authorized Users without the Licensee's express written permission or as required by law."

Confidentiality of Personally Identifiable Information. "The Licensor agrees that no personally identifiable information, including but not limited to log-ins recorded in system logs, IP addresses of patrons accessing the system, saved searches, usernames and passwords, will be shared with third parties, except in response to a subpoena, court order, or other legal requirement. If Licensor is compelled by law or court order to disclose personally identifiable information of Authorized Users or patterns of use, Licensor shall provide the Licensee with adequate prior written notice as soon as is practicable, so that Licensee or Authorized Users may seek protective orders or other remedies. Licensor will notify Licensee and Authorized Users as soon as is practicable if the Licensor's systems are breached and the confidentiality of personally identifiable information is compromised."

Notice of the Use of Digital Rights Management Technology. "In the event that Licensor utilizes or implements any type of digital rights management (DRM) technology to control access to or usage of the Licensed Mate-

rials, Licensor will provide to Licensee a description of the technical specifi-
cations of the DRM and how it impacts access to or usage of the Licensed
Materials. *If the use of DRM renders the Licensed Materials substantially
less useful to the Licensee or its Authorized Users, the Licensee may seek to
terminate this Agreement for breach pursuant to the termination provisions
of this Agreement.*"[142]

The language used in the model license highlights the trend toward equitable agreements between libraries and vendors that reflect the ingrained
norms of the profession while still allowing the vendor to conduct their
business.

When contracting, many libraries, especially smaller public and academic
libraries, may find that they are constrained in their negotiations with larger
vendors. Libraries want to provide access to the best materials for their users,
and despite the inequity that can exist between libraries and vendors, library
administrators should advocate for the highest level of security for patron
privacy. To aid those efforts, ALA has promulgated "Library Privacy Guidelines for E-book Lending and Digital Content Vendors." The guidelines aim
to aid vendors and libraries in negotiations with respect to the management
and security of usage analytics and personally identifiable information of
library patrons. Key components of the guidelines put the library in control
of patron privacy and confidentiality:

- Agreements should address restrictions on the "use, aggregation, retention, and dissemination of patron data."
- Agreements should clearly state that libraries retain ownership of all data
  gathered, and vendors must observe all library polices regarding patron
  privacy, data security, and retention.
- All federal, state, and local privacy laws must be observed.
- Vendors are required to provide users with options as to how much of
  their information is gathered and how it is used. Users should also be able
  to change their minds and have the data scrubbed.
- Users must be provided with easy access to their data to verify its accuracy.
- Security of user data must be integrated into the "design, implementation,
  and day to day practices" of the vendor's operations, and both technical
  and administrative measures should be taken to ensure against loss, unauthorized access, or disclosure of patron data, including encryption, anonymization, and retention policies.
- User consent or a court order is required to share data with third parties.[143]

When negotiating with vendors, libraries must think about the privacy considerations that we, as a profession, want to advocate for our patrons. Providing access to digital resources is an important function of a library, but not at

the cost of our users' confidentiality and privacy. A library should be willing to strike through offending clauses and vigorously negotiate terms that comply with its privacy policies. Libraries should also be aware of the many organizations[144] that advocate for privacy and confidentiality in all aspects of digital media and seek out help and guidance when they need it. Finally, librarians need to empower our users. Patrons are becoming savvier about who is tracking them online, and most are not happy about it. Making patrons aware of the tracking implicit in DRM technologies allows the user to determine if they want to use that resource. By educating users of privacy concerns, libraries are putting the user in control of how their personal information is being gathered and used. As a negotiating tactic, users abandoning a product because they fear for their security may make a vendor more inclined to negotiate privacy terms.

Working Together to Achieve a More Perfect Union

Up to this point, most if not all of the reader privacy and user data principles and practices have been created by library organizations with little to no input from vendors, publishers, and content providers. Whether this was intentional or because there was a lack of interest by either party is unclear. However, in December 2015, the National Information Standards Organization (NISO) promulgated the first set of user data privacy principles that collaboratively created "a balanced set of principles, which achieve the common goal of providing the best possible user experience built from its core with respect for privacy."[145] Working together, libraries, publishers, and systems providers set forth twelve principles that provide a foundation to "support a greater understanding for and respect of privacy-related concerns in systems development, deployment, and user interactions."[146] These twelve areas include shared privacy responsibilities, transparency and facilitating privacy awareness, security, data collection and use, anonymization, options and informed consent, sharing data with others, notification of privacy policies and practices, supporting anonymous use, access to one's own user data, continuous improvement, and accountability.[147]

These principles are a step in the right direction for libraries and content/software providers because they recognize the role of each player in the expanded universe of electronic systems in the digital age. The NISO principles put the onus on libraries, publishers, and software providers to acknowledge there is a "shared obligation to foster a digital environment that respects library users' privacy as they search, discover, and use those resources and services."[148]

A Very Brief Note on Technology

Technology may hold an answer for libraries that are concerned about the impact of DRM on the privacy of their patrons. Requiring encryption and anonymization of all data gathered by vendors and negotiating IP authentication instead of individual passwords are two ways that libraries are currently utilizing technology to protect patron privacy. Other technological methods may exist for libraries who want to provide access to DRM-restricted e-resources while protecting their patrons. One way is to work with e-resource distributors to integrate the vendor's systems with the library's catalog.[149] This way the e-resources can be "treated as just another format patrons could specify in their search," which keeps the patron within the library's digital ecosystem.[150] Another option is for libraries to advocate for a universal format for e-resources, especially e-books.[151] A universal format would allow an e-book to be read on any device, thereby limiting the need to use third parties such as Amazon's Kindle. Currently, many libraries are creating their own workarounds for DRM, including utilizing open source e-book software and choosing not to contract with vendors who restrict access to their materials or track personally identifiable user information.

CONCLUSION

The privacy implications of DRM software are among the many issues that libraries must be aware of when licensing e-resources. The demand for digital resources is growing, while users maintain their expectations that libraries are bastions of confidentiality. An interesting paradox exists in that libraries themselves collect user data and need to use that data to develop services and collections in order to stay relevant in the digital environment. The difference between library collection of personally identifiable patron information and that of a third party using DRM software is control. Libraries can control how the data is collected, used, stored, and ultimately deleted. When a third party collects this type of information, the library cannot control its use or dissemination or keep it secure. Most library patrons are unaware of the implications of using resources licensed through third parties; they assume that if they are using a resource in the library, the library controls that resource and everything that goes along with it. However, that is not the case, and libraries must do their best to safeguard their patrons' privacy by communicating with their patrons about privacy issues, informing them of third-party practices, and negotiating stricter privacy terms with vendors.

NOTES

1. Morgan, "Simple Explanation of 'The Internet of Things.'"

2. For general discussion of the right to privacy in the United States, see Solove, "Origins and Growth of Information Privacy Law," 29; Alderman and Kennedy, *Right to Privacy*.

3. Cohen, "DRM and Privacy," 588–89; and Richards, "Intellectual Privacy," 387.

4. Solove, "Privacy and Power," 1407–9.

5. Solove, *Digital Person*.

6. Brownlee and Waleski, *Privacy Law*.

7. Etzioni, "Cyber Age Privacy Doctrine," 1263.

8. Ibid., 1282–83.

9. Kim, "Three's a Crowd," 325–26.

10. Etzioni, "Cyber Age Privacy Doctrine," 1307.

11. Richards, *Intellectual Privacy*, 166.

12. Sloan and Warner, "Beyond Notice and Choice," 373–74.

13. Ballon, *E-commerce and Internet Law*, 26:01.

14. Solove, "Privacy and Power," 1407–9.

15. *Griswold v. Connecticut*, 85 S.Ct. 1678 (1968), and *Roe v. Wade*, 93 S.Ct. 705 (1973).

16. Warren and Brandeis, "Right to Privacy," 211.

17. Solove, "Origins and Growth," 19.

18. *Olmstead v. United States*, 277 U.S. 438 (1928).

19. Ibid., 455.

20. Ibid., 478 (Brandeis dissenting).

21. *Roberson v. Rochester Folding Box Co.*, 64 N.E. 442 (N.Y. 1902).

22. *Pavesich v. New England Life Insurance Company*, 50 S.E. 68 (Ga. 1905), and see Adams, *Georgia Law of Torts*, §29:3.

23. Former 7 U.S.C. §605.

24. *Katz v. United States*, 389 U.S. 347 (1967).

25. Ibid., 361 (Harlan concurring).

26. *Whalen v. Roe*, 429 U.S. 589 (1977).

27. Stokes, "Apple a Day," 312.

28. S. Rep. No. 105–190 at 2–8 (1998).

29. Digital Millennium Copyright Act of 1998, Pub. L. No. 105-304, 112 Stat. 2860 (1998).

30. 17 U.S.C. §1201(a)(1)(A).

31. Tussey, "UCITA, Copyright, and Capture," 365.

32. Ibid.

33. Seringhaus, "E-book Transactions," 166.

34. Ibid., 166.

35. Electronic Frontier Foundation, "Unintended Consequences."

36. Tussey, "UCITA, Copyright, and Capture," 348–49.

37. Garon, "What If DRM Fails?," 115–19.

38. Richards, *Intellectual Privacy*, 134.

39. Singer, "American Quilt of Privacy Laws."

40. Etzioni, "Cyber Age Privacy Doctrine," 1280.

41. 18 U.S.C. §1030.

42. Pub. L. No. 105-147, 111 Stat. 2678 (1997), *amending* 17 U.S.C. §506.

43. Uniform Computer Information Transactions Act, §103(b)(2)(2002).

44. Ibid., §§102(43), (44).

45. 100 F. Supp. 2d 1058 (N.D. Cal. 2000).

46. Ibid.

47. OverDrive, "Public Libraries Evolving."

48. Gellman and Dixon, *Online Privacy*, 61.

49. 15 U.S.C. §1681 et seq.

50. See Pub. L. 108-159, 111 Stat. 1952.

51. Financial Services Modernization Act of 1999 (the Gramm-Leach-Bliley Act), 15 U.S.C. §6801 et seq.

52. Reader Privacy Act, Cal. Civ. Code §§1798.90, 1798.90.05 (West 2013).

53. Cal. Civ. Code §1798.90(b)(5)(A).

54. Ibid., §1798.90(b)(5)(B).

55. Ibid., §1798.90(b)(5)(C).

56. Ibid., §1798.90(b)(1).

57. Proia, "New Approach," 1596.

58. Azer, "Three-Tiered Public Policy Approach," 105.

59. 307 F. Supp. 2d 1085 (N.D. Cal. 2004).

60. 69 U.S.P.Q. 2d 2023, 2004 WL 402756 (S.D.N.Y. 2004).

61. No. C-11-3309, 2012 WL 3166798 (N.D. Cal. Aug. 2, 2012).

62. 747 F.3d 445, 448 (6th Cir. 2014).

63. Abdo, "Keeping Princess Peach," 1470.

64. *Chamberlain Group, Inc. v. Skylink Techs., Inc.* (*Chamberlain I*), 292 F. Supp.2d 1023, 1024-25 (N.D. Ill. 2003), and *Chamberlain II*, 292 F. Supp. 2d 1040, 1041 (N.D. Ill. 2003), aff'd, 381 F.3d 1178 (Fed. Cir. 2004), cert. denied, 544 U.S. 923 (2005).

65. *Lexmark Int'l, Inc. v. Static Control Components, Inc.* (*Lexmark I*), 253 F. Supp. 2d 943, 947 (E.D. Ky. 2003), and *Lexmark II*, 387 F.3d 522, 530 (6th Cir. 2005).

66. Elkin-Koren, "Making Room for Consumers," 1132–33.

67. Federal Trade Commission, "Third-Party Services."

68. The FIPPs' origins are largely attributed to a 1973 report, U.S. Department of Health, Education, and Welfare, *Records, Computers, and the Rights of Citizens*.

69. See Office of the Chancellor, "Fair Information Practice Principles": "Although these principles are not laws, they form the backbone of privacy law and provide guidance in the collection, use, and protection of personal information."

70. U.S. Department of Health, Education, and Welfare, *Records, Computers, and the Rights of Citizens*.

71. Ibid., xxiv.

72. Ibid.

73. For a good discussion of the fair information practices, as set out by the FTC, see Federal Trade Commission, "Privacy and Data Security Update."

74. Federal Trade Commission, "Protecting Consumer Privacy."

75. Ibid.

76. White House, "Consumer Data Privacy."

77. Burdond, "Contextualizing the Tensions," 94.

78. Federal Trade Commission Act, §5, 15 U.S.C.A. §45, "Unfair Methods of Competition Unlawful; Prevention by Commission."

79. *In the Matter of Twitter, Inc.*, FTC File No. 0923093 (June 24, 2010) (agreement containing consent order), https://www.ftc.gov/sites/default/files/documents/cases/2010/06/100624twitteragree.pdf.

80. *In the Matter of Twitter, Inc.*, FTC File No. 0923093 (June 24, 2010) (complaint), 4 https://www.ftc.gov/sites/default/files/documents/cases/2010/06/100624twittercmpt.pdf.

81. *In the Matter of Myspace, LLC*, FTC Docket No. C-4369 (August 30, 2012) (consent order), https://www.ftc.gov/sites/default/files/documents/cases/2012/05/120508myspaceorder.pdf.

82. *In the Matter of Facebook, Inc.*, FTC Docket No. C-4365 (July 27, 2012) (consent order), https://www.ftc.gov/sites/default/files/documents/cases/2011/11/111129facebookagree.pdf.

83. *In the Matter of TRENDnet, Inc.*, FTC File No. 092 3184 (January 16, 2014) (consent order), https://www.ftc.gov/sites/default/files/documents/cases/2013/09/130903trendnetorder.pdf.

84. *In the Matter of Snapchat, Inc.*, FTC File No. 132 3078 (May 8, 2014) (consent order), https://www.ftc.gov/system/files/documents/cases/140508snapchatorder.pdf.

85. White House, "Consumer Data Privacy."

86. Kim, "Three's a Crowd," 345.

87. Ibid., 344–45.

88. Center for Copyright Information, "Center for Copyright Information Announces."

89. Cohen, "DRM and Privacy," 588–89.

90. Godwin, "Digital Rights Management," 1.

91. American Library Association, "Digital Rights Management."

92. Ard, "Confidentiality and the Problem of Third Parties," 52–58.

93. Such measures would be similar to the structures that were put in place when the Video Privacy Protection Act of 1988 (VPPA) went into effect (18 U.S.C. §2710 [2002]) .

94. Richards, *Intellectual Privacy*, 124.

95. Blitz, "Constitutional Safeguards," 818.

96. Gallagher, "Adobe's E-reader Reader Sends Your Reading Logs Back to Adobe."

97. Ard, "Confidentiality and the Problem of Third Parties," 1, 3–5.

98. Richards, "Intellectual Privacy," 135.

99. *Griswold v. Connecticut*, 381 U.S. 479 (1965).

100. Ibid., 482.

101. For a list of cases involving the right to reader privacy, see Cohen, "Right to Read Anonymously," 1003–19.

102. *United States v. Rumley*, 345 U.S. 41 (1953).

103. *Lamont v. Postmaster General*, 381 U.S. 301 (1965).

104. *Stanley v. Georgia*, 394 U.S. 557, 565 (1969).

105. *Grand Jury Subpoena to Kramer-books & Afterwords, Inc.*, 26 Med. L. Rep. 1599 (1998).

106. *Tattered Cover v. City of Thornton*, 44 P. 3d 1044 (Colo. 2002).

107. *Grand Jury Subpoena to Amazon.com*, 246 F.R.D. 570 (2007).

108. Ibid., 573.

109. 5 U.S.C. ch. 5 §552a.

110. 20 U.S.C. §1232g.

111. 15 U.S.C. §6501 et seq.

112. American Library Association, "State Privacy Laws." The remaining states, Hawaii and Kentucky, have Attorney General opinions confirming the confidentiality of library records.

113. E.g., Vt. Stat. Ann. Tit. 1 §171(3), La. Rev. State Ann. §44-13(2), N.H. Rev. Stat. Ann. §201-D:11(I), Cal. Gov't Code §6267(1)(c)(2), 50 Ill Comp. Stat. 205/3 (2011).

114. Cal. Civ. Code §1798.90 (2013).

115. ACLU of Northern California, "Reader Privacy Act Signed into Law."

116. Proia, "New Approach," 1612.

117. Klinefelter, "Library Standards for Privacy," 558.

118. R.I. Gen. Laws §11-18-32 (2009) and Mich. Comp. Laws Ann. §445.1712 (2009).

119. National Conference of State Legislatures, "State Laws Related to Internet Privacy."

120. American Library Association, "Library Bill of Rights."

121. American Library Association, "Code of Ethics."

122. American Library Association, "Intellectual Freedom Principles."

123. American Library Association, "Privacy."

124. Ibid.

125. American Library Association, "Guidelines for Developing."

126. Ibid.

127. Cohen, "DRM and Privacy," 575.

128. Ibid., 580.

129. Sturges et al., "User Privacy," 44, 45.

130. Ozer, "Digital Books," 4.

131. Zimmer, "Librarians' Attitudes," 123, 130.

132. Ibid., 123; 95 percent of respondents agreed or strongly agreed that people should be able to control who sees their personal information, while 90 percent of respondents agreed or strongly agreed that companies collect too much personal information; 95 percent of respondents agreed or strongly agreed that information given to a company should only be used for the purpose it was given.

133. Ibid., 123, 131, 138.

134. Ibid., 123, 138. Public libraries do a better job of sharing privacy policies, whereas academic libraries do a worse job communicating with their patrons.

135. Ibid., 123.

136. Xiaozhao and Jianhai, "Users' Privacy Issues."

137. American Library Association, "Privacy Toolkit."

138. The ALA privacy policies sections mimic those articulated in Federal Trade Commission, "Privacy Online."
139. American Library Association, "Privacy Toolkit."
140. Ibid.
141. American Library Association, "Library Privacy Guidelines."
142. Center for Research Libraries, "LIBLICENSE Model Licensing Agreement," §§Q–S (italics added).
143. American Library Association, "Library Privacy Guidelines."
144. Postigo, *Digital Rights Movement*, 188.
145. National Information Standards Organization, "NISO Releases a Set of Principles."
146. Ibid.
147. National Information Standards Organization, "NISO Consensus Principles."
148. Ibid.
149. Dobruse, "Redesigning the Library E-lending Experience," 182.
150. Ibid.
151. Ibid.

REFERENCES

Abdo, Jacob M. "Keeping Princess Peach Locked in Her Castle: Criminal Liability for Trafficking Circumvention Technology—*United States v. Reichert.*" *William Mitchell Law Review* 41 (2015): 1470–99.
ACLU of Northern California. "Reader Privacy Act Signed into Law." Press Release, October 3, 2011. https://www.aclunc.org/blog/reader-privacy-act-signed-law.
Adams, Charles R., III. *Georgia Law of Torts.* Suwanee, GA: Harrison Company, 2014.
Alderman, Ellen, and Caroline Kennedy. *The Right to Privacy.* New York: Alfred A. Knopf, 1995.
American Library Association. "Code of Ethics of the American Library Association." January 22, 2008. http://www.ala.org/advocacy/proethics/codeofethics/codeethics.
———. "Digital Rights Management (DRM) & Libraries." http://www.ala.org/advocacy/copyright/digitalrights.
———. "Guidelines for Developing a Library Privacy Policy." http://www.ala.org/advocacy/privacyconfidentiality/guidelines-developing-library-privacy-policy.
———. "Intellectual Freedom Principles for Academic Libraries: An Interpretation of the Library Bill of Rights." July 1, 2014. http://www.ala.org/Template.cfm?Section=interpretations&Template=/ContentManagement/ContentDisplay.cfm&ContentID=8551.
———. "Library Bill of Rights." January 23, 1980. http://www.ala.org/advocacy/intfreedom/librarybill.
———. "Library Privacy Guidelines for E-book Lending and Digital Content Vendors." June 29, 2015. http://www.ala.org/advocacy/library-privacy-guidelines-e-book-lending-and-digital-content-vendors.
———. "Privacy: An Interpretation of the Library Bill of Rights." July 1, 2014. http://www.ala.org/Template.cfm?Section=interpretations&Template=/ContentManagement/ContentDisplay.cfm&ContentID=132904.
———. "Privacy Toolkit." http://www.ala.org/advocacy/privacyconfidentiality/toolkitsprivacy/privacy.
———. "State Privacy Laws Regarding Library Records." http://www.ala.org/advocacy/privacyconfidentiality/privacy/stateprivacy.
Ard, BJ. "Confidentiality and the Problem of Third Parties: Protecting Reader Privacy in the Age of Intermediaries." *Yale Journal of Law & Technology* 16 (2014): 1–58.
Azer, Sandy. "A Three-Tiered Public Policy Approach to Copyright Misuse in the Context of Tying Arrangements." *Fordham Law Review* 81 (2013): 81–125.
Ballon, Ian C. *E-commerce and Internet Law: Treatise with Forms.* 2nd ed. Minneapolis: West, 2015.

Blitz, Marc J. "Constitutional Safeguards for Silent Experiments in Living: The Right to Read and a First Amendment Theory for an Unaccompanied Right to Receive Information." *UMKC Law Review* 74 (2006): 799–882.

Brownlee, Charlene, and Blaze D. Waleski. *Privacy Law.* New York: Law Journal Press, 2012.

Burdon, Mark. "Contextualizing the Tensions and Weaknesses of Information Privacy and Data Breach Notification Laws." *Santa Clara High Technology Law Journal* 27 (2010): 63–129.

Center for Copyright Information. "Center for Copyright Information Announces Three Major Steps towards Implementation." Press Release, April 2, 2012. http://www.copyrightinformation.org/press-release/center-for-copyright-information-announces-three-major-steps-towards-implementation/.

Center for Research Libraries. "LIBLICENSE Model Licensing Agreement." November 2014. http://liblicense.crl.edu/licensing-information/model-license/.

Cohen, Julie E. "DRM and Privacy." *Berkeley Technology Law Journal* 18 (2003): 575–617.

———. "A Right to Read Anonymously: A Closer Look at 'Copyright Management' in Cyberspace." *Connecticut Law Review* 28 (1996): 981–1039.

Cooper, Scott P., et al. "State Privacy Laws." In *Proskauer on Privacy: A Guide to Privacy and Data Security Law in the Information Age,* edited by Kristen J. Matthews. New York: Practicing Law Institute, 2014.

Dobruse, Kathleen. "Redesigning the Library E-lending Experience to Ensure Accessibility and Patron Privacy." In *SIGDOC '13 Proceedings of the 31st ACM International Conference on Design of Communication.* New York: ACM, 2013.

Electronic Frontier Foundation. "Unintended Consequences: Fifteen Years under the DMCA." March 2013. https://www.eff.org/pages/unintended-consequences-fifteen-years-under-dmca.

Elkin-Koren, Niva. "Making Room for Consumers Under the DMCA." *Berkeley Technology Law Journal* 22 (2007): 1119–55.

Etzioni, Amitai. "A Cyber Age Privacy Doctrine More Coherent, Less Subjective, and Operational." *Brooklyn Law Review* 80 (2015): 1263–1308.

Federal Trade Commission. "Privacy and Data Security Update." January 2016. https://www.ftc.gov/reports/privacy-data-security-update-2015.

———. "Privacy Online: Fair Information Practices in the Electronic Marketplace." May 2000. https://www.ftc.gov/sites/default/files/documents/reports/privacy-online-fair-information-practices-electronic-marketplace-federal-trade-commission-report/privacy2000text.pdf.

———. "Protecting Consumer Privacy in an Era of Rapid Change: Recommendations for Businesses and Policymakers." March 2012. https://www.ftc.gov/sites/default/files/documents/reports/federal-trade-commission-report-protecting-consumer-privacy-era-rapid-change-recommendations/120326privacyreport.pdf.

———. "Third-Party Services." August 25, 2015. https://www.ftc.gov/site-information/privacy-policy/third-party-services.

Gallagher, Sean. "Adobe's E-book Reader Sends Your Reading Logs Back to Adobe—in Plain Text," *Ars Technica,* October 7, 2014. http://artstechnica.com/security/2014/10/adobes-e-book-reader-sends-your-reading-logs-back-to-adobe-in-plain-text/.

Garon, Jon M. "What If DRM Fails? Seeking Patronage in the iWasteland and the Virtual O." *Michigan State Law Review,* no. 1 (2008): 103–51.

Gellman, Robert, and Pam Dixon. *Online Privacy: A Reference Handbook.* Santa Barbara, CA: ABC-CLIO, 2011.

Godwin, Michael. "Digital Rights Management: A Guide for Librarians." *OITP Technology Policy Brief,* January 2006. http://www.cs.yale.edu/homes/jf/Godwin-Libraries.pdf.

Killingsworth, Scott. "Website Privacy Policies in Principle and in Practice." In *eCommerce Strategies for Success in the Digital Economy.* New York: Practicing Law Institute, 2000.

Kim, Natalie. "Three's a Crowd: Towards Contextual Integrity in Third-Party Data Sharing." *Harvard Journal of Law and Technology* 28 (2014): 325–47.

Klinefelter, Anne. "Library Standards for Privacy: A Model for the Digital World." *North Carolina Journal of Law & Technology* 11 (2010): 553–63.

Morgan, Jacob. "A Simple Explanation of 'The Internet of Things.'" *Forbes*, May 13, 2014. http://www.forbes.com/sites/jacobmorgan/2014/05/13/simple-explanation-internet-things-that-anyone-can-understand/.

National Conference of State Legislatures. "State Laws Related to Internet Privacy." August 28, 2015. http://www.ncsl.org/research/telecommunications-and-information-technology/state-laws-related-to-internet-privacy.aspx.

National Information Standards Organization. "NISO Consensus Principles on Users' Digital Privacy in Library, Publisher, and SoftwareProvider Systems (NISO Privacy Principles)." December 10, 2015. http://www.niso.org/apps/group_public/download.php/15863/NISO%20Consensus%20Principles%20on%20Users%C2%92%20Digital%20Privacy.pdf.

———. "NISO Releases a Set of Principles to Address Privacy of User Data in Library, Content-Provider, and Software-Supplier Systems." Press Release, December 14, 2015. http://www.niso.org/news/pr/view?item_key=678c44da628619119213955b867838b40b6a 7d96.

Office of the Chancellor, University of California, Berkeley. "Fair Information Practice Principles (FIPPs) Privacy Course." https://ethics.berkeley.edu/privacy/fipps.

OverDrive. "Public Libraries Evolving to Meet Readers' Needs in the Digital Age." Press Release, September 30, 2015. http://company.overdrive.com/news/press-releases/public-libraries-evolving-to-meet-readers-needs-in-the-digital-age/.

Ozer, Nicole A. "Digital Books: A New Chapter for Reader Privacy." ACLU of Northern California, March 2010. http://www.aclunc.org/sites/default/files/asset_upload_file295_9047.pdf.

Postigo, Hector. *The Digital Rights Movement: The Role of Technology in Subverting Digital Copyright.* Cambridge, MA: MIT Press, 2012.

Proia, Andrew A. "A New Approach to Digital Reader Privacy: State Regulations and Their Protection of Digital Book Data." *Indiana Law Journal* 88 (2013): 1593–1618.

Richards, Neil. "Intellectual Privacy." *Texas Law Review* 87 (2008): 387–445.

———. *Intellectual Privacy: Rethinking Civil Liberties in the Digital Age.* New York: Oxford University Press, 2015.

Seringhaus, Michael. "E-book Transactions: Amazon 'Kindles' the Copy Ownership Debate," *Yale Journal of Law & Technology* 12 (2010): 147–207.

Singer, Natasha. "An American Quilt of Privacy Laws, Incomplete." *New York Times*, March 30, 2013. http://www.nytimes.com/2013/03/31/technology/in-privacy-laws-an-incomplete-american-quilt.html?_r=0.

Sloan, Robert H., and Richard Warner. "Beyond Notice and Choice: Privacy, Norms, and Consent." *Journal of High Technology Law* 14 (2014): 373–74.

Solove, Daniel J. *The Digital Person: Technology and Privacy in the Information Age.* New York: New York University Press, 2004.

———. "The Origins and Growth of Information Privacy Law." *PLI/PAT* 748 (2003): 1–51. dx.doi.org/10.2139/ssrn.445181.

———. "Privacy and Power: Computer Databases and Metaphors for Information Privacy." *Stanford Law Review* 53 (2001): 1393–1462.

Stokes, Alexis Brown. "An Apple a Day Keeps Shareholder Suits at Bay: An Examination of a Corporate Officer's Legal Duty to Disclose Health Problems to Shareholders." *Texas Wesleyan Law Review* 17 (2011): 303–24.

Sturges, Paul, et al. "User Privacy in the Digital Library Environment: An Investigation of Policies and Preparedness." *Library Management* 24 (2003): 44–50.

Tussey, Deborah. "UCITA, Copyright, and Capture." *Cardozo Arts and Entertainment Law Journal* 21 (2003): 319–80.

U.S. Department of Health, Education, and Welfare. *Records, Computers, and the Rights of Citizens: Report of the Secretary's Advisory Committee on Automated Personal Data Systems.* Washington, DC: U.S. Department of Health, Education, and Welfare, 1973. https://www.justice.gov/opcl/docs/rec-com-rights.pdf.

Warren, Samuel D., and Louis D. Brandeis. "The Right to Privacy." *Harvard Law Review* 4 (1890): 193–220.

White House. "Consumer Data Privacy in a Networked World: A Framework for Protecting Privacy and Promoting Innovation in the Global Digital Economy." February 2012. https://www.whitehouse.gov/sites/default/files/privacy-final.pdf.

Xiaozhao, Deng, and Ruan Jianhai. "Users' Privacy Issues with E-Learning in Library 2.0." Paper presented at International Conference on Multimedia Information Networking and Security, Hubei, China, November 18–20, 2009.

Zimmer, Michael. "Librarians' Attitudes regarding Information and Internet Privacy." *Library Quarterly* 84, no. 2 (2014): 123–51.

Chapter Eight

Digital Rights Management and Copyright Law

What Librarians Need to Know

Renate L. Chancellor and Heather A. Wiggins

Given the relationship between copyright law and digital rights management (DRM), librarians need to know the general principles and basic concepts that govern copyright law in order to successfully respond to DRM issues. For libraries, navigating copyright law is about creating a balance between fundamental library principles, such as access to information and user privacy, and the rights of copyright holders. The development of DRM technologies in the early 2000s following the rise of Napster and the explosion of online file sharing further complicates this balancing act. [1]

DRM technology enables rights holders to control the use of digital content and impose restrictions on how digital files are used. Both copyright holders and scholars propose the use of DRM as a means to protect against piracy of copyrighted content. However, DRM presents several challenges for librarians. This chapter aims to provide a basic overview of copyright law that will assist librarians in responding to DRM challenges. It will also provide an analysis of common issues that librarians may face with regard to DRM, as well as a list of resources for addressing and resolving these issues.

Where does a librarian begin when trying to understand copyright law? One of the first questions that a librarian may have is whether a work is even subject to copyright law. Not all works are subject to federal copyright protection. So what makes a work protected? The starting point is the 1976 Copyright Act, the federal law that protects the creative expressions of authors, creators, artists, and other rights holders. [2] (In this chapter, Copyright

Act will generally refer to the 1976 act; however, it may also cover previous iterations of the Copyright Act.)

Section 102(a) of the 1976 Copyright Act states, "Copyright protection subsists, in accordance with this title, in original works of authorship fixed in any tangible medium of expression, now known or later developed, from which they can be perceived, reproduced, or otherwise communicated, either directly or with the aid of a machine or device."[3] Copyright extends to all varieties of literary, artistic, and musical works.

The United States Copyright Law requires that a work be based on "original authorship."[4] To be considered original authorship, the courts and Copyright Office regulations have determined that the work must show some "modicum of creativity." Federal regulations explain original authorship by listing examples of works that are not eligible for copyright protection:

> The following are examples of works not subject to copyright and applications for registrations for such works cannot be entertained:
>
> (a) Words and short phrases such as names, titles and slogans; familiar symbols or designs; mere variations of typographic ornamentation, lettering or coloring; mere listing of ingredients or contents;
>
> (b) Ideas, plans, methods, systems, or devices, as distinguished from the particular manner in which they are expressed or described in writing;
>
> (c) Blank forms, such as time cards, graph paper, account books, diaries, bank checks, scorecards, address books, report forms, order forms and the like, which are designed for recording information and do not in themselves convey information;
>
> (d) Works consisting entirely of information that is common property containing no original authorship, such as, for example: Standard calendars, height and weight charts, tape measures and rules, schedule of reporting events, and lists of tables taken from public documents or other common sources. Words and short phrases such as names, titles, and slogans; familiar symbols or designs; mere variations of typographic ornamentation, lettering or coloring; mere listing of ingredients or contents.[5]

In addition, the United States Copyright Law does not protect facts, materials that were created by infringing another copyright, and any works of the United States government.[6]

EXCLUSIVE RIGHTS

Copyright protection is available to both published and unpublished works. Section 106 of the 1976 Copyright Act generally gives the owner of copyright a bundle of five exclusive rights. There is a sixth; however, it is only applicable to sound recordings. These exclusive rights constitute a monopoly over the work. It is illegal to violate the rights provided by copyright law to the owner of copyright.

Specifically, section 106[7] authorizes the rights holder to do and to author-ize others to do the following:

- Reproduce the work in copies or phonorecords
- Prepare derivative works based on the work
- Distribute copies or phonorecords of the work to the public by sale or other transfer of ownership, or by rental, lease, or lending
- Perform the work publicly, in the case of literary, musical, dramatic, and choreographic works, pantomimes, and motion pictures and other audio-visual works
- Display the work publicly, in the case of literary, musical, dramatic, and choreographic works, pantomimes, and pictorial, graphic, or sculptural works, including the individual images of a motion picture or other audio-visual work
- Perform the work publicly (in the case of sound recordings) by means of a digital audio transmission

The 1976 Copyright Act also established limitations on these rights. In some cases, these limitations are specified exemptions from copyright liability. One major limitation is the doctrine of fair use, which is codified in section 107. Another limitation, the exemption for libraries and archives, is codified at section 108.[8] Fair use and the library-archive exemption are discussed below.

OWNERSHIP

It is also important for librarians to know who owns the copyright of a particular work. Copyright initially vests in the author or authors of the work.[9] Under the 1976 Copyright Act, the author of a work is also the initial claimant or owner. Joint authors are co-owners of a work, and under the principle of work made for hire, the employer is considered to be the author and the copyright owner of a work. With a collective work (a work in which separate and independent works are collected into a whole), the various copyright holders retain the copyright to their respective contributions, and the author of the collective work has a copyright limited to reproducing the entire work and its revisions.[10]

There are other important concepts that relate to ownership. First, copy-right ownership is distinct from ownership of the physical object in which the copyrighted work is embodied.[11] As such, the "transfer of ownership of any material object, including the copy or phonograph in which the work is first fixed, does not of itself convey any rights in the copyrighted work embodied in the object; nor, in the absence of any agreement, does transfer of ownership of a copyright or of any exclusive rights under a copyright convey property rights in any material object."[12] In short, the sale of a work does not implicitly include the copyright.

Second, copyright ownership may be transferred in whole or in part. Section 201(d)(1) of the U.S. Copyright law states, "The ownership of a copyright may be transferred in whole or in part by any means of conveyance or by operation of law, and may be bequeathed by will or pass as personal property by the applicable laws or intestate succession." This means that for the transfer to effective, it must be in some form of writing or by inheritance.[13]

DURATION

Admittedly, the provisions contained within the copyright law regarding duration can be difficult to understand.[14] This is because there are standards that apply to the duration of a copyrighted work, and it depends on whether federal statutory copyright protection was secured on or after January 1, 1978 (the date on which the current law took effect). There are also several amendments to the law that occurred after January 1, 1978, which may affect duration. In general, a librarian should pay attention to the year in which the work was created.

For works created on or after January 1, 1978, the law automatically protects a work that is created and fixed in a tangible medium of expression. The duration for these classes of work are for the author's life plus an additional seventy years. For a joint work prepared by two or more authors who did not work for hire, the term lasts for seventy years after the last surviving author's death. For works made for hire and anonymous and pseudonymous works, the duration of copyright is ninety-five years from first publication or 120 years from creation, whichever is shorter. If the author's identity is later revealed in Copyright Office records, the term of the duration would then become the author's life plus seventy years.[15]

Although to some the duration for copyright may be lengthy, there are important limitations on the rights of copyright holders. The big two are the first sale doctrine and the concept of fair use.

FIRST SALE

The first sale doctrine is an important limitation on a copyright holder's exclusive rights of public distribution and display. The first sale doctrine was first established by the United States Supreme Court in 1908 in the *Bobbs-Merrill Co. v. Straus*[16] case and later codified in the 1976 Copyright Act. The first sale doctrine gives permission to the purchaser of a copyrighted work to transfer (i.e., sell or give away) a copy of the copyrighted work once it has been acquired. Originally, the legislation applied only to copies that had been sold. However, the 1976 Copyright Act expanded the first sale doctrine's applicability to any "owner" of a lawfully made copy or phonorecord whether or not it was first sold. This permission is codified in section 109 of the U.S. Copyright Act and gives the owner of a lawfully made copy of the work the right to sell, rent, donate, or put the copy on display.[17] Section 109 allows a library to loan books and other resources to its users.

Copyright law distinguishes between ownership of a physical copy of a work and ownership of the copyright. Since sale of the physical object does not include transfer of the copyright, this section is important for giving the owner of the physical copy some rights. Under section 109(a), "the owner of a particular copy or phonorecord lawfully made under this title, or any person authorized by such owner is entitled, without the authority of the copyright owner, to sell or otherwise dispose of the possession of that copy or phonorecord."[18] Under section109(c), "the owner of a particular copy lawfully made under this title, or any person authorized by such owner, is entitled without the authority of the copyright owner, to display that copy publicly."[19]

There are also special protections for music and software copyrights. Section 109 does not authorize the owner of a phonorecord or a person in possession of a copy of a computer program to rent or lend the phonorecord or computer program for commercial advantage. The provision does contain a specific exclusion for nonprofit schools and libraries that permits them to loan music and software.[20]

Additionally, with regard to the display right under section 109(c), the first sale doctrine does not apply to all displays. A display over the Internet, for example, would not be authorized. It also does not authorize a public performance of the work. Showing a film is considered to be a performance of the work, so section 109 does not authorize the owner of a copy of a film to show the film to the public.[21]

Under the first sale doctrine, content creators receive payment for their work only on the first sale of each copy. This doctrine allows libraries to lend resources to patrons. Initially, this started with books, but in today's information age, it has broadened to include other media found in libraries. Library patrons can now download materials on their laptops, iPods, iPads, smart phones, and other technological devices. Gigabytes are transferred directly from subscription databases, such as ProQuest and Academic Search Premier (which store scholarly journals and newspapers), and accessed for personal use. Technically, libraries have not purchased these resources but rather are licensed to use and share them with patrons.

The first sale doctrine is based on the idea that ownership of the material object in which the copyrighted work is embodied (such as a CD, DVD, or book) is distinct from ownership of the copyrighted work.[22] For example, when an individual purchases a book, he or she owns that particular copy of the book but does not have any ownership interest in the copyrighted arrangement or wording. E-readers, smart phones, and tablets have enabled libraries to provide greater access to information to their patrons. However, e-book publishers, fearing massive file sharing, have imposed a number of restrictions on e-book sales through the use of DRM and licensing agreements that e-book retailers claim govern e-book purchases.[23] In so doing, libraries are restricted from loaning lawfully acquired materials to patrons, thereby diminishing the American Library Association's ultimate goal of providing free and unrestricted access to information to all.

FAIR USE

Fair use lies at the heart of copyright law. The doctrine of fair use has evolved over many years and as a result of a number of court decisions.[24] It was codified in section 107 of the copyright law and is one of the most important limitations on the copyright holder's exclusive rights. Copyright law prohibits the duplication of copyrighted works by someone other than the copyright holder; however, the fair use provision of the Copyright Act allows for the making of limited copies.[25] Fair use allows users of copyrighted materials to make copies for "purposes such as criticism, comment, news reporting, teaching (including multiple copies for classroom use), scholarship, or research."[26] Under the federal copyright law, fair use applies to both published and unpublished works.[27] The following four factors[28] are taken into account when determining fair use:

1. The purpose and character of the use, including whether such use is commercial or for nonprofit educational purposes.
2. The nature of the copyrighted work.
3. The amount and substantiality of the portion used in relation to the copyrighted work as a whole.
4. The effect of the use on the potential market for, or value of, the copyrighted work.

It is important to note that fair use under section 107 is a defense that can be employed when an individual has been found to have infringed a copyright. Fair use is not an exception to copyright. Rather, it is an argument that is presented in order to avoid liability for violating copyright. This is an important distinction since the fair use argument can only be employed if in the first place the person admits to violating copyright restrictions (or has been judged in violation by a court).[29]

Fair use is always a fact-based determination; however, the four factors are interdependent.[30] The following sets out the analysis typically used to determine whether an action would qualify for fair use.

Purpose and Character of the Use. In determining whether there was a fair use, courts typically look at whether the work was used for a commercial or noncommercial purpose. Commercial uses are less likely to qualify for fair use because there is likely to be market harm and a commercial user is able to bear the cost.[31] Private, nonprofit uses are thus more likely to qualify, but that is not a guarantee. The statute mentions uses that are favored, such as "criticism, comment, news reporting, teaching (including multiple copies for classroom use), scholarship, or research."[32] Courts are also likely to consider the good faith of the defendant's actions. Where the defendant made a good faith attempt to get permission to use the work, the court may weigh that in favor of fair use.[33]

Nature of the Copyrighted Work. The more creative expression in a work, the more protection it has against fair use.[34]

Amount and Substantiality of the Portion Used. The portion copied is important, and also whether the amount is appropriate to the favored use. There are three key factors here: (1) whether the copier took an amount that fit the proposed use, (2) whether there was an alternative to taking the portion copied, and (3) whether the amount taken was likely to diminish the market for the copyright owner.[35]

Effect of the Use on the Potential Market or Value of the Copyrighted Work. The copyright owner has to show market harm. There are several ways to show market harm, which include lost sales of the copyrighted work, potential market—showing harm in a market that the copyright owner was likely to enter—and also presumption of market harm.[36]

In addition to understanding the four factors that determine fair use, librarians should also be cognizant of section 108 of the federal statute. Section 108 outlines exceptions for libraries and archives in which they may make reproductions without obtaining permission from, or providing compensation to, the copyright holder.

EXEMPTIONS FOR LIBRARIES AND ARCHIVES

In the case *Williams & Wilkins Co. v. United States*, a publisher of medical books and journals brought an action against the United States for copyright infringement stemming from massive photocopying of journal articles by the National Institutes of Health (NIH) and the National Library of Medicine (NLM) due to their participation in a large-scale interlibrary loan program. In addition, NIH and NLM often let the requesting parties keep the photocopies.[37]

A sequence of events including the publisher's victory before the trial judge, the close decision on appeal, and the pendency of review by the Supreme Court convinced the library community that congressional action was the only sure way to achieve protection for photocopying practices and that the general terms of section 107 on fair use were an uncertain shelter.[38] When Congress did take up the issue, they adopted the intricate set of statutory exemptions in section 108.[39] Congress also recognized the unique social and educational functions that libraries perform. Although at least some of the copying in which nonprofit libraries engage might well qualify for the fair use exemption, section 108 explicitly requires library copying to be considered separately (though not necessarily exclusively) from the section 107 fair use factors.[40]

Therefore, when assessing the ability of a library to copy a protected work, the relationship between sections 107 and 108 should be properly understood. There is a library position that section 108 merely identifies certain copying situations that are conclusively presumed to be legal without affecting the right of fair use, which continues as a general and flexible concept of law.[41] In short, section 108 sets forth the requirements for the exemption, but section 107 is still available for those acts exceeding the exemption.[42]

AN OUTLINE OF WHAT LIBRARIES AND ARCHIVES CAN DO UNDER §108

Libraries and archives may[43] make up to three copies of a work or phonorecord if the following conditions are met:

- Noncommercial purpose
- Collection is accessible to those doing research in a specialized field
- Work has a copyright notice, or a legend states that the work may be protected by copyright if no copyright notice can be found
- Copying is unrelated and isolate
- Copy becomes the property of the user
- Copy's purpose is educational
- A copyright warning is displayed prominently at the desk
- Work is in the last twenty years of its copyright term, provided that the work is not commercially exploited (unless the copyright owner objects)

To qualify, a library must:

- Be unaware of related or concerted copying, not engage in systematic copying, and not engage in interlibrary arrangements in which the receiving library's purpose is to substitute for subscription or purchase.
- Make a copy of a work in its collection and distribute it if (1) it is done for preservation or security; (2) it is for deposit for research use in another nonprofit library or archives; (3) it is to replace a work or phonorecord that is damaged, deteriorating, lost, stolen, or is commercially exploited if, after reasonable effort, a replacement cannot be obtained at a reasonable price; or (4) the equipment on which it is to be used is no longer commercially available.
- Make a digital or other copies of unpublished works for preservation or security; digital or other copies of published works for replacement of lost, stolen, or deteriorating works that can't be obtained at a reasonable price; interlibrary loan copies of one article or other contribution to a copyrighted collection or small part of a phonorecord; interlibrary loan copies of works unavailable at a reasonable price; or audiovisual news program copies.
- Determine a "reasonable price" test for an impartial observer to see the decision as equitable based on standard library acquisition procedures.
- Determine a "reasonable investigation" to use common trade sources or an authorized reproduction service.
- Treat reserve room copies as an extension of classroom copying guidelines.
- Place multiple copies on reserve when the amount of the material is reasonable in relation to the total amount, the number of copies is reasonable, material contains copyright notice, and photocopying is not detrimental to the market for the work.
- Make use of section 108.
- Copy the table of contents of a newsletter if first requested by employees.
- Purchase a journal subscription and then route the journal to employees.
- Make electronic copies to fax for interlibrary loan.
- Place copies of works on electronic reserve when access is restricted through password or other means.
- Make up to three copies of a work in a format for which the equipment is no longer commercially available.
- Display a copyright warning prominently at the desk.
- Display a copyright warning on unsupervised photocopying equipment and other equipment capable of copying.
- Digital copies made for preservation replacements of published works must not be "made available to the public in that format outside the premises of the library or archives."
- Display a copyright legend on all copies of works.

Libraries may not:[44]

- Copy musical works; pictorial, graphic, or sculptural works; and motion pictures.
- Reproduce or distribute copies of works when there is a "substantial reason to believe" that the copying is related or concerted.
- Reproduce or distribute in order to substitute for a subscription individually or in the aggregate.
- Library networks may not make use of section 108.
- Copy to the same extent with newsletters as with other periodicals.

William Patry, a prominent copyright attorney and former counsel to the U.S. House of Representatives on copyright, made two important points.[45] First, copying that may be fair use, if done by a library user, may be "related or concerted" if done by the library. Second, library users do not qualify for section 108 copying privileges and therefore are liable for photocopying beyond fair use. The library in which such copying is done may also be liable unless the copying is unsupervised and it occurs on a machine that bears the required copyright warning notice.[46]

It is important to note that in 2006 the Copyright Office and the Library of Congress convened a committee to recommend ways to update section 108 of the 1976 Copyright Act. A report released in 2008 concluded that section 108 failed to meet the needs of "libraries, archives, and other entities in dealing with born-digital works, digital preservation, and uses and lending of digital copies of works." More work with regard to this is planned for the future.[47]

ALA'S POLICY PRINCIPLES AND CONCERNS FOR LIBRARIES

The ALA has identified four primary library policy principles that DRM challenges: elimination of the first sale doctrine, enforcement of a pay-per-use model of information dissemination, enforcement of time limits that prevent preservation and archiving, and elimination of fair use and related policy issues that undermine education and scholarship.[48]

Enforcing a Pay-per-Use Model of Information Dissemination. DRM can be used to enforce a pay-per-use model of access or limit libraries' ability to archive or access items. In other words, DRM enforces license agreements that libraries make with e-book vendors and publishers. Thus, even if technologies are hacked by outside patrons, libraries could be held in violation of license agreements. Employing a pay-per-use model of information dissemination goes against the core principles of librarianship. It should be noted that ALA asserts that "it should not be the business of government to favor or enforce any particular business model in the information market-place, particularly one that raises major issues of equity and potentially severe economic consequences for public institutions."[49]

Enforcing Time Limits or Other Limitations of Use That Prevent Preservation and Archiving. Many DRM distribution systems place time limits on the content, which can essentially vanish after a specific period of time or number of uses. This prevents libraries, archives, and museums as well as other cultural institutions from preserving and providing long-term access to information in society.

Eliminating Fair Use and Other Exceptions in Copyright Law That Underpin Education, Criticism, and Scholarship. For information professionals, the doctrine of fair use is the most important limitation on the rights of copyright owners. It protects libraries and other information centers as well as their users from liability when they reproduce copyrighted works for scholarship or educational purposes. Eliminating fair use and other exceptions to the copyright law undermines educational efforts and scholarship.

DRM AND THE DIGITAL MILLENNIUM COPYRIGHT ACT

In 1998 Congress passed the Digital Millennium Copyright Act (DMCA) under pressure from rights holders. The growth in digital technologies that made it easier to pirate copyrighted materials caused many rights holders to want to exercise more control over access to content. However, as Pamela Samuelson contends, "the main purpose of DRM is not to prevent copyright infringement but to change consumer expectations about what they are entitled to with digital content."[50] Similarly, McJohn points out,

> Ideally (from the point of the copyright holder), DRM would permit products to be efficiently licensed on different terms to different classes of users (one fee for individuals, one fee for companies), while preventing any use not authorized by the copyright owner. DRM would control how many times a work could be used and what levels of work could be accessed, and allow the copyright holder to remotely monitor or control use of the work. Users could benefit from these controls. By allowing copyright holders to tailor the products they offer, works could be made more widely available and consumers would have more choices.[51]

The Copyright Office summarized DMCA as follows:

> The Digital Millennium Copyright Act was enacted to implement certain provisions of the WIPO Copyright Treaty and WIPO Performances and Phonograms Treaty. It established a wide range of rules for the digital marketplace that govern not only copyright owners, but also consumers, manufacturers, distributors, libraries, educators, and online service providers. Chapter 12 of

Title 17 of the United States Code prohibits the circumvention of certain technological measures employed by or on behalf of copyright owners to protect their works "technological measures" or "access controls." Specifically, Section 1201(a)(1)(A) provides, in part, that no person shall circumvent a technological measure that effectively controls access to a work protected by the Copyright Act.[52]

There are also many arguments against digital rights management schemes. Some in opposition have pointed out that DRM schemes may prevent legitimate uses, such as fair use. McJohn identified the following issues with DRM:

DRM may lock up noncopyrightable elements of work, by controlling access to them. DRM monitoring raises issues of privacy. Price discrimination between users may be unfair. The promises of DRM makers have not always withstood scrutiny by technologists. Various DRM systems have failed to work as promised, or have prevented users from getting promised content, or have even introduced potential bugs or security flaws to the user's systems. DRM systems may also discourage innovation, by discouraging adaptations and development of products that work together with existing products (although they may encourage innovation by hackers, both good and bad).[53]

New protections for copyright owners were added to the Copyright Act in 1998 as part of the DMCA.[54] These protections included more restraints on the circumvention of technological measures that a rights holder has put in place to prevent unauthorized access to the content.[55] Gathegi defines circumvention as "descrambling a scrambled work, decrypting an encrypted work, or otherwise avoiding, bypassing, removing, deactivating, or impairing a technological measure that effectively protects a copyright owner's right, without the copyright owner's permission."[56]

The law, codified in section 1201, provides legal protection for two types of technological measures that copyright owners might use. These two measures are anticopying technology and antiaccess technology.[57] Anticopying technology is used by a copyright owner to prevent copying of the work. Antiaccess technology prevents access to the work without permission. Such technology enables copyright holders to control the conditions under which works can be used.[58]

Although there were many protections already in place, further legal protections were deemed necessary because of the ease with which digital works can be copied and distributed. Proponents of the law also justified the need for these legal protections as conforming to the World Intellectual Property Organization Copyright Treaty (WIPOC Treaty).[59] The United States is a member of the World Intellectual Property Organization and a signatory of the WIPOC Treaty.

Article 11 of the WIPOC Treaty on Obligations Concerning Technological Measures requires members to "provide adequate legal protection and effective legal remedies against the circumvention of effective technological measures that are used by authors in connection with the exercise of their rights under [the WIPOC] Treaty or the Berne Convention and that restrict acts, in respect of their works, which are not authorized by the authors concerned or permitted by law."[60]

Section 1201 also includes two additional prohibitions: an anticircumvention rule that prohibits the circumvention of antiaccess technology, and antitrafficking rules that prohibit the making and selling of devices or services that can be used to circumvent either antiaccess technology or anticopying technology.[61]

Circumventing an antiaccess measure violates the statute, but circumventing an anticopying measure does not. The distinction was made on the theory that making unauthorized copies is often permitted by fair use, but fair use does not sanction unauthorized access. By contrast, the antitrafficking rules apply to both antiaccess and anticopying technology. Making or selling devices or services to circumvent either type of technology is prohibited.[62]

The anticircumventing provisions may increase the copyright owner's legal control over copies no longer under her direct control. Under traditional copyright law, once an authorized copy was in the hands of others, the copyright owner's legal control over it was limited. The anticircumvention provisions extend to the copyright owners some legal control over the terms governing the manner in which copyrighted works are accessed.

The courts are interpreting and applying section 1201.[63] Some courts may read the protections narrowly to apply only to the extent that someone seeks to defeat antiaccess or anticopying measures in order to infringe copyright. Other courts may construe the protections more broadly to find section 1201 violations even where the purpose of circumvention was to use noncopyrighted aspects of works or to make fair use of works. Section 1201 is intended to allow copyright owners to determine the extent to which their copyrighted works are used. If someone purchases or uses a work subject to restrictions imposed by the copyright holder, they must respect those limitations.[64]

Exemptions

Section 1201 contains a number of exemptions from liability. This is comparable to the activities that are protected by fair use. One exemption applies to nonprofit libraries, archives, and educational institutions. These exemptions are very narrowly drawn. The exemption for nonprofit libraries, archives, and educational institutions allows circumvention of antiaccess measures under extremely limited circumstances. If such an institution wanted to acquire a copy of a work but could not otherwise acquire a copy of the work to examine prior to purchase, it may circumvent antiaccess measures in order to obtain a copy to examine. The organization could use the copy only to decide on whether or not they permanently wanted to acquire a copy, and they must not retain the copy.[65]

The exemption applies only to the antiaccess prohibition; it would still violate the antitrafficking provisions for someone to provide software or services in order for the library to gain access to the copy. Rather, the library must presumably rely on the software hacking abilities of its staff to make use of the exemption. It is unlikely that if the library did this they would be sued. The argument with this exemption is that it does little to protect the library from actual situations that they are likely to encounter. If the library owns a copy of an encrypted work and wishes to get access for a purpose such as education, archival presentation, or research, the exemption would be of little use.[66]

Under section 1201, the Librarian of Congress makes a ruling at three-year intervals on whether the users of copyrighted works are likely to be adversely affected in their ability to make noninfringing use of copyrighted works in a particular class. The Librarian of Congress publishes the findings on a list of works that are exempt from prohibition. There are several factors[67] that the Librarian considers:

- Availability of copyrighted works for use
- Availability for use of works for nonprofit preservation, educational, and archival purposes
- Impact on news reporting, criticism, and scholarship
- Effect of circumvention of technological measures on value or marker for copyrighted works
- Other facts the Librarian may consider appropriate

Section 1201 also raises issues of fair use and freedom of speech. The DCMA has been challenged in the courts on numerous occasions as being inconsistent with the Intellectual Property Clause of the United States Constitution. First Amendment challenges include restrictions on speech and claims that the DCMA is overly broad. Gathegi points out that most court challenges to the DCMA have been unsuccessful. Section 1201 is seen as departing widely from traditional copyright protection. The section grants broader rights than traditional copyright without the traditional safeguards of copyright.

The Copyright Office recently concluded the sixth triennial rulemaking proceeding pursuant to 17 U.S.C. §1201.[68] The 2015 exemptions are numerous—there are seventy-two measures, and they include some key points for librarians.[69] The exemptions can be found here: http://copyright.gov/1201/

2015/fedreg-publicinspectionFR.pdf. Ultimately, the courts will determine the reach of section 1201.[70]

TECHNOLOGY, EDUCATION, AND COPYRIGHT HARMONIZATION (TEACH) ACT

Close on the heels of the DCMA was the Technology, Education, and Copyright Harmonization (TEACH) Act. Although the DCMA addressed numerous copyright-related issues, Congress was not able to agree on how to deal with the use of copyright as it pertained to distance education. The TEACH Act was signed into law on November 2, 2002, with the goal of promoting distance education through digital technologies.

The TEACH Act provided numerous benefits for educational institutions engaged in distance education. The benefits of the TEACH Act include expansion of the scope of materials that may be used, the ability to deliver content to students outside of the classroom, the opportunity to retain archival copies of course materials on servers, the authority to convert some works from analog to digital formats, and the ability to display nearly all types of works.[71] In sum, the TEACH Act redefined the terms and conditions on which accredited, nonprofit educational institutions throughout the United States could use copyright-protected materials in distance education—including on websites and by other digital means—without permission from the copyright owner and without payment of royalties.[72]

In order for the use of copyrighted materials in distance education to qualify for the TEACH Act, the following criteria must be met.[73] First, the institution must be an accredited, nonprofit, educational institution. Second, the use must be part of the mediated instructional activities. Third, the use must be limited to a specific number of students enrolled in a specific class. Fourth, the use must either be for "live" or asynchronous class session. Fifth, the use must not include the transmission of textbook material, materials "typically purchased or acquired by students," or works developed specifically for online uses.[74]

Additionally, the exemptions under the TEACH Act do not extend to electronic reserves, course packets (electronic or paper), or interlibrary loan; commercial document delivery; textbooks or other digital content provided under license from the author, publisher, aggregator, or other entity; or conversion of materials from analog to digital formats, except when the converted material is used solely for authorized transmissions and when a digital version of a work is unavailable or protected by technological measures. The act also does not supersede fair use or existing digital license agreements.

Nothing in the TEACH Act mentions the duties of librarians, but the growth and complexity of distance education throughout the country have escalated the need for innovative library services. Fundamentally, librarians have a mission centered on the management and dissemination of information resources. Distance education is simply another form of that pursuit. More pragmatically, distance education has stirred a greater need for reserve services and interlibrary loans in order to deliver information to students in scattered locations. Librarians are also often the principal negotiators of licenses for databases and other materials; those licenses may grant or deny the opportunity to permit access to students located across campus or around the world.

The TEACH Act sets out to strike a balance between allowing educators, students, and librarians the opportunity to utilized copyright-protected materials, while also realizing the rights of copyright owners and the ease in which technology has offered opportunities for their rights to be infringed. This topic highlights the importance for librarians of keeping up with technological trends and making sure that they are equipped to apply their knowledge based on changes in society and changes due to the passage of time.

CONCLUSION

DRM has had a profound effect on a broad range of information policy initiatives, and arguably copyright is at the forefront of these issues. Because DRM technology is intended to provide a broad range of options for content providers, and not the patron of the licensee of these agreements, it can present challenges for librarians. It is important for librarians to understand the complexity of issues like exclusive rights, first sale, and fair use in order to help their patrons make informed decisions about the information they are seeking. However, if courts and Congress would carefully consider the impact of DRM on copyright, it would make life a lot easier for the libraries and those who work for them.

ADDITIONAL RESOURCES

ALA's Advocacy and Issues page on DRM: http://www.ala.org/advocacy/copyright/digital-rights
American Bar Association—Section of Intellectual Property Law: http://www.americanbar.org/groups/intellectual_property_law.html
American Intellectual Property Law Association: http://www.aipla.org/Pages/default.aspx
American Libraries E-content blog: http://americanlibrariesmagazine.org/e-content
American Library Association: http://www.ala.org/
Boing Boing on DRM: http://boingboing.net/tag/DRM
Copyright Clearance Center: http://www.copyright.com/
Copyright Society of the USA: http://www.csusa.org/
Cory Doctorow's *Content*, a free e-book of essays about technology, copyright, and DRM: http://craphound.com/content/download/
Council on Library and Information Resources: http://www.clir.org/

Creative Commons: http://creativecommons.org/
Electronic Frontier Foundation: https://www.eff.org/issues/drm
iCopyright: http://www.icopyright.com/
UNESCO Collection of National Copyright Laws: http://portal.unesco.org/culture/en/ev.php-
URL_ID=14076&URL_DO=DO_TOPIC&URL_SECTION=201.html
United States Copyright Office: http://www.copyright.gov
World Intellectual Property Organization: http://www.wipo.int/portal/en/index.html

NOTES

1. Ericsson, "Recorded Music Industry."
2. Russell, *Complete Copyright*, 12.
3. Pallante, *Copyright Law of the United States*.
4. Russell, *Complete Copyright*, 12.
5. "Patents, Trademarks, and Copyrights," *Code of Federal Regulations*, Title 37. Sec. 202.1.
6. McJohn, *Copyright*, 118.
7. 17 U.S.C. §106 (2011).
8. U.S. Copyright Office, *Copyright Law of the United States*.
9. 17 U.S.C. §201 (a).
10. Ginsburg and Gorman, *Copyright Law*, 59.
11. Ibid., 59.
12. 17 U.S.C. §202; see also U.S. Copyright Office, "Copyright Basics."
13. Ibid.
14. U.S. Copyright Office, "Duration of Copyright."
15. Ibid.
16. 210 U.S. 339.
17. McJohn, *Copyright*, 219.
18. 17 U.S.C. §109.
19. Ibid.
20. McJohn, *Copyright*, 219.
21. Ibid.
22. See Patry, *Fair Use Privilege*, §13:15.
23. American Library Association, "Digital Rights Management."
24. Rubin, *Foundations of Library and Information Science*, 337.
25. Carson, *Law of Libraries and Archives*, 79.
26. Ibid.
27. Ibid.
28. Leaffer, *Understanding Copyright Law*, 475.
29. Carson, *Law of Libraries and Archives*.
30. McJohn, *Copyright*.
31. Ibid.
32. 17 U.S.C. §107.
33. McJohn, *Copyright*, 248.
34. Ibid.
35. Ibid.
36. Ibid.
37. Latman and Gorman, *Copyright for the Nineties*, 495.
38. Ibid.
39. Ibid.
40. Gorman and Ginsburg, *Copyright*, 807.
41. Ibid.
42. Leaffer, *Understanding Copyright Law*, 489.
43. Talab, *Commonsense Copyright*, 118–22.
44. Ibid.

45. Patry, *Fair Use Privilege*.
46. Ibid.
47. U.S. Copyright Office, "Revising Section 108."
48. American Library Association, "Digital Rights Management."
49. American Library Association, "Digital Rights Management Tip Sheet."
50. Samuelson, "DRM."
51. McJohn, *Copyright*, 272.
52. *Federal Register*, "Exemption to Prohibition."
53. McJohn, *Copyright*, 272.
54. Ibid.
55. Gathegi, *Digital Librarian's Legal Handbook*, 104.
56. Ibid.
57. 17 U.S.C. §1201.
58. *Federal Register*, "Exemption to Prohibition."
59. World Intellectual Property Organization, "WIPO-Administered Treaties."
60. Ibid.
61. McJohn, *Copyright*, 272.
62. Ibid., 273.
63. Ibid.
64. Ibid.
65. McJohn, *Copyright*, 3290.
66. Ibid.
67. Gathegi, *Digital Librarian's Legal Handbook*, 108.
68. 17 U.S.C. §1201.
69. *Federal Register*, "Exemption to Prohibition."
70. McJohn, *Copyright*, 290.
71. Strickland, "Copyright's Digital Dilemma."
72. Crews, *Technology, Education and Copyright Harmonization (TEACH) Act*.
73. Ibid.
74. Strickland, "Copyright's Digital Dilemma."

REFERENCES

Agnew, Grace, and Mairead Martin. "Digital Rights Management: Why Libraries Should Be Major Players." In *The Bowker Annual: Library and Book Trade Almanac*, 48th ed., edited by Dave Bogart, 267–78. Medford, NJ: Information Today, 2003.
American Library Association. "Digital Rights Management (DRM) & Libraries." http://www.ala.org/advocacy/copyright/digitalrights.
———. "Digital Rights Management Tip Sheet." July 2012. http://connect.ala.org/files/94226/DRM%20Library%20Education%20Tip%20Sheet_DEFINITIVE_7_11_12.pdf.
Bracha, Oren. "The Adventures of the Statute of Anne in the Land of Unlimited Possibilities: The Life of a Legal Transplant." *Berkeley Technology Law Journal* 25 no 3 (2010): 1427–73.
Carson, Bryan M. *Comments of the American Library Association on the Report of the Register of Copyrights to Congress—Library Reproduction of Copyrighted Works (17 U.S.C. 108)*. Washington, DC: American Library Association, 1983.
———. *The Law of Libraries and Archives*. Lanham, MD: Scarecrow Press, 2007.
Copyright Clearance Center. "About Copyright." http://www.copyright.com/learn/about-copyright/.
Coyle, Karen. *Coyle's Information Highway Handbook: A Practical File on the New Information Order*. Chicago: American Library Association, 1997.
Crews, Kenneth D. *The Technology, Education and Copyright Harmonization (TEACH) Act*. Washington, DC: American Library Association, 2003.

Ericsson, Seth. "The Recorded Music Industry and the Emergence of Online Music Distribution: Innovation in the Absence of Copyright (Reform)." *George Washington Law Review* 79 (2011): 1783–1813.

Federal Register. "Exemption to Prohibition on Circumvention of Copyright Protection Systems for Access Control Technologies." September 17, 2014. https://www.federalregister.gov/articles/2014/09/17/2014-22082/exemption-to-prohibition-on-circumvention-of-copyright-protection-systems-for-access-control.

Gathegi, John N. *The Digital Librarian's Legal Handbook.* New York: Neal-Schuman, 2012.

Gorman, Robert A., and Jane C. Ginsburg. *Copyright: Cases and Materials.* 7th ed. New York: Foundation Press, 2006.

Ginsburg, Jane C., and Robert A. Gorman. *Copyright Law.* New York: Foundation Press, 2012.

Ginsburg, Jane C., and Edouard Treppoz. *International Copyright Law: U.S. and E.U. Perspectives; Text and Cases.* New York: Cheltenham, 2015.

Latman, Alan, and Robert A. Gorman. *Copyright for the Nineties: Cases and Materials.* 3rd ed. Charlottesville, VA: Michie, 1989.

Leaffer, Marshall A. *Understanding Copyright Law.* 4th ed. Newark, NJ: LexisNexis, 2005.

Library of Congress. *Copyright Basics.* Washington, DC: Copyright Office, 2000.

McJohn, Stephen M. *Copyright: Examples and Explanations.* New York: Aspen, 2006.

Pallante, Maria A. *Copyright Law of the United States: And Related Laws Contained in Title 17 of the United States Code, Circular 92.* Oxford: City Press, 2011.

Patry, William F. *The Fair Use Privilege in Copyright Law.* Washington, DC: Bureau of National Affairs, 1985.

———. "Introduction: The Constitutional Clause." In *Copyright Law and Practice.* Washington, DC: Bureau of National Affairs, 2000. http://digital-law-online.info/patry/patry4.html.

Rubin, Richard. *Foundations of Library and Information Science.* 3rd ed. New York: Neal-Schuman, 2010.

Russell, Carrie. *Complete Copyright for K–12 Librarians and Educators.* Chicago: American Library Association, 2012.

Samuelson, Pamela. "DRM (and, or, vs.) the Law." *Communications of the ACM* 19, no. 4 (2003): 41–45.

Stanford Copyright and Fair Use Center. "The Basics of Getting Permission." March 27, 2013. http://fairuse.stanford.edu/overview/introduction/getting-permission/.

Strickland, Lee S. "Copyright's Digital Dilemma Today: Fair Use or Unfair Constraints?" *Bulletin of the American Society for Information Science and Technology* 30, no. 1 (2004): 7–11.

Talab, R. S. *Commonsense Copyright: A Guide for Educators and Librarians.* Jefferson, NC: McFarland, 1999.

U.S. Copyright Office. "Copyright Basics." Circular 1, May 2012. http://www.copyright.gov/circs/circ01.pdf.

———. *Copyright Law of the United States.* Washington, DC: Copyright Office, n.d.

———. "Duration of Copyright." Circular 15a, August 2011. http://www.copyright.gov/circs/circ15a.pdf.

———. "Revising Section 108: Copyright Exceptions for Libraries and Archives." Washington, DC: Copyright Office, n.d.

World Intellectual Property Organization. "WIPO-Administered Treaties: WIPO Copyright Treaty." December 20, 1996. http://www.wipo.int/treaties/en/text.jsp?file_id=295166.

Chapter Nine

DRM Redux

Dana Neacsu

Digital rights management (DRM) is a legal structure purporting to do three things: protect the rights of the owner, support access to the source, and preserve the integrity of the resource. This chapter revisits this structure and asks: Is DRM necessary in the library environment?

Before we start that discussion in earnest, let's make sure that we all understand the legislation that DRM promoters support: select copyright provisions and the Digital Millennium Copyright Act (DMCA) of 1998.[1]

Copyright exists because Congress deemed it important to encourage the creative process. Accordingly, Congress limited public access to creative work to protect the content owner's economic rights. Copyright builds a fence around the creative work, but it is a temporary fence. If Article I, Section 8, Clause 8, of the Constitution gives Congress the power "To promote the Progress of Science and useful Arts, by securing for limited Times to Authors and Inventors the exclusive Right to their respective Writings and Discoveries," it does so by using the "limited" qualifier. Over time, Congress has passed copyright legislation and multiple amendments that lengthened the time of the economic monopoly content creators and their proxies enjoy. Still, the copyright fence remains temporary.

As worry grew that any person could obtain a perfect copy of digital copyrighted content with just a click of a mouse, content creators and their proxies—often referred to as content owners—unsatisfied with the existing "limited" protection successfully manipulated the discussion and added another fence to copyright-protected works. Under this expanded protection, the information is wrapped up electronically and cannot be used without the proper key to unlock the "technological wrapping."

Before data could prove the worriers wrong, the narrative about what could happen and its potential nefarious impact on content owners won the day. High on the list of vocal advocates for more protection were the entertainment industries. Convinced of the possibility described, Congress passed the DMCA, which replaced the view of knowledge and information as a public good whose creation needs temporary privileged access with a more sinister look at knowledge as a "luxury good." In accordance with this new view, Congress approved unlimited "technological fences." Scholars define them as "any technological means of controlling public access to, and manipulation of, digital resources."[2]

The DMCA makes any and all attempt at circumventing, canceling, or bypassing the protections, at any point, illegal. This includes all anticircumvention activities, prohibiting both the act of circumventing technology embedded in the content to prevent unspecified access to the work and the so-called preparatory activities that could enable or facilitate the act of circumvention. The protective technologies and the way to manage them are often labeled as digital rights management, or DRM. In other words, DRM operates to lock access to content. DRM tells users what can and cannot be done, ignoring the copyright tenets of overall progress and knowledge production. As of now, DRM technologies are left unchecked by the traditional copyright limitations utilized by libraries. They are also susceptible to becoming a tool for censorship and market control and have become a tool for keeping track of readers' preferences, thus violating basic privacy rules.

First, DRM encroaches on a user's legitimate rights. If once upon a time a reader could buy a print book and gift it or read it as many times as the print copy physically permitted, users now are forced to limit their expectations. They have limited rights when they purchase an e-book. There are platform limitations. When users purchase an e-book for the Kindle platform from Amazon.com, they actually purchase a "time-share" of content residing on the Amazon cloud. Furthermore, until a few years ago, the Kindle cloud did not permit delivery of the digital copy to multiple devices. Recently, the delivery restrictions between a laptop and a mobile device have been abandoned and users can access the licensed copy from multiple devices. Still, there remain glitches between Amazon and Mac devices, and it is quite cumbersome to sync an iPad Kindle library with that account's Kindle cloud library. In short, DRM encourages a lack of interoperability of mobile devices.

DRM's purpose is to restrict and individualize access to digital content. DRM technologies remain business tools, which have changed the market and customer by focusing on individualized access instead of information sharing. The only legitimate DRM-approved uses of a digital work are those that have been given to each user at the outset, and everything else is presumed illegal. If e-books make the first sale doctrine irrelevant—buyers of a time-share do not own the content—DRM makes the fair use doctrine inoperable: there is no legal use outside the explicit use of the work. Fair use assumes any use within the spirit of copyright protection is legal. DRM excludes such possibility.

Such unrestricted DRM power is dangerous for libraries. It threatens our very existence. As E. H. Walters recently argued,

> There is no need for e-book use of the content to be clunky, when e-journals remain easily accessible and profitable to their aggregators. But it is the libraries' duty to stop growing accustomed to extensive restrictions on use, because if librarians do nothing to protest these restrictions, they give implicit consent that the use restrictions are acceptable and [forget that] customers—not suppliers—determine the success or failure of any business model.[3]

This chapter advocates that together libraries have the economic influence to work against DRM, which has hindered their ability to fulfill their missions for nearly two decades. Part of the problem is the very existence of DRM, and part of the problem is that many libraries ignore its impact: DRM technologies are embedded in the purchased work, and libraries seem reluctant to fight back against such embedded technologies. Agreements with the various publishers and aggregators, whether Overdrive, Freading, NetLibrary, or MyiLibrary, could be less restrictive or even less expensive. Let's see how.

DRM TECHNOLOGIES: SOCIAL AND ECONOMIC CONCERNS

DRM limits information sharing beyond traditional copyright protections. It may seem normal that those less affluent find themselves at the bottom of the information boom, but libraries are meant to balance inequality, and DRM is interfering with the library equalizing role. Worse even, along the way DRM stifles innovation.

The cell phone is one example of the impact of the price discrimination DRM imposes. As of January 2014, 90 percent of American adults owned a cell phone, with 58 percent owning a smart phone.[4] Data showed that five years earlier, 71 percent of American teens owned a smart phone,[5] so the current numbers of teens using mobile devices may be approaching 100 percent. Smart phones tend to be expensive, and the only affordable way for most Americans to get them is to accept a plan and a carrier—in other words, they purchase a "locked" phone. Thus, a user who likes a specific technology, for example, the iPhone, can afford it only if she accepts a contractual plan with a specific carrier, say AT&T. Such a "locked" phone comes with a piece of software that makes it impossible to switch carriers. If users want to switch carriers before their plan expires, they need to unlock their phone. But unlocking the "policing" software is a DMCA violation. Of course, for those who could afford the technology, say an "unlocked" iPhone, the market price is often up to five times the price of a locked iPhone.

The DMCA makes no explicit provision for fair use with regard to the anticircumvention right itself. It provides only that fair use in the underlying work remains available if the work can be accessed. DMCA provides a very limited bridge between fair use and accessibility to the work in the shape of the exceptions established by the Librarian of Congress. Under the DMCA, the Librarian of Congress has the task of identifying "the equitable role played by fair use."[6] Let's look at the role of the Librarian of Congress in our cell phone example.

The DMCA, pursuant to subsections 1201(a)(1)(C) and (D), allows the Librarian of Congress to support exceptions. From 2006 until 2012, the Librarian of Congress successfully argued that unlocking your phone was legal because the evidence showed that the "primary purpose of the locks [was] to keep consumers bound to their existing networks, rather than to protect the rights of copyright owners in their capacity as copyright owners [in the locking software]."[7] Interestingly, in 2012 the Librarian of Congress reviewed the exemptions and no longer promoted the exception allowing the unlocking of cell phones. He found that the market offered unlocked phones. What the librarian forgot to consider was the price of such unlocked phones and the cost to younger people, the ones most technologically savvy and inclined to unlock phones.

This is only one example of the discriminatory economic effects DRM imposes on consumers. Below are further examples of DRM's stifling effect on innovation.

DMCA provides for strike suits that can be filed preemptively. These suits act as a challenge to any new or competing information technology that could be developed and used to circumvent access restrictions. For example, in 2010 Sony used the DMCA to obtain an injunction against the manufacturers of a game enhancer designed to allow legitimately purchased PlayStation games to be played on a PlayStation console purchased in a separate geographical area.[8]

Perhaps even more restrictive is the possibility to sue researchers who communicate results and exchange code with other researchers with respect to computer security and cryptography. Princeton Computer Science Professor Ed Felten was threatened with liability under the DMCA when two music industry associations successfully attempted to suppress the publication of his research that disclosed weaknesses in new watermarking technology. Another computer programmer, Ben Edelman, needed ACLU backing "to research possible flaws in blocking software made by a Seattle company, N2H2 Inc.," without fear of liability under the DMCA.[9]

DRM functions similarly in the e-book environment because everything is perceived to be illegal if not expressly approved at the outset. DRM has dictated to libraries how users can access their collections. As many academic libraries invest 20 percent or more of their budget in digital content because content is either only available digitally or their users have requested digital access to content, the power of digital content owners is increasing.[10] In a world that becomes exclusively digital at a pace impossible to predict, however, it is the content owners who dictate who accesses what and for how long, instead of libraries on behalf of the public.

DRM AFFECTS LIBRARIES IN MULTIPLE WAYS

Libraries are meant to ensure information sharing and community enlightenment. DRM has hindered successful execution of our mission because "unchecked technological fences" have no place in information sharing. DRM is described and promoted as a way to protect copyrighted work from infringement.

Copyrighted works are not bars of gold to be put in a safe and distributed at auctions to the highest bidder. The law has always enabled access to copyrighted works:

> use by reproduction in copies or phono records or by any other means specified by that section, for purposes such as criticism, comment, news reporting, teaching (including multiple copies for classroom use), scholarship, or research, is not an infringement of copyright. In determining whether the use made of a work in any particular case is a fair use the factors to be considered shall include:
>
> (1) the purpose and character of the use, including whether such use is of a commercial nature or is for nonprofit educational purposes;
>
> (2) the nature of the copyrighted work;
>
> (3) the amount and substantiality of the portion used in relation to the copyrighted work as a whole; and
>
> (4) the effect of the use upon the potential market for or value of the copyrighted work.
>
> The fact that a work is unpublished shall not itself bar a finding of fair use if such finding is made upon consideration of all the above factors.[11]

Because of its ubiquitous nature, scholars have persuasively argued that DRM technology is capable of controlling, monitoring, and metering almost every imaginable use of a digital work. As such, DRM has encroached upon the law of copyright and rendered it meaningless. Furthermore, the DMCA ignores both copyrighted content as knowledge meant to advance progress and the role of libraries. In its relevant section, the DMCA provides only an unsatisfactory exception:

> (d) Exemption for nonprofit libraries, archives, and educational institutions.
>
> (1) A nonprofit library, archives, or educational institution which gains access to a commercially exploited copyrighted work solely in order to make a good faith determination of whether to acquire a copy of that work for the sole

purpose of engaging in conduct permitted under this title shall not be in violation of subsection (a)(1)(A). A copy of a work to which access has been gained under this paragraph: (A) may not be retained longer than necessary to make such good faith determination; and (B) may not be used for any other purpose.

(2) The exemption made available under paragraph (1) shall only apply with respect to a work when an identical copy of that work is not reasonably available in another form.

(3) A nonprofit library, archives, or educational institution that willfully for the purpose of commercial advantage or financial gain violates paragraph (1): (A) shall, for the first offense, be subject to the civil remedies under section 1203; and (B) shall, for repeated or subsequent offenses, in addition to the civil remedies under section 1203, forfeit the exemption provided under paragraph (1).

(4) This subsection may not be used as a defense to a claim under subsection (a)(2) or (b), nor may this subsection permit a nonprofit library, archives, or educational institution to manufacture, import, offer to the public, provide, or otherwise traffic in any technology, product, service, component, or part thereof, which circumvents a technological measure.

(5) In order for a library or archives to qualify for the exemption under this subsection, the collections of that library or archives shall be: (A) open to the public; or (B) available not only to researchers affiliated with the library or archives or with the institution of which it is a part, but also to other persons doing research in a specialized field. [12]

In the history of man's cultural development, as Elmer D. Johnson wrote in his history of the book, "the communication of ideas ranks as one of his most significant achievements."[13] But, he added, in time, that communication needs recorded information, and only libraries have proved to be effective systems for recorded information. [14]

The Internet is raising the bar on sharing organized recorded information because it has encouraged both information communication and sharing. It can be something as well defined as the neatly parceled free access to the BBC archives, [15] which anybody can research for noncommercial use. Or it can be Google's more nebulous portfolio, which lets users identify relevant works they want to access in or at close-to-home libraries. Project Gutenberg, possibly the oldest digitized archival project, which has an archive of over forty-five thousand books online, available at no cost, is another example of information sharing. [16] Finally, the HathiTrust is another digital effort of academic and research institutions, offering a collection of millions of titles digitized from libraries around the world. [17]

As the world of organized recorded information becomes more digital, what is the social and economic impact DRM technologies have on the world of free-floating information? DRM restrictions are not easy to spot because they are part of the transaction between libraries and content providers, and unlike "delivery" costs, they are not clearly itemized. When the DRM restrictions are visible, libraries may still choose not to act for many reasons. For instance, librarians may feel uncomfortable defending the public right of access versus the writer's limited economic interest in the work. But that is not a real choice. In the library environment, content owners are rewarded by the money libraries pay for a copy of the content and the exposure libraries offer to the work. Alternatively, libraries may feel powerless in negotiations with large content owners.

DRM has no role in a library environment. While promising a more efficient way of disseminating information,[18] DRM impedes fair use. The DRM default is "to deny access not expressly permitted"[19] and to facilitate price discrimination. Libraries have to choose between one-copy/one-use plans with a certain number of checkouts and annual plans (with as many checkouts within that year and then it expires). DRM technologies circumvent constitutional limitations imposed by the Intellectual Property Clause. In addition, DRM allows information providers to scale prices to reflect the types or number of usages any given consumer needs. Such a pay-per-use world allows content providers to exploit the full potential of the market. That much control is challenging. By its own reasoning, Congress would have been better advised to ban all types of DRM technologies rather than grant them virtually unconditional protection.[20]

Collection Development: Budgetary Decisions

There are libraries whose budgets are large enough that they can dictate trends in academic publishing. There are libraries that cannot. Those who can pay provide their users with immediate, uninterrupted access to content. Those who cannot pay have no choice but to wait for content to become more widely accessible. In this latter case, access happens when copyright restrictions, usually known as "moving walls," disappear and allow databases to include the previously embargoed content and provide the information through less restrictive licensing agreements.

Despite the assertions that DRM technologies do not block access to works but streamline access to them, the truth is that DRM polices dominate our "cultural and social behavior as to copyrighted works."[21] DRM dictates the usage rules, including the number of copies and the number of viewings. In the past, a library user did not have to indicate the time she spent with a print resource. Even the most intrusive way of using a book, by annotating it, was considered an added advantage to reading a library book. Today, purchased content itself can disappear without any prior notice. In addition, content user annotations are at risk of being lost even when digitally allowed in the first place. That happens when the platform provider changes the terms of its licensing, or when it changes the platform entirely by upgrading it.

Of course, DRM is not static, and libraries have formed consortia to respond to some of the more egregious aspects of DRM implementation. As a result, DRM has become more flexible and some digital assets have become accessible through a variety of different distribution channels and devices. For example, the Open Mobile Alliance (OMA) has promoted a set of DRM technologies for cellular phone applications that include such capabilities as "Forward-Lock," which allows content to be downloaded to a specific handset and played unlimited times. Unfortunately, until very recently content was locked to the specific device. Moreover, "Flexible Preview" allows content to be forwarded to any other device, but only for a specified preview of digital content.

The clunkiness of access often tends to keep users at bay. That is perhaps why a growing number of mostly independent publishers are doing the unthinkable. According to Hugh McGuire and Brian O'Leary, independent publishers are releasing e-books without any form of copy restriction, and their business is thriving. That business decision is mostly dictated by the high cost of DRM. For instance, Adobe uses DRM technology that costs $0.22 per item, not including hardware costs, network costs, or professional services.

> Compared to Adobe's ACS technology, Amazon and Apple's DRM might seem like a bargain. There are no licensing costs, no maintenance fees, and no professional service or consumer support overhead. . . . Of course, this "free" DRM comes at a cost . . . 30% of each sale, limited access to each marketplace, and no information about consumers who purchase books.[22]

Staff Implications

E-books have grown extremely popular in recent years, and in response libraries are experiencing a major increase in their e-book lending. The problem is that patrons want the same rights with e-books that they have with their print counterparts. DRM-restricted e-books make that impossible. A majority of e-book publishers have very restrictive licensing agreements. For each e-book title, libraries are forced to accept the terms negotiated with the vendor. Not only does this mean high prices that are subject to increase if an e-book ends up being more popular than expected, but the purchase of an e-book is essentially more like a lease, one in which most of the terms are dictated by the vendor.[23] This is an example of a "Terms of Use" provision:

> S&S grants you a limited, personal, non-exclusive, revocable, non-assignable and non-transferable license to view, use and/or play a single copy of the Materials and download one copy of the Materials on any single computer for your personal, non-commercial home use only.[24]

Although unproved by facts, publishers fear that with the rise of e-books, unrestricted borrowing in libraries will hurt their business. As a result, many e-book vendors went through periods when they avoided doing business with libraries. Penguin withdrew its e-books from OverDrive (one of the largest e-book vendors to libraries) in February 2012. Thus "the remaining publishers who do offer e-books to libraries either place heavy restrictions on lending or make libraries pay hefty increases for subscriptions. Random House has raised its price for e-books to libraries, and HarperCollins now demands that their e-books be removed from the library's digital collection and be repurchased after they have been checked out 26 times."[25] Such lending restrictions make interlibrary loan difficult and require new skills of a library's staff.

User Satisfaction

Digital content can be accessed in a variety of ways via libraries. Libraries use subscription models, leasing models, purchased content, and sampling. Aggregator platforms prevent users from working effectively with whole books. Users may be able to print a chapter or two, but may not be able to save chapters as portable PDF files. Furthermore, DRM restrictions often make it impossible to copy and paste graphics (i.e., tables and figures). Often a need to print content from more than a chapter or two requires a digital rights workaround like logging out of a browser session and logging back in to get the next needed chapter or chapters. Although some aggregators tout downloadablity, downloads are often limited to a particular proprietary software environment that is effectively an accommodation of "offline" use rather than the true portability conferred on PDFs of electronic journal articles.

Simultaneous Use

Early functionality on the NetLibrary platform resulted in a lag time between closing a book on one computer and being able to open it on another. Thus librarians were forced to predict the possible number of uses for each book offered in the package and purchase the appropriate model. That required acquisition librarians to go with certain aggregator models, such as Ebrary's Single or Multiple User Purchase. As imagined, such a demand was very onerous on libraries with a limited budget, and thus impractical.

Archivability

Even when libraries own the e-books they purchase on an aggregator platform, there is currently no provision for archiving them if the aggregator goes out of business or a library chooses to end its business relationship with the particular aggregator. If purchased e-books were DRM-free, they could be delivered to libraries or archives and provided to users in the case of these eventualities.

One option is to purchase directly from publishers because most e-books that are hosted on publisher sites are DRM free. They are fully downloadable (at least at the chapter level), and many publishers are providing their content to independent archives like Portico or LOCKSS (Lots of Copies Keep Stuff Safe). The main problem is that a piecemeal publisher-by-publisher approach requires a lot of research and time for the acquisition librarian. At the same time, users want in e-books the same freedom they have with electronic journals. Most publisher platforms provide this freedom—aggregator platforms don't. Without DRM, these challenges would not exist.

Authenticated Access

The e-book system works in various ways. Most often a book is downloaded or checked out, or a book's chapter is viewed or printed. Where one patron checks out the book, the patron has to authenticate her legal access, and when she does it, the copy is not available for use by any other patron. While DRM is supposed to help with authenticated access, it actually causes more problems. For instance, placing e-books on reserve becomes impossible. The purpose of reserves is collective accessibility, but DRM authentication is so cumbersome that when users check out e-books for a limited amount of time, they accidentally create havoc among library staff and users. It is easier to check out print books for two hours than to check out e-books:

> Two days ago, a student came to the reference desk looking for a copy of a book for which their professor had given them (and every person in their class) a syllabus which instructed them to locate the library's ebook copy of an assigned text. This professor had probably looked in the catalog, discovered that the electronic copy of the text was listed and therefore not placed a print copy on reserve. The problem was that when this student came and asked for guidance in opening this ebook at the reference desk, the librarian went into the catalog with him, and opened up the electronic copy of the book. They could see/view/read the ebook for that moment. However, when the librarian hit the back button and tried to open it again, the ebook was no longer available. It said the book was "checked out" and could not be used. They hadn't logged in to any accounts nor had the two realized they were "checking out" this title upon clicking. And since no one had logged in, essentially the book had been checked out to the ether.[26]

Privacy

To the extent that DRM is used to keep tabs on how digital content is used, it enables privacy violations. For example, Adobe's e-book software, Digital Editions, logs every document readers add to their local library and tracks what happens with those files, essentially tracking a user's reading habits. Originally, Adobe then placed this information at risk when it transmitted it in plain text. In doing so, it undermined decades of efforts by libraries and bookstores to protect the privacy of their patrons and customers. Adobe never denied transmitting the information, only stating that it collected it for licensing purposes.[27]

Libraries encourage their patrons to use such software because it helps the library comply with the restrictions publishers impose on electronic lending. Yet, as noted, there are privacy risks:

> In 2011 EFF and a coalition of companies and public interest groups helped pass the Reader Privacy Act, which requires the government and civil litigants to demonstrate a compelling interest in obtaining reader records and show that the information contained in those records cannot be obtained by less intrusive means. But if readers are using Adobe's software, it's all too easy for folks to bypass those restrictions [i.e., the content is already given].[28]

Preservation

HathiTrust is an important component of the digitization efforts that have taken place to date, as is the Internet Archive, but these efforts apply primarily to preservation and access for works that were initially released in print. Libraries need to make different arrangements for works that exist only in electronic form.

> Given that libraries' relationship with serials, especially electronic journals (e.g., the pricing practices that have resulted in a widespread boycott of all journals published by Elsevier), can be seen as a lesson in how not to work with commercial interests, it may be worth noting the recent report by university libraries at Columbia and Cornell which notes that only "15–20% of the e-journal titles in the libraries' collections are currently preserved" by libraries' two leading digital preservation initiatives, LOCKSS and Portico. One way for libraries to avoid these kinds of difficulties is to find ways now, while ebooks are still relatively new, to begin preserving copies of ebooks in ways that will ensure their availability for future readers.[29]

But how can that be done when budgets shrink because libraries don't own authorized copies? DRM does not allow such copies, unless under the DMCA the Librarian of Congress promotes such a library exception. To the extent libraries rent instead of own e-books, they can be recalled at any time by publishers. But even when they own the books, "Digital Rights Management (DRM) restrictions often prevent libraries from downloading or printing copies of e-books for archival purposes."[30] Of course, most libraries prefer to rent because even if publishers were prepared to sell e-books, the majority do not have adequate infrastructure to store them. At this time, most do not have a "robust information technology infrastructure (institutional repository) in which to store eBook files, [or] have a plan in place to migrate eBook files (or any other kind of digital files) from the current generation technology platform to the next."[31] Nevertheless, the choice for having access to a digital copy should remain with the libraries and not with DRM technologies.

THE VERY EXISTENCE OF A LIBRARY IN A DIGITAL ENVIRONMENT

Today, libraries collect both print and digital materials. Very soon content will be predominantly available only in a digital format, and that goes to the core of our mission: information sharing. The first sale doctrine was the basis for print library lending. But in a thoroughly digital world, content providers dictate use: how many digital copies libraries need in order to "rent" content to patrons for a specified number of readings. DRM keeps track of every conceivable use, and the library becomes a business cipher advertising content rather than sharing it. Our main tools, the first sale doctrine and fair use, are becoming obsolete. If we do not come up with a plan, then libraries risk becoming obsolete.

Today, the percentage of people who own e-book readers and tablet computers is increasing rapidly. According to a January 16, 2014, report by the Pew Research Center,

> Overall, 50% of Americans now have a dedicated handheld device—either a tablet computer like an iPad, or an e-reader such as a Kindle or Nook—for reading e-content. That figure has grown from 43% of adults who had either of those devices in September. In addition, the survey found that 92% of adults have a cell phone (including the 55% of adults who have a smartphone), and 75% have a laptop or desktop computer—figures that have not changed significantly from our pre-holiday surveys.[32]

Thus, if libraries wish to serve people who own these devices while also upholding the core values that best serve all readers (e.g., intellectual freedom and preservation), it becomes very clear that they need to develop e-book practices and software that complement one another. All libraries, academic or not, purchase e-books from a portfolio of different vendors. In order to select the books and packages that they acquire, they apply a number of criteria. DRM restrictions dominate other criteria, such as the license, price, platform, interface, and subject coverage. DRM affects all the criteria librarians care about because it dictates the business model publishers offer and the price they ask for digital content.

The only e-book options that promote libraries' core values either provide libraries with ownership rights for the authorized copies they purchase and circulate or are free of DRM software—ideally, both. Many library scholars, such as Levy, have noted that DRM is an inherently flawed technology that can be replaced by creating better software or licensing terms. For instance, OverDrive does not provide DRM-free downloads, but it changed the provision in its contracts and supports library ownership of the copies that libraries purchase through OverDrive. Safari has a consumer product that allows for DRM-free downloads. However, it only allows access to the titles in Safari's library product and is only online. These are only imperfect solutions without library input. Are there any additional solutions?

LIBRARY ADVOCACY

This chapter concludes with some suggestions focused on the information-sharing role of libraries.

The Role of the Librarian of Congress

The Librarian of Congress has the legislative powers bestowed by Congress to promote progress through information sharing. The current proposals for DMCA exceptions incorporate already implemented exceptions, such as the *Authors Guild v. HathiTrust* decision,[33] which held that searching e-books and making them accessible to the disabled is covered by fair use. Among the exceptions the Librarian of Congress makes is "literary works distributed in ebook format when all existing ebook editions of the work (including digital text editions made available by authorized entities) contain access controls that prevent the enabling of the ebook's read-aloud function and that prevent the enabling of screen readers to render the text into a specialized format."[34] Thus, first on the advocacy list is an encouragement, a plea for the new Librarian of Congress to use the DMCA legislative powers to promote progress rather than business interests. Robinson Meyer explained the Librarian of Congress's role explicitly:

> The Librarian has the power to grant exemptions that enable people to copy or remix otherwise protected works. (Technically, the Librarian's authority is to exempt the Digital Millennium Copyright Act's ban on opening digital locks—like an encrypted DVD, for instance. Which means that people can still unlock and access such works for legal purposes, like copying a clip of a DVD as part of a remix.) The idea is to be sure there's a way around locks or encryptions that would prevent lawful use of a class of locked works.
>
> This is a big deal. As Jessamyn West, a librarian and the former Chief Operating Officer of the legendary web community Metafilter, put it: "The Librarian of Congress gets to say, these things you could go to jail for? They're okay." And he or she does this every three years.[35]

On October 28, 2015, the final rules from the most recent triennial proceeding were announced and consisted of the ten exemptions listed below:

1. Motion pictures (including television shows and videos)
2. Literary works, distributed electronically, protected by TPM interfering with assistive technologies
3. Computer programs that enable devices to connect to a wireless network ("unlocking")
4. Computer programs on smart phones and all-purpose mobile computing devices ("jailbreaking")
5. Computer programs on smart TVs ("jailbreaking")
6. Vehicle software to enable diagnosis, repair, or modification
7. Computer programs to enable good faith research of security flaws
8. Video games requiring server communication
9. Software to limit feedstock of 3D printers
10. Patient data from implanted networked medical devices

As noted above, the Librarian of Congress included on the proposed list of DMCA exceptions "(3) Unlocking of cellphones, tablets, mobile hotspots and wearable devices to allow connection to a new wireless network provider."[36] And this year, the exemption became reality for the next three years. This suggests that library advocacy is and remains a tremendous tool for promoting progress and information sharing.

Of course, there is more that can be done, and Maria Scheid, rights management specialist at the Copyright Resources Center of Ohio State University Libraries, persuasively explained that the DMCA exemption process, as designed, is in need of reform:

> The process is time-consuming, involving multiple rounds of public comments, hearings, and opportunities for response. The result is a handful of exemptions that only remain valid for a relatively short amount of time. In [the 2015] rulemaking round, for example, multiple exemptions were sought to simply renew already existing exemptions."[37]

At a minimum, as the Register of Copyright has suggested, a presumption needs to be made in favor of the renewal of exemptions when no meaningful opposition to the renewal has been raised.

The Role of Library Associations

DRM restrictions have created a series of reactive library responses that can be grouped under (1) lending initiatives, (2) preservation initiatives, and (3) embracing new technologies that promote greater access to content irrespective of the e-reader platform.

Comprehensive surveys currently underway ask library patrons about preferred device usage, preferences for print or digital formats, collection assessment, and other issues that affect the use and distribution of published content in public libraries. For instance, the Book Industry Study Group (BISG) and the American Library Association have announced a partnership to produce a major survey of public library patrons' use of digital content. The survey seeks to understand the behavior of library patrons, including their use of digital resources and other services offered by public libraries. It will examine the impact of digital consumption behaviors, including the adoption of new business models, on library usage across America. In a comprehensive survey, library patrons will be asked about preferred device usage, preferences for print or digital formats, collection assessment, and other issues that affect the use and distribution of published content in public libraries. While such a survey is welcome, it looks like a timid step—a far cry from a deliberate movement to replace or restrain DRM technologies. What is needed is a well-crafted movement to ask Congress for a library exemption, because DRM hinders the work of libraries.

The Role of Library Consortia

The size of a library's budget dictates its power. This means that if you are not one of the top academic or public libraries, a consortium to fight problems is the best strategy. In 2011, librarians were fighting for their readers. The result was the Readers' Bill of Rights for Digital Books.[38] The Bill of Rights specifies the following:

1. Ability to retain, archive and transfer purchased materials
2. Ability to create a paper copy of the item in its entirety
3. Digital books should be in an open format (reading on a computer, not just a device)
4. Choice of hardware to access books (in three years when your device has broken, you can still read your book on other hardware)
5. Reader information will remain private (what, when, and how we read will not be stored, sold, or marketed).

This anti-DRM movement promoted the following ideas:

- Consumers should not bear the risk of technological obsolescence. Users of content should not bear the risk of piracy. Those who claim the lion's share of the benefit of technological innovation and creation of content should bear the associated risks.
- The content industry wants the benefits of digital distribution of content with none of the associated risks.

- The cost of ameliorating the content industry's risk is the freedom of the public to use content in ways that have been traditionally guaranteed in our society.
- The cultural works from the 20th century are at risk of being lost in an "intellectual purgatory," as scholars have already explained, unless large users' associations, such as library consortia, step up their advocacy to force the content providers' industry to reflect the truth that content, recorded information, which was never meant to be a commodity, is a different type of goods. It does not grow on anybody's farm.
- It grows out of the free exchange of ideas. Without sharing information there is no content to create and protect, and no democracy where a market for such content can exist.[39]

Unfortunately, the Readers' Bill of Rights is not law but a set of guidelines for use by libraries and other purchasers of digital content.

Also in 2012, Brett Bonfield published a very thorough review of what libraries can do right now to push back the unnecessary DRM encroachment. Bonfield found eleven ways to improve the current state of the library-DRM relationship.[40] They are listed below and then briefly summarized:

Open Library

Open Library, which has been endorsed by all fifty state librarians in the Chief Officers of State Library Agencies (COSLA), partners with libraries to create a nationwide, shared e-book collection. Participating libraries contribute at least one print-based book to the shared collection, which Open Library digitizes and then locks away in long-term storage. The print-based copy of the book does not circulate. Instead, Open Library circulates the digital copy of the item. In return for contributing a book to the Open Library collection, participating libraries' cardholders are given access to all of the e-books in the collection. Open Library retains ownership of the authorized copies of e-books on behalf of the participating libraries.

Open Source/DRM Hybrid Model

Under this model libraries deal directly with copyright holders, have them sign a simple Common Understanding license, and host the e-books either on an open-source server if the rights holder is willing or, if the rights holder wants more restrictions, e-books can be held on the library's own Adobe Content Server.

Unlimited Content License Model

Under the Unlimited Content License Model, which was created by the Ann Arbor District Library, publishers agree to allow the library to distribute unlimited, unencrypted copies to their cardholders, and libraries agree to pay the publishers a flat annual fee. If the library chooses not to renew its payment, it must remove the files from its servers when the term is up.

Portability Model

Under this model the library negotiates with the aggregator to allow it to transfer the titles purchased through one aggregator to a different platform if that platform is more advantageous to the library. This model is perhaps best associated with the state librarian in Kansas, Jo Budler. The issue arose when the library signed its first contract with OverDrive, but the platform did not work. OverDrive's contract locked the library to its platform.

Publisher Hosting Model

This model is most prevalent in contracts between academic libraries and scholarly publishers, though this is more a matter of convention and of large libraries' buying power.

Unglue.it

Unglue.it uses a Kickstarter-like crowd-funding model but focuses solely on working with rights holders to set prices for "ungluing" their books—that is, releasing an e-book versions of the work under a Creative Commons license. The rights holders set a price, and Unglue.it helps them get it digitized. Ownership of authorized copies of e-books in the Unglue.it model is universal.

Library License

Library License, proposed by Jeff Goldenson of the Harvard Library Innovation Laboratory, is similar to Creative Commons, but it is directed solely at authors who want their work to have a special, companion license that allows libraries to own and circulate the work. The initial draft calls for three possibilities, including an embargo, where libraries could have the work for free only after the work has been commercially available for a specified number of years.

Sneakernet Model

Using the Sneakernet Model, libraries would buy e-books like any other purchaser and place the authorized copy on a read-only flash drive. The copy would circulate like any other physical object, such as books, DVDs, and CDs, using existing software.

DIY Model

DIY, which stands for "do it yourself," is an homage to the members of the indie/punk music scene of the 1980s and 1990s, who believed bands could and should avoid major record labels, and even published guides/zines describing how to put out their own records. Specifically, the DIY Model uses Open Library's model as a precedent and gives individual libraries control of their own authorized copies. Open Library's interpretation of copyright is that libraries, upon purchasing an item, also purchase the right to circulate one copy of that item at a time, even if the library elects to transform that item into another format, such as digital.

Steampunk Model

Like the Sneakernet Model, the Steampunk Model is another technological step back—in this case, from digital back to print. The key is to work directly with rights holders who value libraries or who see the library as a useful market for increasing their sales and promoting their work, especially if they would not otherwise consider printing their books at all.

The State Redistribution Model

This model involves significant legislative changes. Richard Stallman of the Free Software Foundation originally proposed the idea in a letter to the Brazilian government. Under Stallman's proposal, the author or publisher would retain ownership of the copyright but agree to share the work noncommercially. Copying and redistributing authorized copies would be legal and authors would be reimbursed based on the popularity of their work. Popularity would be measured not by counting downloads or monitoring use of the work in other ways, but by responses to voluntary surveys in which readers would report what they have read. Rights holders, authors, and artists would be paid from a pool of funds set aside by the government to pay authors for their work.[41]

In other words, big library organizations usually set the trend and establish the parameters of negotiation with the publishers. While the American Library Association (ALA) as well as the American Association of Law Libraries (AALL) and other library organizations provide resources on legislative tracking and other advocacy activities, they have also been problematic. AALL, for instance, includes both vendors of content and librarians. Therefore, their advocacy is inherently tainted. If the organizations are inherently weak, should we expect individual librarians—from the small public to the large public, from the small liberal arts college librarian to a large university system—to set the tone of the resistance to DRM encroachment? We should, because our profession requires us to preserve the public's right to accessing information. For librarians, accessing information is tantamount to a human right. We are neither in the business of policing copyright, nor are we in the business of enabling copyright infringement. But short of that, librarians cannot side with those who make money by setting unnecessary fences around information. The only legal fence is that established by the Constitution, and that fence is clear, even if in 1998 Congress chose to ignore it. The public's access to information is limited only to the extent it interferes with the promotion of progress through the author's creative effort. Historically, that has been limited to a few decades at most. It is now a century and yet nobody is writing ten times as much as they used to. Making the law clear to individual librarians, we encourage them to set the tone of their professional organizations.

CONCLUSION

For libraries and schools to serve their educational, research, and information roles, the public must be able to use works in the full range of ways envisioned by the Copyright Act and its limitations and exceptions.[42] The DMCA prohibits freeing copyrighted works from the restraining powers of DRM. The only entity allowed to present exemptions to the DMCA is the Librarian of Congress. That power is limited to "classes of works" that adhere to fair use. The exemptions include "compilations consisting of lists of websites blocked by filtering software applications" and "literary works, including computer programs, and databases." This chapter argues that libraries should not limit themselves to this status quo and should use their associations and consortia to fight back for better ways to promote the sharing of information within the limits of the copyright clause. DMCA is an imperfect piece of legislation, and it is our role as librarians to point out what needs to be changed and how we should do it.

NOTES

1. Digital Millennium Copyright Act of 1998, codified in 17 U.S.C. §1201(a)(1)(C).
2. Weinberg, "Hardware-Based Id," 1256.
3. Walters, "E-books in Academic Libraries," 93.
4. Hasenfus, "Unlocking Will Get You Locked Up," 301.

5. Patel, "Taking It Easy."
6. Burk, "Anti-circumvention Misuse," 1138.
7. Hasenfus, "Unlocking Will Get You Locked Up," 324.
8. *Sony Computer Entertainment America LLC v. Hotz*, CV 11 0167, 2011 WL 347137 (N.D. Cal., January 27, 2011).
9. Brown, "Digital Rights Management," 823.
10. See Goertzen, "E-book Program Development Study."
11. 17 U.S.C. §107.
12. 17 U.S.C. §1201(d).
13. Johnson, *Communication*, 10.
14. Ibid.
15. See http://www.bbc.co.uk/archive/.
16. See https://www.gutenberg.org/.
17. See https://www.hathitrust.org/.
18. Armstrong, "Digital Rights Management," 61.
19. Ibid., 71.
20. Brown, "Digital Rights Management," 804.
21. Dusollier, "DRM at the Intersection," 303.
22. Biglione, "Analyzing the Business Case."
23. See Norris and Humphries, "Ebooks."
24. "Terms of Use," Simon & Schuster.
25. Norris and Humphries, "Ebooks."
26. Alycia, "Sad Reports from the Field," Reader's Bill of Rights for Digital Books, February 13, 2016, http://readersbillofrights.info/ReportfromField, quoted in Norris and Humphries, "Ebooks."
27. Digital Book World, "Adobe Confirms."
28. McSherry, "Adobe Spyware Reveals."
29. "Ebook Options for Libraries."
30. Goertzen, "E-book Program Development Study," 52.
31. Yale University Library, "The Ebook Strategic Plan Task Force," March 3, 2013, http://www.library.yale.edu/departments/collectiondevelopment/Yale-ebook-task-force-rpt.pdf, quoted in ibid.
32. Zickuhr and Rainie, "E-reading Rises."
33. 755 F.3d 87 (2d Cir. 2014).
34. "Statement of the Librarian of Congress."
35. Meyer, "How a New Librarian of Congress."
36. "Long Comment regarding a Proposed Exemption."
37. Scheid, "New DMCA Exemptions."
38. "Readers' Bill of Rights."
39. Ibid.
40. Bonfield, "Ebook Cargo Cult."
41. Ibid.
42. American Library Association, "Digital Rights Management."

REFERENCES

Books

Brousseau, Eric, Meryem Marzouki, and Cécile Méadel, eds. *Governance, Regulations and Powers on the Internet*. Cambridge: Cambridge University Press, 2012.

Crews, Kenneth D. *Copyright Law for Librarians and Educators: Creative Strategies and Practical Solutions*. Chicago: American Library Association, 2012.

Johnson, Elmer D. *Communication: An Introduction to the History of Writing, Printing, Books and Libraries*. Metuchen, NJ: Scarecrow Press, 1973.

Lindey, Alexander, and Michael Landau. *Lindey on Entertainment, Publishing and the Arts.* Minnesota: Thomson Reuters, 2015.

Zeng, Wenjun, Heather Yu, and Ching-Yung Lin, eds. *Multimedia Security Technologies for Digital Rights Management.* Boston: Academic Press, 2006.

Articles

Armstrong, Timothy. "Digital Rights Management and the Process of Fair Use." *Harvard Journal of Law & Technology* 20 (2006): 49–121.

Balaban, David. "Battle of the Music Industry: The Distribution of Audio and Video Works via the Internet, Music and More." *Fordham Intellectual Property, Media and Entertainment Law Journal* 12 (2001): 235–88.

Biglione, Kirk. "Analyzing the Business Case for DRM." In *Book: A Futurist's Manifesto,* edited by Hugh McGuire and Brian O'Leary, chap. 5. Sebastopol, CA: O'Reilly Media, 2012. http://book.pressbooks.com/chapter/drm-kirk-biglione.

Brown, Kristin. "Digital Rights Management: Trafficking in Technology That Can Be Used to Circumvent the Intellectual Property Clause." *Houston Law Review* 40 (2013): 803–36.

Burk, Dan I. "Anti-circumvention Misuse." *University of California Los Angeles Law Review* 50 (2003): 1095–1140.

Chiarizio, Matthew. "An American Tragedy: E-books, Licenses, and the End of Public Lending Libraries?" *Vanderbilt Law Review* 66 (2013): 615–44.

Dusollier, Severine. "DRM at the Intersection of Copyright Law and Technology: A Case Study for Regulation." In Brousseau, Marzouki, and Méadel, *Governance, Regulations and Powers on the Internet,* 297–317.

Hasenfus, Nicholas. "Unlocking Will Get You Locked Up: A Recent Change to the DMCA Makes Unlocking Cell Phones Illegal." *Journal of High Technology Law* 15 (2015): 301–28.

Levy, David M. "Digital Libraries and the Problem of Purpose." *D-Lib Magazine,* January 2000. http://www.dlib.org/dlib/january00/01levy.html.

Montagnani, Maria Lilla. "A New Interface between Copyright Law and Technology: How User-Generated Content Will Shape the Future of Online Distribution." *Cardozo Arts & Entertainment Law Journal* 26 (2009): 719–73.

Murck, Patrick. "Waste Content: Rebalancing Copyright Law to Enable Markets of Abundance" *Albany Law Journal of Science & Technology* 16 (2006): 383–422.

Patel, Ronak. "Taking It Easy on Teen Pornographers: States Respond to Minors' Sexting." *Journal of High Technology Law* 13 (2013): 574–612.

Price, Jason, S. "Patron Driven Acquisition of Publisher-Hosted Content: Bypassing DRM." *Against the Grain* 23 (2011): 16–18. http://docs.lib.purdue.edu/atg/vol23/iss3/7.

Vasileiou, Magdalini, Richard Hartley, and Jennifer Rowley. "Choosing E-books: A Perspective from Academic Libraries." *Online Information Review* 36 (2012): 21–39.

Walters, William H. "E-books in Academic Libraries: Challenges for Sharing and Use." *Journal of Librarianship and Information Science* 46 (2014): 85–95.

Weinberg, Jonathan. "Hardware-Based Id, Rights Management, and Trusted Systems." *Stanford Law Review* 53 (2000): 1251–81.

Weisera, Philip J. "The Internet, Innovation, and Intellectual Property Policy." *Columbia Law Review* 103 (2003): 534–613.

Born-Digital Sources

American Library Association. "Digital Rights Management (DRM) & Libraries." http://www.ala.org/advocacy/copyright/digitalrights.

Bonfield, Brett. "The Ebook Cargo Cult." *In the Library with the Lead Pipe,* July 11, 2012. http://www.inthelibrarywiththeleadpipe.org/2012/the-ebook-cargo-cult/.

Digital Book World. "Adobe Confirms It's Gathering Ebook Readers' Data." October 7, 2014. http://www.digitalbookworld.com/2014/adobe-confirms-its-gathering-ebook-readers-data/.

Goertzen, Melissa. "E-book Program Development Study: Annual Report." Columbia University Libraries, June 30, 2014. http://academiccommons.columbia.edu/catalog/ac%3A178009/.
Kellogg, Carolyn. "HarperCollins' 26-Checkout Limit on Libraries' Ebooks Starts Today." *Los Angeles Times*, March 7, 2011. http://latimesblogs.latimes.com/jacketcopy/2011/03/harper-collins-library-ebook-checkout-limit.html.
McSherry, Corynne. "Adobe Spyware Reveals (Again) the Price of DRM: Your Privacy and Security." Electronic Frontier Foundation, October 7, 2014. https://www.eff.org/deeplinks/2014/10/adobe-spyware-reveals-again-price-drm-your-privacy-and-security.
Meyer, Robinson. "How a New Librarian of Congress Could Improve U.S. Copyright." *Atlantic*, June 19, 2015. http://www.theatlantic.com/technology/archive/2015/06/could-a-new-librarian-of-congress-fix-us-copyright-law-dmca/396080/.
Norris, Bryan, and Michelle Humphries. "Ebooks." Digital Rights Management. http://drm.web.unc.edu/libraries/ebooks/.
Price, Jason S., and John D. McDonald. "Beguiled by Bananas: A Retrospective Study of the Usage and Breadth of Patron vs. Librarian Acquired Ebook Collections." *Proceedings of the Charleston Library Conference 2009.* http://docs.lib.purdue.edu/cgi/viewcontent.cgi?article=1027&context=charleston.
Rosenblatt, Bill. "Public Library E-book Lending Must Change to Survive." *Copyright and Technology*, December 4, 2011. https://copyrightandtechnology.com/2011/12/04/a-bleak-future-for-public-libraries-and-e-books/.
Scheid, Maria. "New DMCA Exemptions." Ohio State University Libraries, December 30, 2015. https://library.osu.edu/blogs/copyright/2015/12/30/new-dmca-exemptions/.
Zickuhr, Kathryn, and Lee Rainie. "E-reading Rises as Device Ownership Jumps." Pew Research Center, January 16, 2014. http://www.pewinternet.org/2014/01/16/e-reading-rises-as-device-ownership-jumps/.

Miscellaneous

"The Digital Media Manifesto." September 30, 2003. http://manifesto.chiariglione.org/.
"Ebook Options for Libraries." http://lisinfo.org/ebooks/latest/index.html.
"Long Comment regarding a Proposed Exemption under 17 U.S.C. 1201." http://copyright.gov/1201/2015/comments-020615/InitialComments_LongForm_CCA_Class14.pdf.
"Readers' Bill of Rights for Digital Books." http://readersbillofrights.info/.
"Statement of the Librarian of Congress Relating to Section 1201 Rulemaking." http://www.copyright.gov/1201/docs/librarian_statement_01.html.
"Terms of Use." Simon & Schuster, October 21, 2008. https://www.pimsleurdigital.com/termsofuse.html.
"WIPO Copyright Treaty." December 20, 1996. http://www.wipo.int/treaties/en/ip/wct/.

Index

About the Editors

Catherine A. Lemmer is director of the Lake Forest Library, Lake Forest, Illinois. Previously she was assistant director of information services at the Indiana University Robert H. McKinney School of Law. In addition to library administrative duties, she is a research instructor in both the JD program and the LLM program in American law for foreign lawyers. Her research interests include information technology in law and legal education, information literacy, knowledge governance, and library leadership and administration.

Her international work includes serving as a senior library fellow for six months in 2013–2014 with the Legal Resources Centre of South Africa, the oldest and largest public interest law firm in South Africa, working to modernize their law libraries. She has served three times as an NGO observer at the 9/11 Military Commission hearings held in Guantanamo Bay as part of her work with the Military Commission Observation Project established by the IU McKinney program in international human rights law.

She was the editorial director of *AALL Spectrum*, the professional journal of the American Association of Law Libraries, and a regular blog contributor to *RIPS Law Librarian*, *Ruth Lilly Law Library Blog*, and *The Gitmo Observer*. Lemmer has written a number of articles on teaching and librarianship and regularly presents at regional, state, and national library conferences.

Prior to her appointment to the law library faculty, she was the project manager for Evergreen Indiana, responsible for implementing a statewide open-source ILS initiative in partnership with the Indiana State Library. She also practiced law, specializing in corporate and financial institutions law, at a major Chicago law firm and has held management positions in a public library.

Lemmer has a BA from Lawrence University, a JD from the University of Wisconsin Law School, and an MSLIS from the University of Illinois. She is a fellow of the Harvard University Graduate School of Education Leadership Institute for Academic Librarians, a fellow of the American Association of Law Libraries Leadership Academy, and a member of the Order of the Coif, Phi Beta Kappa, and Beta Phi Mu.

Carla Wale is the head of public services at the Temple University Beasley School of Law Library. Prior to joining the Temple Law Library, she was reference librarian at Georgetown University Law Center and research and electronic technologies librarian at Northern Illinois University College of Law. She teaches advanced legal research courses at Temple Law and was an instructor at Georgetown Law and Northern Illinois University Law.

Wale was previously a contributing editor for Esquire Books, has written several articles focused on technology in libraries, has presented at regional and national conferences, and is the coauthor of two forthcoming books on legal research. She has a BA in political science from Washington State University, a JD from Loyola University New Orleans School of Law, and an MLIS with a certificate in law librarianship from the University of Washington. She is a fellow of the Harvard University Graduate School of Education Leadership Institute for Academic Librarians, a fellow of the American Association of Law Libraries Leadership Academy, and an MBA candidate at Johns Hopkins University.

About the Contributors

Alex Berrio Matamoros, JD, MSLIS, is emerging technologies librarian and library associate professor at CUNY School of Law. His current research interests include copyright protection of digital media and legal education reform, focusing on adapting educational technologies to enhance lawyering skills development throughout the law school curriculum. Professor Berrio Matamoros received his law degree from Boston College and his master's in library and information science from Drexel University.

Renate L. Chancellor, PhD, MLIS, is an assistant professor at the Department of Library and Information Science at the Catholic University of America. She is the director of the Law Librarianship Program of Study and the University's pre-law advisor. Dr. Chancellor's research focuses on legal-information-seeking behavior and multicultural library and information services. She is widely published and has presented her research at international and national conferences. She is recipient of the Association for Library and Information Science Education Excellence in Teaching Award in 2014. Dr. Chancellor received her master's and PhD in information studies from the University of California, Los Angeles.

Ashley Krenelka Chase, JD, MLIS, is the associate director and an adjunct professor of law at the Dolly & Homer Hand Law Library at Stetson University College of Law. She is responsible for the administration, planning, management, and supervision of reference and outreach services, acquisitions, library systems, and web page development, as well as teaching advanced legal research. Her scholarly interests include the development of leadership and management skills in millennial librarians, the evolution of student and faculty research habits, and finding clever ways to incorporate

212 About the Contributors

emerging technologies into those habits. She received her bachelor's in English from Bradley University, her law degree from the University of Dayton School of Law, and her master's in library and information science from the University of South Florida.

Frederick W. Dingledy, JD, MALIS, is senior reference librarian at Wolf Law Library, William & Mary Law School. He is a former president of the Virginia Association of Law Libraries. He has presented a continuing legal education course sponsored by the Law Library of Louisiana and the Supreme Court of Louisiana Historical Society on the *Corpus Juris Civilis*. Dingledy has also contributed to *Virginia Lawyer*'s "Law Libraries" column, the second edition of *Law Librarianship in the Twenty-First Century*, and multiple editions of *A Guide to Legal Research in Virginia*. Dingledy received his law degree from the University of Minnesota and his master's in library and information studies from the University of Wisconsin–Madison.

Brian R. Huffman, JD, MLIS, is the electronic services librarian at the William S. Richardson School of Law Library, University of Hawai'i at Mānoa. He has published and presented on topics including digital self-publishing and open educational resources. His duties include managing library database accounts and coordinating and marketing the law library's e-resources, website, LibGuides, archival collection, and digital institutional repositories, in addition to teaching advanced legal research. Huffman is an active member of the American Association of Law Libraries (AALL) and its Western Pacific chapter (WestPac) and serves as the current president of the Hawai'i Library Association (HLA). He received his law degree from the Drake University Law School and his master's of library and information science from Saint Catherine University.

Jordan A. Jefferson, JD, MLIS, is the coordinating librarian for reference services at the Lilian Goldman Law Library at Yale Law School. Her responsibilities include managing the daily operations of the reference desk, providing research services to the Yale community, and teaching. She is a founding member of the Professional Engagement, Growth, and Advancement special-interest section of the American Association of Law Libraries; the cofounder of Beer & Edits, an annual scholarly networking event held at the AALL conference; and the vice president of the Southern New England Law Librarians Association. Ms. Jefferson received her law degree from the University of La Verne College of Law and her master's in library and information science from the University of Washington.

Benjamin J. Keele, JD, MLS, is a research and instructional services librarian at the Ruth Lilly Law Library, Indiana University Robert H. McKinney

School of Law. He provides legal research assistance and instruction and advises student law journal editors. He is coeditor of *Law Library Journal*'s column "Keeping Up with New Titles" and a coauthor of the *Librarian's Copyright Companion*, second edition (W.S. Hein, 2012). He earned his law degree from the Indiana University Maurer School of Law and his master's in library science from Indiana University.

Dana Neacsu, PhD, is reference librarian and lecturer in law at Columbia Law School, Arthur W. Diamond Law Library, in New York City. She holds a PhD in philosophy from Rutgers University, a master's in library science from CUNY, and various law degrees, including an LLM from Harvard Law School. Since she immigrated to the United States, Neacsu has practiced law as a junior associate in a private law firm and then for the New York City Law Department, and practiced librarianship at Columbia Law School. Since 2003 she also co-teaches in the Barnard College Environmental Studies Department as an adjunct faculty member. Neacsu wrote the introductory legal research book for LLM students (*Introduction to U.S. Law and Legal Research*, Transnational, 2005), which she subsequently updated and published on Columbia University's Academic Commons, where most of her work can be freely accessed. In her spare time, Neacsu writes political satire for ThePotholeView.com.

Jere D. Odell, MA, MLS, is a scholarly communications librarian working in IUPUI's University Library Center for Digital Scholarship, Indianapolis, Indiana. He supports the implementation of IUPUI's open access policy, open access publishing fund, and open journal publishing service. Odell received his master's in English from the University of Notre Dame and his master's in library and information science from Indiana University.

Roberta F. Studwell, JD, MLS, is associate dean for information services at the Euliano Law Library of the Barry University Dwayne O. Andreas School of Law. She writes in the areas of privacy, technology, process improvement, and library management. Studwell received her law degree from the University of Miami and her master's in library science and information from the University of Washington in Seattle.

Victoria J. Szymczak, JD, LLM, MSLIS, is the law library director and an associate professor of law at the University of Hawai'i, Richardson School of Law. At Richardson, she is responsible for managing library services, including collection development decisions and database contract negotiations. She is also responsible for coordinating legal research programming for first-year and upper-class students. Professor Szymczak serves on the AALL Copyright Committee and is the co-chair for the International Legal Research

Interest Group at the American Society of International Law. She is an active member of the American Association of Law Libraries (AALL) and its Western Pacific chapter (WestPac), the Chinese and American Forum on Legal Information and Law Libraries (CAFLL), the Society of American Law Library Directors (SALLD), and the Hawaii-Pacific Islands Laws Initiative. She received her law degree in comparative and international law from the Duke University School of Law and her master's in information and library science from the Pratt Institute.

Jasper L. Tran, JD, is a law clerk to U.S. District Judge Raymond Moore for the District of Colorado. Previously he practiced patent litigation with Faegre Baker Daniels, prosecuted patents at various intellectual property boutiques, and taught legal writing at the University of Minnesota. He received his bachelor's in chemistry and neurobiology from the University of California, Berkeley, and his law degree from the University of Minnesota. After law school, he was a Google policy fellow and a Humphrey policy fellow.

Amanda T. Watson, JD, MIS, is associate director of the Law Library and adjunct lecturer in law at Tulane University School of Law. In addition to teaching advanced legal research, she is responsible for all library operations, taking specific interest in electronic resource management. Watson received her law degree from the University of Mississippi and her master's in information studies from Florida State University.

Heather A. Wiggins, JD, MLIS, is a copyright specialist at the Library of Congress. She received her bachelor's from the University of Wisconsin–Madison, where she triple majored in Spanish, international studies, and LACIS. She received her law degree from the University of Wisconsin Law School and her master's in library and information science from the Catholic University of America. She has researched libraries and cultural institutions abroad, including research trips to the Vatican Secret Archives and to the Capitoline Museum in Rome. She is also a frequent volunteer at the National Book Festival, fielding questions about copyright and about the Library of Congress.